THE FORGOTTEN ARMY

THE FORGOTTEN ARMY

ARMY

A BURMA SOLDIER'S STORY IN LETTERS, PHOTOGRAPHS, AND SKETCHES

JAMES FENTON

FONTHILL

To my father and my mother for the forethought in saving these letters from the very first, never knowing where they would lead me, and what they might tell of the future, or if there would be a successful conclusion. Also, to Lilian my wife, who kept my letters for sentimental reasons.

First published 2012

British Library Cataloguing in Publication Data.
A catalogue record for this book is available from the British Library.

ISBN 978-1-78155-047-2 (PRINT)
ISBN 978-1-78155-133-2 (E-BOOK)

Typesetting and origination by
Printed and bound in Great Britain

Connect with us
 facebook.com/fonthillmedia   twitter.com/fonthillmedia

Contents

Foreword   7

Primary Training   9

Joining the Royal Artillery   20

Posted to a Regiment   43

Sailed from Liverpool   53

Arrival in India   59

The Regiment is Given a New Role   69

Into Action Against the Japanese   91

A Well-Earned Rest   108

Preparing for Action   122

The Campaign in Central Burma   136

A New Move   161

Alandi Camp, Poona   173

The Far East   198

Homeward Bound   219

Royal Artillery Barracks, Woolwich   225

Postscript   247

Appendix – The Home Guard   251

Endnotes   254

Abbreviations   256

FOREWORD

The letters sent home to my parents, James Arthur, and Annie Fenton, living in Oswaldtwistle, Lancashire, have been numbered and bound in nine volumes. Call-up documents, medical certificate, service pay book, discharge papers, letter index, family tree, news cuttings and leaflets have been preserved in a tenth volume. There are a total of 440 letters spanning military service in the army at home, India, Burma, and Malaya during the Second World War.

Copies of sketches, illustrations, photographs and paintings have been placed with the original letters where reference is made. Very few letters were lost in transit, or misplaced. The whereabouts of a series of humorous cartoons about the Royal Artillery is not known. Scenes in sepia watercolour of actions against the Japanese during the Burma campaign sent for publication to UK and USA were not returned. Sketches of the attack on Myitson, and copies of illustrations printed in the magazine *Soldier* are the only drawings of wartime actions that have survived. Original portraits in watercolour, pictorial scenes, and photographs have been exhibited at various venues, a larger number have never been on show.

In addition to the letters sent to my home, many more were written to my brother Harry serving with the Royal Corps of Signals, and to a large family of relatives and friends. Strict censorship regulations on leaving England prohibited the disclosure of troop ships, military activities, locations and place names, or information that may be of value to an enemy during the conflict. Hostile encounters with Japanese forces during the Burma campaign were not allowed to be reported until the closing days of the war. Unimportant details concerning only the family, and reference to other matters that could be confusing, have been omitted. The last of my experiences as a soldier serving in uniform is related in letters to my wife. This is a continuous account of military service during the Second World War, from my very first day in the army, to my last.

CHAPTER 1

Primary Training

I joined the Local Defence Volunteers when it was formed during the early part of the war to act as a military unit manned by civilians trained to defend Britain against an invasion by the enemy, but the name soon changed to the 'Home Guard'. The barracks and drill hall occupied previously by the East Lancashire Regiment, Territorial Army, became the command post for operations. Tactics were to patrol the surrounding isolated moors and vulnerable parts of the town to obstruct a landing by airborne troops. Strategic defence positions were guarded by groups of sentries during the hours of darkness, a duty I fulfilled regularly until called for military service in 1942.

Carlisle Castle, Cumbria

Pte. J. Fenton 14237694
8 Squad
2 Coy. 18 I.T.C.
Bitts Camp
Carlisle, Cumbria

16 July
Dear Mother and Dad
Please excuse the pencil, I am not quite settled making the best of life writing this letter on my case sat on my bed. I would like you to know I arrived OK and am feeling fine. The train left Preston this morning about 10.10 getting to Carlisle two hours later. There were quite a few fellows travelling from Manchester with me coming here, we have parted since arriving, some have been sent to a camp nearby. I made friends with one of the men in the new batch and we may decide to get out together

tonight. The sergeant told us we would be allowed out until one minute to twelve, I do not intend cutting it so fine my first night here.

I have been given most of my army kit, shirts, towels, socks, and vests, but have not yet been issued with a uniform. About half an hour ago I enjoyed a bath and shower. I expect the worst days will come when we start kicking chunks out of the parade ground. I had dinner as soon as I arrived, potatoes, meat and cabbage with nice gravy for the first course. My favourite pudding to follow, jam roll.

The weather is unsettled, never fine for more than half an hour, the rain has not been too heavy. I had better close this letter, there are many things to arrange before tea. This should convince you I am not gloomy. Cheerio. Your loving son, Jim.

PS. I was asked to turn in my new ration book which I left behind at home. I have allotted you seven shillings a week mother.

17 July

This morning we rose like larks when we heard melodious notes blown on the bugle at 6.15, the first task was to make our beds, wash, shave and be ready to parade for breakfast at 7.0. For breakfast we had mashed potatoes, sausage meat cooked in batter, tea, bread and plenty of butter. We have been issued with battle dress and this afternoon I was given a medical check, the doctor could not mark a grade as my medical papers are not here. Next came dinner, mashed potatoes, meat, carrots and as usual bread was served. The second course was a tasty chocolate raisin and date pudding with custard, but would have wished for more. The afternoon was spent receiving the last of our kit and a rifle, the Short Lee Enfield.

We paraded at 5.15, for tea to relieve the cooks of one and a half slices of bread, plenty of butter, jam, cheese, a slice of sausage meat roll and tea. Afterwards I undertook the boring job blancoing all my webbing equipment which was no mean task. It was 10.30 when I finished, too late to venture out of camp so I decided to write this letter. I learned from our corporal we are to be inoculated tomorrow.

Saturday, 18 July

This morning I went to a nearby camp to take a hearing test, learning nothing about the result. I am to undergo six weeks preliminary training in the General Service Corps, and granted 48 hours leave when it has been completed, then posted to a regular unit. Earlier this afternoon I had an inoculation in each arm, they are not troubling me at the present moment except for a slight headache. I felt no discomfort when I received the injections, putting on my shirt I was overcome with a sickly feeling, sweating like a bull for about twenty minutes. How I walked from the medical room I hardly remember, and later learned three of my group passed out. The corporal warned us not to call out for his attention during the night if anyone should feel ill. We are excused 48 hours duties and not allowed out of the barracks.

Thank you for your letter, mother, along with the ration book. I shall do my best to write to relatives and friends whenever I can, I don't want to spend all my time indoors writing letters every night. I am billeted in the barrack room Gallipoli, within the famous Carlisle Castle.

Sunday, 19 July
You see I am managing to write OK, the left arm is most affected and I slept well lying on my back. We paraded at 9.0am for the reading of the Army Act by the sergeant major, during which time two guys suffering the effects of the inoculations fainted. It happened to one lad three times. I was next at the mercy of the army barber getting my hair cut – it is a really close one, you would not know me. Sunday dinner was very nice, if I get no worse than this I shall not mind. We had roasted potatoes, Yorkshire pudding, cabbage, meat and again nice gravy, followed by blancmange. Today the weather is as good as it was yesterday.

22 July
Thank you for sending on the letter from a girl at art school congratulating me on my recent successful Board of Education art examination results. We were given a series of ability tests this morning on squares, mathematics and a third test constructing simple objects. A small lock, a light bulb holder, spanner, picture chain, vice, wood plane and a door knob, to be assembled in a limited period of time. Two items I did not quite complete, a bicycle hub and a pump. Tonight we must stay in barracks to carry out maintenance on our respirators. Soon I shall let you know what regular duties and training we have to face. Would you please get me a nail file, and send it along with a kit bag lock?

24 July
This afternoon I had an interview with the Personnel Selection Officer, about which task and branch of the army would be best suitable for me. He was interested to know Harry was serving in the Royal Corps of Signals, and seemed to dwell on the subject of my knowledge, and ability in photography, and although we spent time talking about my artistic talents, nothing whatever was advised.

On my first pay parade which was none too soon, I drew ten shillings. I must watch my spending with no spare money in my pocket, if I should get 48 hours leave a train ticket to travel home will cost about eighteen shillings.

25 July

All work parades finished at dinner time today (Saturday), until Monday. Yesterday I received your very welcome parcel of handkerchiefs, cigarettes, nail file and kit bag lock, the latter is very serviceable. Registered letters must be collected in person from the Orderly Sergeant. Today I received 40 State Express cigarettes from the Observer Cigarette Fund and enclosed was a label printed with the fund's logo, a design I produced at art school for the newspaper.

Sunday

I have just returned from Sunday morning church parade and I think it was a service held especially for us at 9.30, I did not see any civilians there at all. We found four of the lads absent when we got up this morning. I suspect they have gone home. It was expected of one of the group but no doubt they will be in trouble when they return, if ever they do. They are volunteers as are most of the lads in my room.

Last night I went to a dance costing sixpence for armed forces held at a Sunday school, and there was supper included, teacake and a cup of tea. Somehow I missed out on the cake, perhaps there was not quite enough to go around. What can you expect to get for sixpence? One good thing can be said about this town, the Y.M.C.A. and canteens are very reasonable. At the N.A.A.F.I. in camp, cakes are one penny each, a cup of tea the same and coffee is three halfpence. We are allowed to purchase 35 cigarettes at the price they cost before the last increase, or as many as we wish to buy at the normal price.

26 July

In one of your letters you ask, "What are my duties?" At 6.15 we hear a melodious tone on the bugle, wash, shave, lay out army kit on our beds, sweep and tidy the room before parading at 7 o'clock for breakfast. On Sunday breakfast is a half hour later. Weekday parades are at 8.0am for P.T., foot drill, or whatever training has been planned for that period. The whole morning is marked in periods for different purposes. One hour each might be spent on the Bren gun, rifle drill, or hand grenades, a variety of different subjects throughout the whole day. At 10.15 we take a break for tea and cake costing two pence. We continue at 10.45 until about 12 o'clock, dinner is served at 12.30pm. Dinner on Sunday is 15 minutes later. We parade again at 1.30 until 5 o'clock, with a break for ten minutes during the afternoon. Tea at 5.15 is the last meal served by the cooks. If you spend the evening in barracks and wish to have supper, it is ready from 7 o'clock, but not on Friday, Saturday or Sunday. I had supper on one occasion and it was very good. Should you want something later it can be bought at the N.A.A.F.I. until 9.30, usually tea and cake, or beans on toast for 5 pence. 'Lights Out' at 10.30 is a rule to be observed in all barrack rooms, at present, lights are not needed during the light evenings. I have never read a newspaper or heard any news since I came here, there might be an armistice signed for all I know about this war.

29 July

Yesterday I was called for dental treatment and had three teeth out and one filled. I am much happier they are gone. I shall have another visit for cleaning and I am looking forward to knowing my teeth will be in better shape when the job is done. The dentist took out two teeth from the top without trouble, the one at the bottom broke into pieces and flew everywhere hitting the window and floor leaving bits scattered in my mouth. He gave me five injections and used three pairs of extractors. I must have recovered from the ordeal romping home on a five mile run before tea, midway in the squad making no effort to be the first!

On Friday I am Room Orderly, my job is to make certain the barrack room is never left unoccupied, the floor clean and the room tidy. The orderly is responsible for looking after the squad's kit, staying in the empty barrack room during meal times until someone returns to take over. The job will keep me in barracks throughout the whole evening, and an inoculation the following day confines me to barracks for the next 48 hours. The way this has turned out I shall be spending three consecutive nights in barracks, Friday, Saturday and Sunday.

At this moment three lads are arguing about the correct manner to conduct foot drill stamping their feet making a row marching up and down the room changing step, and about turn. They are keen to get it right. One of the absentees who signed for seven years and five on reserve returned on Monday morning, getting off lightly with seven days C.B. Two others came back last night and were given the same punishment. The fourth has not returned.

1 August

We were having instruction about the Bren gun this morning, when the Orderly Sergeant ordered us to pack up, get out of battle kit, and report to the M.O. for inoculation. Loud groans came from everyone at this happy news; it was not expected until after dinner. I felt nothing as it was done, straight away grabbing my shirt to dash out of the room into the fresh air suffering no ill effects as I did the last time. Taking a bath a short time later, I found great difficulty getting out of it. Next week we are to be vaccinated.

We have been given ration cards for an allowance of one block of chocolate each week. Speaking of rations, I shall bring home soap coupons or soap; I have four spare coupons and a new tablet of soap. We get one coupon each week which is more than enough using it carefully, and I do not neglect to wash. Mother, you need have no worries how I keep my clothes washed and clean, they are parcelled, labelled, and put into the QM stores to be sent to a laundry. This, too, is a good help with the soap ration. The towel and other items I brought with me in the suitcase are secure in the stores, I shall collect them to take home when I get leave.

A showing of the film, *Next of Kin*, is being arranged at a picture house in Carlisle, and counted a parade duty. I saw this film some time ago at the Empire cinema, Oswaldtwistle, when it was shown to members of the Home Guard.

7 August

During training this afternoon, up came the corporal with the expected news we were to report to the M.O. for vaccination. I hardly knew it had been done and no unpleasant after effects, I can think only about one thing to complain about; we are not excused duties.

I have been given a locker to store my belongings, making life easier to pick out whatever I need immediately, instead of rummaging through a lot of gear in a canvas kit bag. The squad has spent the last two periods of the afternoon cleaning the room for an inspection tomorrow, now it is done. I am writing this letter on my bed as are many other lads, before going for tea.

9 August

Have you ever tried getting dressed wearing a gas mask? You should. As the P.T. period was coming to an end yesterday morning, dressed only in gym vest and shorts, the gas rattle sounded, sending everyone scurrying to put on respirators when Tear Gas was used for practice drill. Returning to our barrack room the sergeant ordered us to get fully dressed. What a surprised look was registered in the eye pieces of every gas mask. It took about fifteen minutes to get out of P.T. kit into battle dress, and it was not easy. After dinner we were given another test; mustard gas was spread on the back of our hands to teach us decontamination procedures. Later that day I noticed one guy with a bandage on his hand.

The church parade this morning was at Carlisle Cathedral. If I can get time off I should like to make sketches of the interior where some of the oldest parts date from the 14th century. Many lads seeing my sketches would like me to draw their portrait, I have already collected one shilling and if the news gets around there could be more opportunities.

Regarding leave I was expecting shortly, you can forget it; all branches of the army are desperate for recruits finishing General Service Corps training. Some squads that began training before us are leaving on Tuesday to allotted units, without a break. These fellows hoping to get a few days leave at home learned the disappointing news on Saturday.

11 August   *Y.M.C.A. headed note paper*
I am writing this letter in the John Peel, Y.M.C.A., and using their note paper. It makes a pleasant break to get outside the confines of camp. There are times when it is too much trouble changing from work denims, to find half the evening has passed before I am washed and properly dressed in uniform ready to leave the barracks.

Thank you for the registered parcel, receiving one in the army is like Christmas morning in the early years of childhood. You begin unwrapping the packages and wonder what surprises are in store. Please thank Auntie Mary for the half crown, tell her it will be used for the good of the stomach. There are three important things in the army, Leave, Grub and Pay. I find it a good life as long as I do not stay on this I.T.C. (Intensive Training Course) for more than the allotted time. I have not the faintest notion where the army will send me from here. The Personnel Selection Officer gave no hint what to expect as he sat at his desk with all the results of my tests, and other papers. He invited me to sit down, beginning a friendly chat talking about life at home, sports, and what I was studying at the art school. Hearing all this he sat back in deep meditation and scratched his head, which is perfectly true. After a period of silence he said with a slight chuckle, "You arty chaps are the most difficult to handle." He has told some fellows what future he selected for them, it depends if vacancies are available in their particular line of work.

Today, I took a bus journey to another camp along with a dozen other guys from here for an eye test. We would not be back in time for dinner and were given haversack rations, two slices of bread and cheese. It was eleven o'clock when we arrived at the camp, and sat around for more than an hour before a nurse kindly told us we would not be seen until 2.30 in the afternoon. Off we went in search of a canteen to get a drink and eat our rations, wondering if we may also find a cookhouse to scrounge a hot meal. Indeed, we discovered there were three, at which point one of the guys declared, "Third time lucky!" We approached the first cookhouse spinning a plausible yarn to the cook, telling him our appointments had been delayed. We of course did not disclose we were given rations that had already been eaten. A nice dinner was served to us, but we were confronted with a serious problem, not one of us had with us any eating irons. Knife, fork and spoon are precious and closely guarded personal items that can never be found lying around. Yet again the cook came to our rescue, offering to lend us utensils borrowed from A.T.S. girls in the mess. Eventually, I had my eye test but was given no indication about the result. That was not a satisfactory conclusion for me. Coming away, I was handed the medical sheet to take from the room; glancing at a note written on the back of the form I saw the words, *Glasses Not Needed*.

14 August

We received our pay today so I feel like a millionaire. There was an inspection to check the results of our recent vaccinations and about half a dozen in my squad have not felt the slightest effect, others have suffered badly. Tonight the weather has turned out to be a perfect evening, and as we were blancoing our gaiters and rifle sling, one fellow made a casual remark in his native tongue, "A think war's cum to an end, sun's shinin' in Carlisle."

I fired a Bren gun yesterday making no attempt to gain a high score, perhaps on purpose!

16 August

Another lovely day, soft white clouds dashed with grey floating slowly along in a blue sky, a perfect day for church parade, attended as usual by military units from other camps. I was out walking last night and visited Carlisle Art Gallery when I found it did not close until 8 o'clock. There were some nice paintings; one or two others I saw failed to impress me. Each week we have to write a short story about Careless Talk, a prize of two shillings and sixpence is offered for the best. I have written two essays on the subject and both have been highly commended, yet I have never seen any reward.

Many of the lads are troubled with effects of vaccination and are stretched out on their beds, two reported to have vaccination fever, some with lumps under the arm and an itching sensation. Mine is OK, a red spot is visible proving it was successful.

18 August

It was such a nice day last Sunday, after dinner I left camp with my paints searching for a scene suitable for sketching. Before settling myself down, as a precaution I had words with a policeman telling him what I planned, knowing the subject I chose would not contravene wartime regulations imposed on photographing, or copying sensitive locations. I made a small simple watercolour and was back in the barracks before tea, showing it to the lads.

The whole of this week we are undergoing more tests; yesterday's test was gym and sports. Tonight we are to be abandoned some distance outside the barracks to check our powers of observation and sense of direction, using common sense and initiative to find a way back. Tomorrow the subject is map reading, Thursday and Friday, shooting on the firing range.

I shall be leaving here a week today, and as yet have been given no details about where I might be posted. If I get placed in the infantry I would not have to go far, there is a training unit nearby. Yesterday I made another visit to the dentist to have three teeth filled; after he had cleaned my teeth he told me one more needed to be filled to complete the job. While confined in barracks on fire picket last night I managed to answer some long overdue letters.

20 August

Would you believe it! Yesterday we were given another inoculation, this one for lockjaw (tetanus), with no unpleasant after effects. I caught the words of a mumbled expression made by one of the lads as he left the treatment room, "We will resemble a pin cushion when we leave here." I understand that is to be the last. Today on a shooting range about five miles from here, we were tested on our ability to handle the Bren gun. Reports on my marksmanship signalled by butt's markers, (hits on the target), my score was very good. We travelled to the range by train spending the whole day there. A really nice dinner had been prepared for us and I enjoyed the best rice pudding I have tasted since joining the army, not as good as yours, mother. Tomorrow will be another full day on the shooting range testing our skill to fire a rifle.

A batch of new recruits arrived today and I have met only three so far, the rest I shall see at breakfast tomorrow. Quite a number are from the Manchester area and I believe one lad is from *Ossy*. Last night was the only time I could freely step outside the barracks this week. Monday I was on fire picket duty, Tuesday night manoeuvres, and fire picket again tonight. Tomorrow night I may go to a dance at a camp nearby, and Saturday night a dance is to be held in the gym hall, the first in the castle since I came here.

The corporal informed us we should get to know on Monday the units to which we are to be posted, and 48 hours leave would be granted soon after our arrival. I hope I am not bound for the far north of Scotland, or far away in the opposite direction – Penzance.

22 August

Well here is the news I have been waiting for, I am going to 'Bonnie Scotland' on Tuesday, or Wednesday, and I hope the posting is as good as I am led to believe. Four of us have been selected to train as signallers with the Royal Artillery, in Edinburgh. I am the only one in my squad chosen to take the course; the other fellows are new to me. We all got together to talk about the move when we learned the news.

Yesterday, an officer checking our kit, along with a sergeant who had seen my cartoons, asked if he might borrow the drawings. A short time later I was called to see Lt. Fisher in the Company Office, and asked if I would produce about half a dozen drawings to illustrate stages of attack, and defence, for training new recruits in bayonet drill. I made one drawing to show him before embarking on the rest in case the technique was unsuitable. I understand prints are to be made from my originals and posted about the camp. I hope to work on the drawings during fire picket tonight; tomorrow I shall carry on doing as much as I can instead of undergoing regular training with the squad.

A large number of pals in my squad are moving to another camp about one mile from here, they are joining the Border Regiment to undergo ten weeks intensive infantry training.

24 August

Just before kit inspection this morning, the Second in Command (Lt. Fisher) asked how I was getting along with the drawings. He was pleased with the ones he had seen and reminded me I would soon be leaving the castle. The squad is revising many of the special training subjects. Not me, I was asked to carry on and finish the drawings before leaving.

Many lads are hopping about like kangaroos; the corporal asked if anyone moving to Durranhill Barracks does not want a 48 hours leave pass from Wednesday, to Friday midnight? How strange, no one refused the offer. Durranhill Barracks is the Border Regiment infantry training unit nearby. I have been told I shall be leaving on Wednesday, and if I understand the sergeant correctly, the squad's final test results are only six points short of a possible maximum!

Thank Harry for his letter; I am pleased he is home enjoying seven days leave. I stayed up until lights out last night, writing him a letter he will not read until he finds it waiting for him when he returns to his unit.

25 August

I collected your parcel and investigated the welcome bag of mystery. Thank you for everything, the cake, money, cigarettes and chocolate.

I don't know what time I expect to be leaving here tomorrow, I shall keep you informed about where I am living and the type of training I am doing.

I handed three more sketches to Lt. Fisher today, making a total of eight to complete the series. Each black and white drawing measures about 10 x 8 inches; unfortunately I won't get to see my final efforts displayed inside the castle, for the benefit of training new recruits.

CHAPTER 2

Joining the Royal Artillery

Redford Barracks, Edinburgh

Gnr. J. Fenton 14237694
B Battery, 3 Squad
38 Signals Training Regiment R.A.
Redford Barracks
Edinburgh 13

26 August

I arrived at the R.A. barracks in Edinburgh about one o'clock along with the three other fellows from Carlisle, and was immediately notified of a change to my rank from 'Private,' to 'Gunner.' Reveille was early this morning at 5 o'clock to hand in our blankets at the stores. We had breakfast at 6.15, and at 7 o'clock left the old historic castle for the last time to catch a train from the station at 8.45. During the journey the lads had a jolly good sing song to well known tunes I played on my mouth organ. We were given a meal before signing in, and collecting bedding. Every night when not on duty we are allowed out of barracks until 10.59pm, one hour earlier than the restrictions imposed at Carlisle. There is no chance whatsoever of getting leave until part of my training has been completed. I learned there is a dance to be held in barracks on Friday; I shall make every effort to get there and be treading on some unfortunate girl's toes. A large number of A.T.S. are stationed here.

I hope you are enjoying your leave at home Harry, please give Major a pat from me and let him know he has not been forgotten.

26 August

The food here is better than meals at the castle. For dinner I lined up in the dining hall to be served steak and chips with two slices of bread. I found afterwards I could also have had a pastry sandwich of sausage meat. For tea there was sausage, lettuce, marmalade, bread and butter, and tea is sweeter served with more sugar.

I have marching drill to learn once again; the orders are very different in the R.A., and some will seem quite strange at first. Commands in infantry regiments are given on the right foot, in the R.A., marching orders are given on the left foot. Training begins learning the workings of the internal combustion engine to turn us into capable mechanics. We are first taught to drive lorries on a large open field behind the barracks. The next stage is learning to drive on country roads, and in the busy town of Edinburgh. After two weeks driving we learn to ride motorcycles. Finally, most important of all, training to be a signaller in the Royal Artillery.

27 August

It is a beautiful morning and from my barrack room window I can see the colourful Scottish hills bathed in glorious sunlight. After breakfast I came to my barrack room with half a mug of cocoa to enjoy, along with a piece of your cake, mother. It would be about 7 o'clock when I got up this morning, the sergeant told us it did not matter what time we get out of bed, we are to be ready for breakfast at 8.0am. At this moment I can hear a Morse buzzer bleeping not very far away. Before dinner I met a squad wearing crash helmets preparing for motorcycle training, and later I noticed one fellow with his arm in a sling, one with a bandage around an eye, and another gunner limping. I can not say if this has any connection with motorcycling but it looks rather suspicious.

Training to be a signaller will take 12 or 16 weeks to complete, followed by a posting to a regular artillery unit. I trust you are now fully aware what is involved with my new assignment.

30 August

I can find many faults and advantages compared to my last unit. Every Wednesday morning there is a gas kit Inspection, and Saturday morning a full kit Inspection; little more than army red tape organised to give the officers reason to earn their pay. There are over keen rules on cleanliness, the wood back of a boots blacking brush handle must be clean and white. How would you like to keep the ones at home like this? The hair brush too must be kept in the same condition. I was told some Big Bug making an inspection not long ago was checking the backs of cap badges to see if they were as clean, and bright, as the front. Until recently there were bugle calls throughout the day marking parade times. There is an abundance of hot water; you could brew tea with it as it comes out of the tap, a luxury we never had at Carlisle except when taking a bath.

The squad sergeant is our driving instructor, and a decent fellow; he has promised to pick out some of the nicest spots when we go out driving on convoy runs. We had our first Morse lesson today and the buzzer was left in the room for everyone to practice sending messages. Besides the telegraph, we are to learn signalling with a flag, and with a lamp. Yesterday I was introduced to 13 pounder, and 18 pounder field guns.

Last night in town with the other lads from Lancashire, we saw a good variety show; the only seats we could get were in the gods. Going into the theatre one of the lads said, "We may not understand these Scottish jokes, so laugh with everyone else." The comic from Blackburn asked me to sketch his portrait to send home to his girl friend.

31 August, Monday

You will be surprised to learn I spent the latter half of yesterday, and evening, with Uncle Joe and his pal. About 3.30 in the afternoon a bombardier (R.A. rank equivalent to corporal, two stripes) came and told me – two sailors at the guardroom gate wanted to see me. After getting over the shock I guessed who it might be, not knowing how Uncle Joe could have found me here. Apparently, he had been home on leave and learned of my address. I was confined to barracks on duty for the afternoon. When I explained the situation to my sergeant, I managed to obtain a pass allowing me to go into town with Uncle Joe and his pal.

On Sunday nights in Edinburgh there is not much entertainment to be found, we listened for a while to the Scottish pipers playing in Princess Street Park, and visited one or two canteens to avoid intermittent showers of rain. I noticed a photographer's studio where I may have a photograph taken wearing my army uniform with official R.A. badges and trimmings. I can buy three post card size portraits for sixpence.

To answer to your questions about my job. If I pass the course, I shall send fire orders to the guns and communications to other units. I may drive a wireless truck; hence the reason to drive. When the guns depend on observations of accuracy of *fire*, I may end up pretty near to Gerry. In other circumstances, I may be expected to career around on a motorcycle, or lay signal lines for communication.

All for now   • — • •   — — —   • • • —   •   (L   O   V   E)

3 September

In future I shall have little spare time counting the amount of work ahead, attending lectures taking notes on motor vehicle engines, wireless and telephones. My Morse is improving; I had a lesson today, one lesson I missed yesterday when I visited the dentist to have two teeth filled.

5 September

On the first day I arrived, I was in conversation with the person writing down my details and discovered our mutual interest in art. He is an ex schoolmaster about 35 years of age. He mentioned he had made enquiries at an art school in Edinburgh about evening classes. He is looking further into the matter.

We were given a Morse test yesterday, not at all fast at three words a minute, achieving marks of 95%. I must tell you about my experiences towing a field gun bouncing about the countryside. On one occasion we skidded on the soft mud, the weight of the gun pushing us down a slope and slewing us around. It was thrilling crossing streams and passing between trees with barely enough room to get between them. In an area behind the barracks, I noticed a cinder roadway winding about like a maze lined with small posts placed along the sides at intervals, designed to test our skill learning to drive lorries. I think it will be a great deal of fun when we begin M.T. training. This afternoon during sports period we had an unusual game of baseball, introduced by an American officer stationed here.

Sunday, 6 September

Over a week ago I was dancing in the open air in Princess Street Gardens to the band of the Highland Light Infantry, while the B.B.C. was making a recording. The programme of music was broadcast on Friday between 1.30, and 2.0pm. A religious service was held in the dining hall today for about ten minutes, long enough to bring to mind memories of home.

8 September

Tomorrow afternoon, I shall go into Edinburgh shopping to buy a good notebook that will be useful for making M.T. notes, and diagrams, explaining the working parts of the internal combustion engine. I shall try to make a good job of it; you never know who may wish to see the final results that might stretch to openings in other activities.

Would you please contact Mr. Hargreaves at Shaw's Pottery, in Darwen, and enquire if the casting of the bas-relief plaque I modelled at art school has been completed. If it is finished I should like you to collect it, and keep it safe for me until it can be framed.

10 September

Tonight I am doing guard duty for the fourth time since I came here. We are the junior squad and it will often occur until a new batch arrives to take over the job. An officer and four men are listed for guard throughout the night. Three men take turns on sentry duty over a period of twelve hours, two hours on sentry and four hours off. I have been selected as the 'attending man.' The attending man is chosen by the officer when the guard report on parade. His job is to collect the men's bedding and take it to the guard room. Fetch supper from the cookhouse during the night, return the bedding in the morning, and clean the room. He does not stand sentry and may get a fair night's sleep if all is quiet. On sentry duty you try to make yourself comfortable in a Bedford truck, or nearby vehicle, more so during cold nights. Great care has to be taken not to be surprised in the darkness by the officer making his rounds of the guard post, while comfortably settled in the cab of a truck enjoying a quick drag from a cigarette.

11 September   *CHURCH OF SCOTLAND headed note paper*
Oh, what an exciting time we had this morning when we took out the guns over the usual switch back countryside to practice coming into *action* quickly and *laying* the gun. On our way back we ran into a bog quite by accident, and one of the wheels sank almost to the hub. The second gun following behind did the same. We spent three quarters of an hour getting them free of the muddy mess. There are six men to a gun and my position, No3, is to *lay* the gun, set the *sights*, select different aiming points and also to *fire* the gun. The task is demanding and I don't think any other men on the team are capable of doing it except No1, and he is the guy in charge giving the fire orders. Gun drill has only recently been introduced in signaller training, a backup if we should ever find ourselves in a position to take over and operate a gun to save our skins.

I have lit one of your cigarettes from the package you sent, which reminds me to tell you, lighter fuel is easily obtained with little fear of running short. The bombardier keeps a bottle in his locker filled with petrol from the vehicle shed for all to use.

I wonder how Dad is managing for sugar, his entire ration allowance from Tuesday will have been used by Thursday and he is in no position to borrow sugar from me.

There is a dance at this canteen tonight, the reason why I am here writing to you on the canteen's headed note paper. I am on the spot, ready and waiting to take to the floor when dancing starts in five minutes time at eight o'clock.

13 September
Last night after tea, I was in town walking along Princess Street when I heard the sweet strains of dance music coming from the direction of

the park, and saw open air dancing in progress. I paid sixpence to get inside; the last time the entrance cost three pence. You would never say it was an ideal dance floor, not a bit slippery but a good size. My partner, whom I had never met, was picked because I noticed she was a good dancer, and we each won two shillings and sixpence in saving stamps. The competition dance was an old fashioned waltz. Three prizes were given away, not merely for dancing; the cheerful attitude of the couple was also a factor to be considered. Three judges picked one couple each from the large number of dancers. When the selection was made, the floor was cleared and the three couples gave an exhibition dance. The audience was asked to hold up handkerchiefs to choose a winner. I can honestly say we were only a few votes short, seeing the number of hands frantically waving for us. Two girls dancing together won first prize; they had many young friends in the audience.

This morning we were given news we are to take gun drill pass out test on Thursday, in readiness to begin the next part of our training on the M.T. course. The first week we shall attend lectures and take notes on the subject before learning to drive. Tonight I am on fire picket; ten men are chosen and sleep in one room, to be on call in an emergency should there be a fire. There is little to do unless someone decides to commit arson.

14 September

You may think I have used the whole of the writing pad you sent to me, this paper I scrounged to write to you in my spare moments on guard, yes, on guard duty again! I exchanged with another fellow to be sure I would be free to attend the dance tomorrow night. Just my luck, since I made the arrangement I have seen orders posted for tomorrow, and I am not on the guard list. The *angles* and the *sight* settings for *laying* a gun are chasing one another around in my head. Gun drill is very nice, and I thoroughly enjoy the complexity of the task training with guns thrown out from the last war. We go through the motions coming into action, and firing at an imaginary target, using dummy rounds. The guns we use for practice may blow apart if ever live shells were used.

I am happy knowing Shaw's Pottery has finished casting and firing the wall plaque, please be sure to pack it well and keep it safely for me.

Tuesday, 15 September

I received a letter from Harry this morning and I must reply to keep up our regular correspondence. It is terribly windy, as it was throughout the night, now the sun is shining making the day much brighter. We are expecting a Brass Hat to inspect the barracks tomorrow. After tea this evening our free time will be spent on the arduous task of spit and polish, making sure our room and kit is glorified in preparation for our important visitor, before getting away to the dance.

16 September

Because of the general's visit today, our usual afternoon off has been postponed until tomorrow. I enjoyed myself at the dance last night; it is really wonderful to leave the hall and walk upstairs and get into bed. Thank you for the letter and stamps, I counted ten stamps you have so far sent to me including two received today. Do I not write to you often enough? I bought a Royal Artillery dress cap that cost 8/9d including the cap badge.

Your recent letter was handed to me when we were messing about in the gun shed and my answer to your question is, "No!" I do not wish to transfer to the position of No.3, gun layer, I shall stick to my work as a signaller. Tomorrow we take our passing out test at the end of training on the guns. I never saw the glittering diamond that was to have visited the barracks today.

18 September

I have been thoroughly enjoying myself trying to wreck a W.D. vehicle, and will be out again this afternoon driving on the field behind the barracks. I am beginning to learn more about the working parts of the engine, with a better understanding after visiting Uncle John, watching him stripping down his motorcycle, and laying all the separate pieces on the kitchen floor.

Saturday, 19 September

I found it easier driving a big Fordson lorry yesterday afternoon, but harder to control when cornering, than the previous vehicle I have been driving. Tonight I shall stay in barracks to draw diagrams of the internal combustion engine in my note book. I need to spend a lot of spare time drawing engine parts and writing notes, instead of writing letters. The next time you send a parcel would you please include a red, and a blue pencil; they would be useful for colouring illustrations. You will find them among my art materials lying about the house. When posting a parcel of no great value, do not register it, parcels arrive here safely without any trouble.

I will find time to write to Uncle Fred in Sweden if you would please send me his address.

22 September

Saturday and Sunday night I spent drawing diagrams, and making notes about petrol engines. We were given more notes to write yesterday, and

I would have done them in the evening if I had not been feeling sick. I had been unwell during the afternoon and was in bed by 7.30. Later that evening I took a couple of aspirin tablets and as feeling a lot better when I awoke in the morning. It is too much trouble to follow the formalities reporting on sick parade. I got through the first two periods in the morning OK, P.T. and reading Morse. The rest of the day passed a little easier sitting in a cab driving around the field on the training track.

24 September

There is very little hard work to do here unless you think attending lectures and driving is hard work. The whole morning was spent carrying out maintenance on vehicles, and this afternoon we were given more driving instruction. Yesterday I went into town with one of the lads to see the film. *The Ghost of Frankenstein*, and enjoyed it considering the type of film it is.

25 September

Winter appears to be with us today in Scotland; it is very cold with occasional bursts of autumn sunshine. Yesterday afternoon it poured with rain during a driving lesson, turning the surface of the field into about six inches of mud, causing the lorries a lot of skidding. Controlling a large motor vehicle on a treacherous surface fills you with confidence to tackle all types of road conditions anywhere. It is not as easy as you may think. Handling a military pantechnicon in that situation was good training for us all. If the officer is in a good mood this afternoon we may be taking our first driving lesson outside the barracks on country roads.

It seems quite a while since I patted Major on the head, and said goodbye to you, mother, at the door, walking down Union Road to the railway station with dad alongside pushing his bike to see me on my way to join the army. From the time I was first weighed at my medical, and until coming here, I have gained the enormous amount of 2½ lbs. Your letter, mother, makes no mention of a 10 shilling note found inside the envelope; did it slip in by mistake? A £1 note has been tucked away safely in my wallet since joining up, a wise decision should I need cash in an emergency.

We had an M.T. test yesterday and I came second in the class. The fellow who was first has eight years driving experience; two more civvy drivers were 4th, and 5th, so I can not be doing too badly. Today our note books were collected to be seen by the major. Later the sergeant said I was treating M.T. very well, my note book and diagrams were very good. A fortnight today I begin learning to ride a motorcycle, and after passing out, my training in this Battery will come to an end, rewarded with the prospects of a few days leave.

The squad is confined to barracks on duty, a precaution the whole area will never be deserted, as if that could ever happen! We must report to check-in at 8.30 this evening. When it has been completed, I may sneak out across the field behind barracks and visit the nearby canteen at Colinton. One of the lads is thinking seriously about joining me.

28 September

On Wednesday, the schoolmaster and I are going to make enquiries about attending night classes at an art school. He has ambitions to start editing a wall newspaper, and asked would I be willing to draw illustrations where they are needed. I don't know when, or even if his idea might ever get off the ground.

Tuesday, 29 September

I was late for dinner today, a lecture about electric currents and coil ignition on I.C. engines ran over time. Pay parade at 5 o'clock, I learned never to get there early. We are paid at different locations in groups by surname, letter 'F' is the last to be paid in my group.

1 October

Last Sunday evening I had taken a few steps crossing Princess Street, in Edinburgh, when someone came behind me in the middle of the road, tapped me on the shoulder and said, "Are you from Lancashire?" Not being sure of himself he asked the question, I immediately knew he was Arnold Jennings. We walked around for about two hours talking about the old home town, and he showing me where he is stationed before parting at 9.30.

This afternoon we were driving around the main streets and centre of Edinburgh, where the squad had a couple of mishaps. One of the lads was testing the resistance of a horse and cart; fortunately all survived. Another of our drivers took a dislike to a tramcar, either that or to the colour; he removed a considerable amount of paint from its side. During the time spent learning to drive I have done quite well, only a couple of scary moments blooming forth and fresher for the experience.

4 October, Sunday

Last Friday I went to night school life class in Edinburgh; it was a wonderful break and much the same set up as the art school in Accrington. The teacher's influence was noticeable on the full-time students, limiting their ability to produce masterpieces of an individual style. I enjoyed a good scribble and hope I shall be able to attend more classes.

I received a letter from Uncle Joe yesterday morning asking if I could meet him in the afternoon at 3 o'clock, failing this, 6 o'clock. We do not have Saturday afternoon's free; however, I managed to get permission to see him. I was making my way to a canteen where he arranged we should meet when I saw he was on his way there. We enjoyed a cup of tea waiting for his pal coming off duty to join us. We planned to have photographs taken at a studio, turning away disappointed when we discovered the limited supplies of materials had run out, and work had ceased for the day. After tea we chose to see a film before parting, to return to our respective units.

Seeing army trucks erratically driving around Edinburgh yesterday and again today Sunday, should be a warning to local citizens about the dangers they may encounter going to church, and be well advised to stay comfortable indoors at home.

7 October, Wednesday

We set out on a night column run at two o'clock on Monday afternoon, driving until 10 o'clock at night, and again from 8.30 next morning, returning a little after midday on Tuesday without accidents. Two persons in each truck along with a qualified driver; our driver never took the wheel at any time. Driving in darkness observing black-out regulations, side lights only, is quite an experience. I was not sorry when it became time for my partner to take over from me. You could never imagine what it was like driving a large heavy vehicle, occasionally reaching 30mph, and more, on a dark country lane with an archway of trees overhead and not a glimmer of light to guide you. Of course I was not on the road the whole time; there were moments when I preferred to drive on the verge.

You seem confused about my training programme so I shall try to explain the whole procedure more fully. Training in B Battery takes about seven weeks, the first weeks learning gun drill, following this M.T. (Motor Transport), learning to drive. We then undergo D.R. (Dispatch Rider), instructions riding motorcycles, after that I hope, a few days leave. When I return from leave, signal training begins in earnest. Signalling, signalling, and more signalling, including Morse buzzer, wireless operator, signalling by lamp, heliograph and flags, over a period of about eight weeks. After qualifying on all these courses I will join a regular Royal Artillery unit. Now after all that as our sergeant would say, "Is that quite clear, any questions?"

8 October

Thank you for the parcel, each one you send appears to get larger. I shall find the torch most useful going to bed at night after lights out, safely climbing the stairs to my barrack room avoiding the risk of a broken neck. We are all ready and waiting to attend a lecture about the progress of the war. My regular army pay has been increased by 3 shillings each week.

9 October

The final part of M.T. training was completed this afternoon when I passed my driving test. The examining officer told me what he had written on my report; it was full of praise about my driving ability but I can not remember the exact wording. After placing his signature at the bottom of the form he said to me, "That is the last M.T. pass out sheet I shall sign in this Regiment." At the week end he is leaving to join the Royal Engineers. Five out of a squad of fifteen failed the test. It was a *lovely* afternoon, rain and strong wind thrashing the sides of the canvas covered trucks. This morning I got through the written test OK, now I can wear an M.T. proficiency badge on my sleeve.

I was weighed in the gym and appear to have gained 7lbs.

11 October, Sunday

Saturday morning we left our old barrack room, moving to a different room to begin lessons with a new sergeant instructor learning how to start a motorcycle engine and use the various controls. In the afternoon we were riding on the field behind the barracks, and again today. One or two lads came off their bikes, picked themselves up uninjured, and laughed it off. I can truthfully declare I did not leave my riding position, I know there is always a first time. When we broke off for dinner I was feeling saddle sore, not to mention a couple of big blisters on each hand that has burst. I wish you could see me in crash helmet and gloves. We have our own machines for the whole week; the one I am riding is a Norton. Tomorrow we are going on a column run, the next day we shall have more difficult terrain to negotiate, riding through streams, specially prepared bomb craters, steep inclines and around trees in a wooded area.

Thank you for the letter card, with it came 40 cigarettes from the Observer Cigarette Fund.

13 October

Today we challenged the rough riding course, everyone came off their motorbike a few times without serious misfortune, including my humble self when it happened twice. Seeing the hazardous course for the first time fills you with trepidation, knowing you are facing the knack of negotiating tricky obstacles, riding through bomb craters and water controlling the engine to prevent it stalling. These are a few of the difficulties we are expected to overcome.

My weekly pay will be boosted to thirteen shillings on pay parade this evening; I shall receive a regular raise not due to proficiency. We have been asked to hand in our home address, and nearest railway station, the signs are quite good to enjoy a few days leave. I may get away Friday night, or it could be Saturday, I can not tell you definitely which day it might be.

Nine days leave with my parents, 17 – 25 October.

25 October
Soon after leaving home, I discovered I had left behind my gas mask. Would you please post it to me as soon as you can? My address has changed to 'C Battery.'

26 October
Spending a few minutes waiting for a bus to take me to the railway station at the beginning of my return journey, I met Uncle Harry, having time only for him to kindly give me two shillings and to shake his hand as I left. At Church station, Arnold Jennings turned up to get the same train, along with a friend to see him off. Changing trains at Blackburn we found a connection for Preston, and looking from one of the windows was the jester from No3 squad. We piled into his carriage talking about the time spent at home, and in spite of our dismal feelings we managed to crack a few jokes to cheer us. Arriving at Preston, I began gathering together my kit to suddenly discover I had left my respirator behind at home. Here another of the clan joined us bringing our strength up to four. The journey was heaven compared with the beginning of our leave travelling from Edinburgh. Never once were we crushed for room, five of us in a compartment until somewhere near Carlisle we lost our odd passenger, I can not say where exactly, I kept falling asleep. Arriving about sixty minutes late near to midnight at Edinburgh, we reported to the R.T.O. to sign our passes, clearing us for the delay and to telephone the barracks for transport. An hour went by before a wagon arrived to collect us and it was half past one in the morning when we finally handed in our passes at the main gate guard room. All the vehicle's radiators had been drained of water for the night, causing a long delay before picking us up. After refilling with water, the driver had difficulty finding an officer to sign a work ticket before any transport could come to our aid. We crept quietly into the barrack room amid snores of contentment coming to our ears from our pals in No3 squad. Some kind person had thought to collect

our blankets from the stores. I was soon asleep dreaming I was once again on a train taking me back home.

At the end of eleven weeks in this Battery we will be due for nine days leave. The signal training course covers nine weeks to *pass out*, followed by an extra two weeks revision. Half way through the course we get a week end break from Saturday dinner time, to Sunday night. Our officer told us *pass out* would be on a Friday, and that turns out to be Christmas Day.

29 October

There was an alert in barracks yesterday morning when poison gas and incendiary bombs were supposed to have been dropped, just my luck I did not have my gas mask. Tear gas was used, but not nearby, and luckily blowing away from my direction. We had been warned to expect the exercise. It was ironic; my gas mask was languishing in the barrack's post room where I could not get it. I was aware it had arrived, trying more than once to collect it, each time I found the office locked. Fortunately I avoided problems over the incident and a short while after the exercise I was able to collect it.

2 November

I should have written you a decent letter earlier having taken the trouble to forward my respirator. The 'Big Bugs' are having fits about awareness of gas attacks, continually dropping gas bombs about the place, scaring everyone to carry their gas mask in barracks at all times.

Wednesday will be my first chance to collect photographs taken recently at a studio in Edinburgh, although they very kindly offered to post them to me.

Continued later

I have not chosen a comfortable seat to continue this letter, trying my best to write on the top deck of a moving tramcar. Uncle Joe called at the guard room this afternoon hoping I could join him on a visit to town. I could not leave barracks that moment; now I am on my way to meet him at six o'clock at the G.P.O., in Edinburgh. This morning I reported sick with a terrible nose bleed, the M.O. gave me menthol to inhale and told me to see him if it started again. It began two days ago on Saturday afternoon, bleeding on and off like a pig. The same evening in a café I had to leave the meal because my nose was bleeding badly. Sunday it began again as I was having a wash, since then I am hopeful it has finally stopped bleeding. I have almost reached my destination and will post this letter when I get off the tram.

4 November

I am on duty with the black-out squad making inspections of barrack rooms, checking all black-out precautions are in place before writing this letter. I spent a marvellous evening at a variety theatre with Uncle Joe and three navy friends serving on his ship docked at Rosyth. We were entertained by Norman Evans, Gipsy Petulengro, and a performing troupe, the Grenadiers. The gipsy, dressed in colourful regalia, forecast the 'German Reich would crack up in May,' and 'September would see the end of the war in Europe, with Great Britain the victors.' To this statement Uncle Joe made a timely remark, "Only another six months to go." Uncle Joe's brothers are a group of entertainers touring the theatres, and friends of Norman Evans. We went back stage and Uncle Joe introduced us to Norman Evans, talking with him in person we found him as amusing as he is on the radio.

6 November, Friday

For the past two hours I have been getting ready for kit inspection tomorrow. In B Battery we had two inspections every week, in C Battery one only each week. The squad that gets the best report is allowed out every night the week following. It never works like that; every squad is given the top marks at some stage. It is comforting to know they come around and make an inspection, a task seldom performed in B Battery. A free half day yesterday when I was able to collect photographs I ordered at a studio in Edinburgh, three copies of which I shall send you. I began looking around at ties for dad and discovered prices in the shops have gone up, the cost varies between 3/11 pence to 4/6 pence each. I have not yet used any of your clothing coupons I borrowed and am aware you will wish me to return them as soon as I can. It is almost 8.0pm, time to leave this letter to get changed ready for the dance tonight downstairs in the main hall at the barracks.

7 November

The day I had my photograph taken, the squad was confined to barracks with no duties scheduled for the whole day. It was such a nice day, a friend and I decided to go into town, taking the risk our absence would go unnoticed. In the light of day we were able to leave surreptitiously by the open area at the back of the barracks; throughout the hours of darkness it is fully protected and guarded by sentries. Crossing the training field in a lazy manner, with dress caps tucked out of sight inside our tunics to conceal our deception, we reached the outside lane to the main road without mishap, and boarded a tram to town.

After taking a leisurely walk around Edinburgh, looking in many of the shops and having my photograph taken, all the while fearful of being spotted by Red Caps, we decided, late in the afternoon, it was to time to return, mindful of an immediate problem. Before nightfall, a sentry would be posted at the rear of the barracks obstructing our only means of sneaking back inside. A decision was made to have tea, wait a while, and slip quietly into barracks during darkness taking care not to alert the night guard. We arrived back safely, having enjoyed a pleasant afternoon and early part of the evening in town, no one the wiser for our escapade.

I am in the N.A.A.F.I. with Ken, the friend with whom I had been out with for the day, waiting for a couple of A.T.S. girls to take to a dance nearby. We are C.B. tonight and must carefully play it smart to skip away. One of the girls pressed my trousers for me this afternoon; the other girl has a great voice and will be singing with the band at the dance. She has recently been invited to join a military unit of performers to entertain members of the armed forces.

8 November

A little before ten o'clock last night, I left the dance to get back to the barrack room in time for roll call. I loosened my tunic, threw a few things around on my bed and waited for the sergeant to come and check off the names on the duty rota. Fifteen minutes later, as soon as the sergeant had left the room, I rushed back to the dance hall buttoning my tunic on the way. It was nice, dancing most of the evening until midnight, without being missed.

13 November

I was on the main gate guard last Tuesday and got very little sleep. In the past it was a 24 hour guard duty; recently it has been reduced to 14 hours, interfering with a normal rest pattern of a few solid hours undisturbed sleep. Wednesday night (last night), I went dancing again in the nearby barracks; by 10.30 the recent lack of sleep began to tell on me. I slept through the night like a log, as the saying goes. This morning I was the last person out of bed, more often I am the second or third to be up and about.

I am sorry a few days have gone by without writing to you, occasionally I come into the N.A.A.F.I. with every intention to write a letter as I have tonight; sitting among friends talking, time slips easily away. Last night Ken and I brought pen and paper here, neither of us wrote a single word. I am waiting for him to join me to go to the canteen at Colinton.

My signal training is coming along fine, the many Morse, wireless signals, and symbols we learn will be the same Harry will use in his mob. In addition, we have special signals to relay fire orders to the guns.

18 November

We have the pleasure of a wireless in the barrack room and I am listening to the Intermezzo from Cavalliera Rusticana as I write. A squad posted to R.A. regiments after completing the signalling course, offered the wireless for sale when they left. All sixteen men in No3 squad clubbed together, each paying two shillings and sixpence towards the cost of the luxury item. There will be no trouble getting it repaired in this outfit with the abundance of wireless technicians available. During the 7.0am news broadcast we are attending roll call, making certain everyone is awake and out of bed. The roll call could never be called a parade, in the true sense of the word; we assemble in a dishevelled state. Later at 8 o'clock, we are fortunate to have an opportunity to listen to the radio and catch up on the war news.

Half day today gave me the chance to go into Edinburgh shopping for your ties, dad, I bought three in Woolworth's, a place I never thought to look for them. I chose two Scotch ties and another one that I rather like, making the choice for you and not myself. The Scotch ties each cost 1/6d, the third 2/9d; I also bought tie pins for 1/4d, making a total of 7/1d. I will pack the ties and tie pins, and send them by registered post. Tell me if you would like to have another tie, I could buy it with the 3 shillings left over from the money you gave me.

Uncle Joe turned up again at the barracks to meet me, unfortunately I had gone into town and nobody could tell him when I would be back. He left thinking he might by chance meet me in town, but I came back early to be given the news. The following weekend, midday Saturday until midnight Sunday, I get 36 hours leave. It is hardly time enough to spend at home. I may book a bed for the night at the N.A.A.F.I. in Edinburgh. I shall write to Uncle Joe telling him about my good luck. I have a date tonight with a Scottish A.T.S. girl and we are going to the dance in the Cavalry Barracks next door. I gave her one of my socks that needed darning; she said she would mend it for me.

At the end of this week we undergo our fourth big test to check progress, sending and receiving messages in Morse code by buzzer, by signal lamp, and procedures on signalling.

21 November, Saturday

Afternoon recreational training today was a gallop up the hills behind the barracks; for my short legs it was a challenge. I think the officer in charge is related to the ornithological ostrich. On arrival at the top I sat down to gaze at a magnificent view. I could see the Forth Bridge, the Firth of Forth, and miles away a light buoy flashing over the water. In the distance, windows of tiny houses glittered like stars reflecting light from the sun's rays. It has been a beautiful afternoon and although I have been there before, the scene was never as exhilarating as it was today.

Tonight at 5 o'clock I report for Fire Pump Crew, and again at 10 o'clock to sleep in the duty room. I am replacing someone from another squad who has been taken off the list; I'm the unlucky guy to get the job. We have to act the instant a fire alarm is sounded, and if by chance the officer's mess catches fire during the night, I could help to burn it down. The rest of my squad was on duty throughout the barracks, checking black-out precautions were in place, and found a dartboard left behind in an empty room where a squad had moved out. The Regimental choir is to hold a sing-song and concert on Wednesday at the canteen in Colinton, in my spare time today I produced a poster for the event.

I should like to write to Harry, would you please forward his new address, he must be feeling a little 'blue' leaving behind all the friends he has made. I am not clear why he has moved from his present unit, is he attending an N.C.O.'s course?

26 November

Fire Crew again tonight, I have been told officially this is a permanent job for me and I will not be expected to do any guard duties. Each time it comes around, I take my bedding into the duty room and almost certainly get a good night's sleep. I am looking forward to tomorrow when we will be taking three cable trucks, and three escort motorcycles, outside the barracks to learn cable laying techniques. I have been detailed to ride one of the motorcycles.

27 November

Thank you for the registered parcel packed with writing pad, cigarettes, sweets, cake and jam. The jar of jam I brought with me from leave I still enjoy. Ken had the same idea and returned with a pot of marmalade. At breakfast we share with each other taking turns to indulge.

I spent the morning riding a motorcycle dashing around the fields, negotiating difficult pathways and climbing hills near to the high point with the wonderful view of the Forth Bridge. My assignment was dispatch rider, happily enjoying myself during the cable laying exercise with the squad.

Thirty-six hours leave, 28 – 29 November. Leave pass, Edinburgh and Rosyth.

29 November Sunday, *Y.M.C.A. Dunfermline*

Last week I chose to visit Rosyth on a 36 hour leave pass, I knew there may be an opportunity to see Uncle Joe if his ship was in port, if not, I could spend my time in Edinburgh on the same pass.

Friday morning I received a letter from Uncle Joe saying he would meet me in Edinburgh on Saturday afternoon, he was granted leave from his ship until 8.0 the following morning, Sunday. I did not have to be back in the barracks until 11.0pm that same night. We met as arranged and straight away booked beds for the night in a forces canteen in Edinburgh. With accommodation arrangements completed we walked to Edinburgh Castle and climbed the battlements for a panoramic view of the city, the scene would have been more interesting if the day had been clearer. After tea we decided to see the film, *Gone With The Wind*; we were unlucky, the picture house was fully booked for ticket holders only. We chose another film to see before supper and it was half past midnight by the time we took to our beds.

Rising early at 6.0 o'clock, we went to the station to get the 7 o'clock train taking sailors with special passes straight into the restricted area of the dockyard. I did not have a dockyard pass and was refused permission to board the special train. An hour later I took the next train to Inverkeithing and was crossing the Forth Bridge as dawn was breaking. At Inverkeithing a bus took me to Dunfermline where I soon found the Y.M.C.A. to begin writing this letter, sharing the latest news about our adventures. Uncle Joe promised he would obtain a pass that would allow me to go aboard his ship, arranging I should meet him after lunch at the dockyard gates in Rosyth.

Continued later in barracks, the same day

At the dockyard gates I was handed a pass by one of Uncle Joe's shipmates and escorted aboard his ship. Uncle Joe was on duty and could not leave his post to meet me; once I was on board he was able to show me around. I spent a few wonderful hours with him seeing the extensive armament and guns she carried, the engines in the boiler room, and above all a very special privilege to be allowed inside the bridge. I had tea with the lads and sat with them peeling spuds preparing their dinner. One of the sailors was the ship's barber and trimmed my hair before saying goodbye to Uncle Joe and thanking the crew for a hearty welcome aboard their ship. I caught a train at 7.30 from Inverkeithing, and here I am in barracks concluding the events of a pleasant week-end leave before I hear the call, "Lights out!" It was an honour to have received such a warm welcome by the lads aboard a R.N. Fighting Ship[1], no name can be mentioned, 'Careless Talk Costs Lives'.

Would you please get me a sketching block, not too large, one that will fit into my pack, and post with it my lettering pen holder and lettering nibs?

3 December

Many Happy Returns mother, I know your birthday is coming soon and I hope you like the card I made for you, I would also like to turn out some Christmas cards for friends but I have very little spare time at the moment. I can visualise an idea for a suitable calendar for the girl that does my mending, she would appreciate something amusing about the A.T.S.

5 December

Thank you for the lettering pens and holder; I recognised what was in the envelope when I saw it. I began using the sketch block and find the paper is very good.

Sunday, 6 December

Yesterday each person had to give a lecture to the squad assessing our ability to speak to an audience; my subject was cable laying. The talks were to last 45 minutes, but as this was not possible during the lecture period, ten minutes only was the limit allotted to everyone.

Wednesday, I took Jean, the A.T.S. girl I have been dating to see a very good film, *The Spoilers*, showing at the Palace cinema, Princess Street. We had tea in a café before dancing at the Palais. The Palais is almost to the standard of the Tower Ballroom at Blackpool, with theatre organ too. Change over between two bands occurs on a revolving stage while couples are dancing to the music. Both bands play the same tune, except the musical arrangement of the new band is different in style as it emerges on the stage replacing the outgoing band. Around the dance area, tables and chairs are arranged to take comfort from dancing, and there is a balcony above where people can look down on the couples on the floor below.

8 December

I was pleased to receive Harry's letters you forwarded to me; now I know more about what he is doing I shall return the letters, and write to him as soon as I can.

I am getting along fine with my work, lamp reading, buzzer reading, radio telephony and the next is wireless telegraphy. I am reading 10s (ten words a minute), normal speed on the buzzer but we sometimes get messages faster than this. Pass out speed is 10 words a minute on

Morse buzzer, 6 on lamp, both these I have no trouble with. We have to repair the instruments if they go wrong like most jobs in the army. We use excellent wireless sets to communicate messages over the air, and to pass carefully plotted fire orders to the guns.

It seems only a couple of weeks since I came into this room to begin the signaller's full training course. There are five signal training regiments in the U.K. This regiment has the reputation to be the best. From here I could be sent anywhere like the Latin motto on my Royal Artillery badge, Ubique (everywhere).

12 December

The weather is dull and changeable, and the nights very cold; this morning was quite the opposite, the sun shining so brightly it was almost impossible to read the signalling lamp.

From Saturday last, until Thursday, it rained continuously and half a gale blowing at times. Thank you for the kind thought about gloves, I have a pair I wear every day on parade and to keep my fingers warm for sending messages by signal lamp in the field. They were issued to me in the Home Guard and never handed in when I left. A month ago the army gave me a new pair that has not been used.

17 December

I shall write as often as I can in the coming week, swatting will occupy every bit of spare time. This morning we were asked if we would like pass out test the day before Christmas Day, or the day afterwards, we all chose the day before, one week today. Two fellows from No1 squad, two weeks ahead of us, failed the classification test last week. They were relegated to join our squad to take the test again. Our wireless has conked out, I think a valve has failed, the squad sergeant said he would fix it.

We received good news yesterday, we could have a short leave pass from 5.30pm on the 24th, to 11.0pm on the 25th, alternatively, the same hours from the 31st, to the 1st; we chose New Year. We shall by then have been classified, anyone not successful is automatically relegated to the next squad. The R.A. is in urgent need of signallers, which may affect future decisions to turn out as many newly trained operators as possible.

This morning we underwent a test covering the first eight weeks training; tomorrow I expect the officer will confront us chewing our ears with the results. After our final test we will carry on revising during the last two weeks, all those who have been successful will be standing by, waiting to be posted to a Royal Artillery Field Regiment, and well earned leave.

21 December

The test results came in this morning, two of us share second place with 75%, Ken on top with 80% and we are busy revising for the final test on Thursday. Four lads at the blackboard are establishing W.T. communications, one chap next to me on a S.U.C. 10 line switchboard (telephone exchange), and under my nose someone fault finding on an S.D.S.R. lamp. The sergeant asked me if the lads at the blackboard have got it right. "Yes they have," I told him.

$$\bullet - \quad \quad - - \quad \bullet \quad \bullet - \bullet \quad \bullet - \bullet \quad - \bullet - -$$
$$- \bullet \bullet - \quad - - \quad \bullet - \quad \bullet \bullet \bullet \quad \quad (A \ M E R R Y \ X M A S)$$

25 December, Friday

All the classification exams were taken yesterday. Lamp reading test in the morning was an ordeal with the wind blowing hard, and before long it started to rain turning to mist in the strong wind. Our officer decided to call off the test and try later. Again the weather was almost as bad but we carried on doing the best we could. My writer taking down messages I was reading recorded 100% accuracy on many of the messages, the highest score is the one accepted for the final results of the test.

The lads were singing carols this morning while making up their beds. It feels like Christmas, but nothing can compare it with the festivities at home. For breakfast we had fried egg, fried tomatoes, bacon and marmalade. Christmas dinner was the traditional menu, roast potatoes, sprouts, pork, turkey, stuffing and gravy. Xmas pudding was first-rate. The colonel gave a short speech and dinner was served by officers and sergeants dashing around, at the same time handing out bottles of beer. During dinner the Regimental band was playing carols, *sticking out* – as the accompaniment might best be described. Still feeling the after effects of Christmas dinner, I did not go to the dining hall for the evening meal of boiled ham, pickles, mince pies, Xmas cake and much, much more that was being served.

At the dance last night there were too many people on the floor before midnight, when the crowd thinned there was more room for dancing until 1.30 in the morning, One of the lads who was quite sober gave me a shot of whisky that would fill about three thimbles, knowing I cared little for it but thinking it would not be Christmas without tasting a tot. Tomorrow night I must not miss the dance to be held in the Cavalry barracks. The squad is C.B. today, with satisfaction knowing the duty should not again come around New Year's Eve when there may be a dance, or concert in the barracks.

27 December, Sunday

Just back from church parade and we are expected to begin revising once again, I expect there will be very little work done today. The squad has achieved 100% passes, crossed flags badges, white and blue signaller's badges were handed out to stitch on our sleeve.

30 December

There have been schemes every day this week. Yesterday I was riding a motorcycle, today driving one of the cable laying trucks, tomorrow I shall again be riding a motorcycle. Not many in the squad care to drive either lorry, or motorbike, which gives me the advantage to enjoy both. I believe we have the whole day free New Year's Day; I shall spend the morning in bed if the major does not catch me. Cheerio, and a Very Happy New Year to all.

− 1943 −

3 January

The first snow of winter began falling on the morning of New Year's Day, melting as it reached the ground. During the afternoon it changed to rain and as night fell began to freeze. Yesterday morning it was snowing again, three inches deep by midday. The squad was on a training exercise using a signalling lamp; gradually the snow fell heavier and the lamp faded as a star at dawn, making it impossible to read any further messages. The surrounding hills are covered with snow transforming the scene into a wonderland picture of winter. Last night I stood on the barrack room balcony, and as I was shaving watched for a while the transformation of a brilliant orange and grey sunset.

No1 squad finished training two weeks ahead of us and some of the lads are being posted today. They are joining a Royal Artillery Field Regiment in Essex. The remainder is going home on leave tomorrow and will be posted to Regiments when they return. If I end up in the same situation without immediate posting, I could be home on leave in about two weeks.

The squad has been hard at work this afternoon shifting snow from the parade ground, a crazy idea that has worsened the situation, making the surface very slippery. The Orderly Officer on his rounds last night, one minute after lights out, found the lights on in our barrack room and decided to make snow shifting a fitting punishment. This has all the

signs of a 'fix', an easy way to find a solution to clear the parade ground
of snow. I was operating the telephone exchange last night and knew
nothing about the incident until I came off duty.

7 January

The A.T.S. girls are C.B. tonight as always on Thursday, not allowed to
visit the N.A.A.F.I., they are expected to do mending and other chores.
Jean has borrowed my fountain pen, the reason I am writing this letter in
pencil, she is meeting me later to return it. I may go to the pictures to see
the film, *Mrs. Miniver*. The correct thing I ought to do would be to sort
out the priority of replies to letters I should be writing instead.

Tomorrow morning, once again more fun on the road driving vehicles
and communicating using wireless sets.

12 January

I have been operating the telephone exchange this morning, and coming
off duty I managed to hide away until the squad were well occupied doing
physical training, before sneaking into the barrack room to write letters.
There is no longer a rigorous training programme keeping us busy; we
spend each day doing odd jobs about the place. If nothing worth while
can be found for us to do, periods of rifle drill, or marching parades are
organized to keep us amused.

I did not sort out my correspondence last night as planned, I offered
to help out one of the lads who was broke and took him to the pictures
to see the film, *Mrs. Miniver*. It was one of the best films I have seen
recently. I bought chips for us to eat on our way back to the barracks, a
warming comfort on a cold night out.

14 January

Yesterday morning and again at night, I was on R.P. duty, standing
at the main gates of the barracks, wearing a red arm band with large
letters R P, and carrying a baton under my arm with authority. When not
checking all comers entering the gates, or answering enquiries, I spent
quiet moments in the nearby guard room.

Leave for the whole squad has been arranged to begin one week
tomorrow, Friday, January 22nd. This will be granted only if I am here
waiting to be posted to a regular Royal Artillery unit.

CHAPTER 3

Posted to a Regiment

178 Field Regiment R.A., Felixstowe, Suffolk

The order to report to a Royal Artillery Field Regiment as a fully qualified O.P. (Observation Post) signaller came suddenly out of the blue; I had no opportunity to write a letter home warning my parents about my new posting to an active army unit.

19 January, Tuesday

I expect my posting will be a shock to you as it is to me. I am travelling on a train taking me to a new destination and a perfectly good reason for using pencil, trying my utmost to scribble a legible letter. At the present moment the train is halted at Bury St. Edmunds, I think the next station is Ipswich where I must change trains to take me to my new Regiment at Felixstowe in Suffolk. A group from my squad, together with others from another squad, left Edinburgh last night about ten o'clock. We have been travelling throughout the night for more than twelve hours with no confirmation of the time we are expecting to arrive. Our carriages have been reserved which helps to make the long journey comfortable.

On Sunday night, it was rumoured there was to be a big posting the next day, I never for one moment thought I would be on it. A number of lads were left behind from other squads, along with six men from my squad up to letter F, making a total of sixteen men on the draft. Please warn all the folks at home and relatives, about my move. Letters turning up at Edinburgh will be redirected. It is midday, and at this very moment the train has arrived at Ipswich station.

19 January, *a later letter*

We reached Felixstowe at 2.0pm and everything so far is fine. The Battery is billeted in one part of the town, in private houses vacated by the owners, or the properties may have been requisitioned because of their proximity to a defensive coastline near the sea.

This afternoon, everyone on the new intake had a personal interview with the Battery major who promised to grant leave from next Monday, the 25th. My billet where I sleep is the house next door to the main Post Office, and mail is collected at 5.30 every evening from the office. Tea will be ready in ten minutes, afterwards, what remains of the day I shall spend taking a brief look at the new surroundings where I am living.

Here is my address, classed as a Signaller (Sig), not a Gunner (Gnr).

B Troop, 366 Battery
178 Field Regiment R.A.
Felixstowe
Suffolk

20 January

My first night and morning has gone down well. Felixstowe looks a nice place, but I am afraid the Regiment will not be here for much longer. Tell Harry I will be home on Monday, he should try to get leave to join me so that we might spend a few days together. The Battery occupies several empty properties, I am living in a combined shop and house with many rooms, located on a main road into the centre of town. We also occupy the house next door.

Last night I walked to the sea front with a fellow from Edinburgh, and stood for a moment listening to the waves breaking on the shore. We heard the sound of a band playing coming from a hall, and looking inside, saw people dancing to the music. Feeling worn out after a long overnight journey we decided not to stay. Every evening we can pop into town, except when on guard duty, and some of our new batch could be picked for guard tomorrow night. I attended a sick parade this afternoon for the usual health check-up, and I should get paid soon having received none for more than a week.

21 January

You can expect me home Monday around tea time! I shall be leaving Felixstowe by train at 7 o'clock in the morning along with other lads. I hope to reach Manchester around 4 o'clock, and change there to catch a train that takes me directly home to the railway station at Church.

Life in Felixstowe is OK, except the whole place is dead compared to Edinburgh, most of the local population has moved away. It is no more than about five minutes easy walking to reach the promenade and sea shore, taking a pleasant stroll there each night beneath a lovely moonlit sky, fascinated, watching and listening to the waves caressing the beach. On Tuesday and Wednesday, I passed away the evenings dancing; tonight I shall go to see a picture show. Tomorrow night, if I have no duties, I shall again be dancing at the Pier Pavilion where the dance floor is not to the standard at the Cavendish, a neighbouring dance hall.

Since arriving here there have been three air raid warnings, yesterday at dinner time, again at night, and during dinner today. A.A. guns are constantly firing at the German bombers flying overhead, crossing the coast to drop their destructive cargo on important targets further inland. My first readdressed letter arrived today; it was from Jean at Redford barracks. I pray that tomorrow will bring a letter from you. I hope you are all OK, with Major in the best of health and happy to greet me when I turn up on Monday.

23 January, Saturday

I do not intend making this a long letter, I shall be home the same day you receive it. I have collected a travel warrant to cover me for the journey, also full pay for the days of my leave. I shall have the company of a pal on the train with me as far as Manchester. Don't plan to take Major out for a walk about the time I am expected to arrive home.

Embarkation leave with my parents, 25 January – 7 February.

7 February

I was back in Felixstowe at 11.20 last night and collected my blankets from the stores. We began picking up more of our boys along the journey as the train moved further south; by the time we got to London there was a crowd of us, and more lads joined us at Ipswich. I enjoyed the sandwiches you packed for me, eating them all with the help of the boys.

This morning I underwent the usual medical inspection. I was issued with a new uniform; it was just my luck handing in battle dress recently dry cleaned while at home on leave.

10 February

At last I have found time to write to you in peace, in the canteen. There has always been something to keep me busy this week. I told you we had been issued with new kit and there are a few minor items which we shall collect as soon as they arrive in the store. I am making packing boxes, and attending lectures about our move. Tonight there was a parade to get the boxes that are packed, loaded and sent away.

As I came off night guard this morning I scrambled around quickly getting organized for an early inspection of the billets by the B.C., leaving no time to roll my gas cape and place it in the small pack we carry. The ends of the cape must be visible, mine was conspicuous by its absence and the B.C. did not notice, or trouble to ask where it was. He discovered my water bottle was not in the correct place when he picked up my pack. If he had looked inside the pack, he would have found several items that should not have been in there. It contained sketching blocks, pastels, paint brushes, a tin of cigarettes, knife fork and spoon; a real junk bag. When he lifted the pack, the contents produced the same metallic sound mess tins would make had they been inside, appearing to satisfy his curiosity. At 9.30 the Battery endured a thorough battle order inspection, standing on parade wearing full equipment until well past eleven o'clock before being dismissed. It was in preparation for a visit by the O.C. on Friday, to be certain we are correctly dressed when we leave here. It would be too late arriving abroad to discover equipment at fault, or not in the best order. A few things came to light that prompted a change.

I was called to the Battery office tonight and found the sergeant holding my letter to the O.C. requesting a transfer for Harry to serve alongside me in my unit. I noticed a typed slip had been attached to the top of the letter with the word, *URGENT*, written in red. The sergeant assured me it would normally go through without any trouble, but time is the governing factor and there is precious little time left. He told me to advise Harry to endorse the application right away, there was nothing more to be done at this end. I am sure it will not be long before we leave and unless Harry can get things moving quickly, it will be too late.

14 February, Sunday

I visited Auntie Molly on a short one day pass and to my surprise found Uncle Arnold was home for the weekend. It may seem expensive for the limited time I was allowed, never the less, very enjoyable. I autographed a photograph and gave it to her.

Is Harry aware he must apply to his office requesting a transfer to my unit to get all the details processed officially? However, it is up to him to act quickly at this late stage to achieve any chance of success, I was told there is little hope because he is a specialist at his job. You will have to be satisfied with this short note until I can tell you more.

16 February

Last Saturday I wrote myself a pass and got it signed for the next day from reveille Sunday to 2359 hours, hoping to visit Auntie Molly at

Woodley. With Saturday afternoon free, I straight away headed for the railway station fully aware I would need my wits about me carrying a pass not yet valid, if I was to avoid trouble with Red Caps. All went well travelling from Felixstowe crossing London to another station to catch a train to take me to Reading. Calmly strolling onto the station at Paddington I was immediately confronted by a guy about 6 feet tall wearing a bright red hat, a white stripe on his sleeve, red armband with distinctive letters MP, looking down on me asking to see my pass. I tried to look innocent as he questioned why the pass was not yet in date. I replied with convincing answers telling him I had been allowed to leave that afternoon because of the length of my journey. He evidently thought my snappy answers genuine, handing back my pass as we parted.

I got to Reading at ten o'clock that evening and found the last bus for Woodley had left half an hour earlier. The only option was to start walking, arriving at the house an hour later. Approaching the back door I could hear someone working on a car in the garage, it was too dark to know who it might be. When I knocked on the door, the person in the garage shone a torch on me as I moved inside the kitchen without getting any answer. Passing to the living room I could hear Auntie Molly talking to friends. In response to more knocking she said, "We are not in!" Without saying a word I stepped inside the room to be confronted by an expression of complete surprise. Her sarcastic response was to Uncle Arnold she thought was knocking on the door. Uncle Arnold had shone the torch, and she asked if he had not recognized me? He replied, "How can I know who comes to see you when I am away?" A remark that caused a great deal of laughter from everyone in the room.

I have been cleaning my rifle I test fired yesterday, we have each been issued with a weapon, a rifle, Sten gun, or pistol.

20 February

I heard someone asking for me when I was upstairs in the bathroom having a bath, from below a reply came back saying I had gone out. Hearing this I gave a loud roar and asked, "Who is calling, and what do you want?" It was quite funny, nobody knew from where my shout had come, until I said I was in the bath. Standing in my birthday suit with one foot in the bath, a guy at the door asked to check my number before handing me a telegram. The message came from Harry's office saying the transfer was going through. Learning the good news at this late stage filled me with happiness, afraid to build my hopes too high. I can not be sure the transfer to my unit would happen until I see him here with me, in person. A letter from Harry this morning said he was to have an interview with his O.C.; the future outlook to join me has improved.

During the time I was on duty in the cookhouse, I could not be present on pay parade, consequently, I had to collect my pay from the sergeant in the Battery Office. When I gave him my name he looked at me and said, "Oh, you are the fellow asking for a transfer for your brother, why you should ever want him to join us I can not think?" When I told him Harry was with an armoured division, he rightly agreed with me. The cookhouse job is great for a day, not like some of the chores which are detested. I was feeding my face the whole time. There are few spare moments, and the cookhouse is not near to my billet, with little chance to slip away to write letters. I am reminded you asked in one of your letters about the quality of food we are served, I can tell you it is good, equal to the meals at Redford Barracks; perhaps even better. At Redford it was pleasing to be served by the A.T.S. girls during mealtimes, and the spacious dining hall was never overcrowded. Everything linked with the Battery operates on a much smaller scale, a lesser number of men to feed and fewer cooks making the best use of rations we are issued.

My group were to been given 48 hour passes this weekend; one fellow who never returned from a break last week provided a good excuse not to grant the passes.

21 February, Sunday

We have no parades today and nothing special to do. I woke about 8.30 lying in bed until forcibly ejected about 45 minutes later by a couple of the lads. After two more disruptions I realized it was useless to get back into bed, the treatment would have continued. I was good fun, and I was not the only one dealt with in this manner. A lance bombardier suffered the same fate. Too late for breakfast, I managed to get something to eat in the Y.M.C.A.

Last night we had a flurry of action around Felixstowe, air raid sirens blaring loud wailing notes and the roaring engines of Gerry bombers overhead, which is not the least unusual on this part of the coastline. The A.A. guns were quickly in action, adding accompaniment to the awful racket repeatedly firing at the planes sending lines of glowing tracers high into the night sky. Unfortunately, I did not witness any direct hits on enemy targets.

Some of the lads who earlier were on embarkation leave are due again for leave. If we are to be here a while longer I may get lucky to enjoy five days leave, every extra day holds a better chance Harry may be in time to join me. We could be serving abroad together for three years, which may seem an awful long time but, it would be comforting for both of us.

23 February

Tomorrow the Battery is going on a route march in full battle order, a diversion the B.C. has introduced to keep us active and pass away time. One chap is moaning, "What do they think we are; this is the artillery not the infantry!"

This afternoon I have been learning to drive a Bren gun carrier, a small open top tank with tracks, I also operate the communication wireless in this sardine tin. The vehicle is mainly used at an O.P. to observe enemy targets, send instructions to the guns directing and correcting the fall of shot. You get more thrills than riding the Big Dipper on the fairground, romping around the countryside, ripping branches off trees or taking half the hedgerow along for a ride. It is very different to driving a Jeep or army truck, painfully uncomfortable, a warm job during cold weather, broiling you alive on a hot day.

Thank you for writing a note to the Observer newspaper reminding them I am a smoker still, I received from them a tin of 40 cigarettes. Be careful if you send more telegrams, the last one came about 7 o'clock in the evening, I might easily have crept away from my billet without informing the guard room and that could have caused me to answer awkward questions.

25 February

Harry's letter yesterday brought me cheerless news saying everything about the transfer was flat, I felt sorry to tears having to accept the outcome as the final answer.

Almost everyone in the Battery undertook a gruelling route march yesterday; more than half the fellows reported sick with foot trouble and my feet are in a pretty poor state as a result. The soldiers of 366 Battery are easily identified by the impediment in their gait ambling around the streets of Felixstowe.

This morning I was messing about with the Bren carrier again, learning about the engine and carrying out maintenance on various parts. I shall be driving tomorrow; the sergeant has promised to scare us showing us what this hulk of metal can really do. Once I was ready to bale out when we were in a precarious situation, I shall be prepared to do the same tomorrow if the need arises. I must pass a driving test and maintenance course on the Bren gun carrier as I did on lorries, and motorcycles.

We shall be here another couple of weeks at least; quoting the proverb, 'Wait and see are not words of progress,' explaining our true situation. I must blanco my gaiters and then to bed.

28 February

After attending church parade we have the rest of the day to ourselves. Some of the lucky lads living in London are again visiting home today. I mentioned Harry had written to tell me the transfer had been called off, he was afraid if he pressed the case harder they would move me, and I would end up with him in his mob. There is no chance that could happen. Perhaps Harry is not aware that a brother can not request an older sibling to join him, and I would not be taken off an overseas draft close to leaving.

I am surprised I am not black and blue all over my body, receiving several hard knocks bouncing about on rough ground, driving the Bren gun carrier during the last couple of days. One of the chaps made a truthful remark, "We haven't much money but we do see life!" Driving on a smooth road surface in traffic adds confidence, fully aware any vehicle you might come in contact with would be the one to suffer in an accident. So far I am doing pretty well with my driving, only once did I have a mishap when I smashed a cast iron drainpipe attached to a house, fortunately the wall is still standing. It was a lovely bright sunny day yesterday, driving along Felixstowe promenade in the carrier was a pleasing sensation, like being on holiday. The tide was high and a light sea breeze caressed the waves along the shore. Wearing a cricket shirt instead of army battle dress would have topped the bill. Friday we were given an unusual exciting job, driving the Bren carrier to Ipswich to collect a double bass, and mute for a trumpet, instruments needed by the band for a farewell dance. Folks along the route stared in wonderment and disbelief at a group of soldiers loose on the road behaving like a troupe of circus clowns. A jovial mob of khaki clad men clinging to an unmistakable big double bass poking high in the air on top of a Bren gun carrier, skidding around corners and dodging cars. Tomorrow is a restricted non travel day to economize on fuel, and carry out maintenance on vehicles.

1 March

I am building up hope to stay here a little longer when I learned a Battery in the Regiment allowed a group of lads home for a short break. A few days leave is beginning to look promising, I'm waiting to hear the slightest whisper of a rumour it might happen.

I have been doing maintenance on the Bren carrier the whole day, tomorrow I will be driving again with perhaps one or two scars to display on my anatomy. A special farewell dance for the whole Regiment has been arranged to take place tonight at the Pier Pavilion; wives and girl friends of the many lads living in and around London will be coming.

5 March

Thanks a million mother for your parcel and the 10 shilling note enclosed. I am away to the shooting range this afternoon to fire my rifle; it may be late when I get back. I was called to the office on Wednesday and told to expect Harry at any time, his transfer has gone through.

7 March, Sunday

We had another route march last Thursday; the lovely blisters on my heels are valid proof of the suffering I endured. The lads had a great laugh when I fell into a river; witnesses to the calamity have been pulling my leg. We were returning from an exercise tramping across a vast area of fenlands, following difficult narrow tracks skirting ponds, and wading through streams very often ankle deep in mud. Crossing one of the rivulets required an energetic leap to reach the other side. The tall guys managed to cross easily, several others landed with one foot in the water, short guys got both feet wet. Someone found a discarded pole from an old bell tent and placed it across the stream to the other bank. I started acting crazy, pretending to crawl across with never any intention of doing so. One fellow placed his foot on the opposite end of the pole. Screaming loudly not to step on it, my cry was unheeded, 'snap – splash!' The extra weight was more than the rotten wood could support and I was flung face down into the stream. I bent to pick up my rifle, water gushing from the two empty ammunition pouches fastened to my belt. In spite of the discomfort endured trudging waterlogged back to my billet, I saw the funny side of the incident.

Friday morning I reported on sick parade with pride, showing the M.O. a nice set of blisters on of my feet. He proceeded to burst each one in turn, and to my pleasure placed me on light duties, excused wearing boots. He said I must report to him again tomorrow when I know he will pass me fit for duty and the short period of bliss will come to an end. I was to have been on guard tonight, placing me on the sick list will surprise a poor unsuspecting soul to take up the duty for me.

There has been spells of nice weather recently, but a change last night when it decided to rain. Coming out of doors this morning on my way to breakfast I found ice on the surface of the roads. The condition did not persist for long, all traces of the frost quickly disappeared.

Commemorative photographs of the whole Battery were taken recently as a lasting souvenir; two prints have been well packed and ready to send home. One of the photographs portrays the whole group of soldiers in 366 Field Battery, the other shows the lads in my section, B Troop. Separate photos were taken of each Troop in the Battery. I wrote a letter to Uncle Fred a fortnight ago, purposely not giving my address because

the long delay exchanging letters would cause problems. I have heard
nothing further about Harry's move or any indication I may be given
home leave. That is all the news I have for you at this moment.

8 March, Monday
Very important information. The Regiment will be leaving Felixstowe
on Thursday night is all I have time to tell you, letters in future are to be
addressed to me as follows:-
B Troop, 366 Field Battery
178 Field Regiment R.A.
c/o A.P.O.4055

10 March, Wednesday
We have been busy preparing for a final inspection before leaving
tomorrow. There is no news of Harry. I know nothing more about plans
that have been made; his position is being held open. A report must go
into the office tonight. There is yet one more day, if Harry turns up at
the last minute I am sure he will be found a suitable position and made
welcome.

The regiment was moved by train to Liverpool Docks where we embarked
on a troop ship, destination unknown.

13 March   *On board a Troop ship prior to sailing*
Tonight I intend getting out my sketch pad, before this war is over there
will be plenty of opportunities to draw portraits; many of the lads would
willingly sit for me. Please send Harry my best wishes and tell him I am
sorry he did not get here. I was so much looking forward to seeing him.
Unfortunately, expectations in life do not always run to plan, I must be
content accepting events as they come. I am quite happy, don't worry
about me, I shall be thinking of you wherever I am.

CHAPTER 4

Sailed from Liverpool

We sailed from Liverpool on Cunard White Star Line, MV *Britannic*, a converted luxury liner crewed by the Merchant Navy and lascars, accommodating a large contingent of military personnel. The *Britannic* joined a convoy of ships under the protection of the Royal Navy, bound for an undisclosed destination, frequently changing course to avert attacks from German submarines and aircraft. At night, strict wartime black-out conditions were enforced; no lights, no talking, and no smoking allowed on the outside decks. From this point onwards, until the final days of the war, all letters were scrutinized to pass strict censorship regulations, with every page initialled by the examining officer. The envelope was then sealed and overprinted with an official stamp to confirm the letter had been inspected.

    March   *AT SEA*
It is a lovely evening writing this letter on deck somewhere at sea, knowing it may not be long before we put into a port where it will be posted. Life has felt lonely, each day passing without receiving news from home. I see only a blur of words where I write and soon it will be dark.

    I have moved below to the mess deck adding a few more lines before hearing the call for 'Lights out,' ready to sling my hammock and climb into it. I find sleeping in a hammock comfortable, but very different to lying on a bed. Throwing yourself into it requires a special technique, easily mastered with practice. The body conforms to the protective shroud like a row of peas in a pod. Sleeping in a hammock becomes less of a novelty and more like a habit. Some lads hate them, saying they are uncomfortable. I have no trouble sleeping. Only once have I been sea-sick, wishing to escape the torture, you feel like jumping into the sea. I was soon relieved of the horrible feeling, certain in my mind the misery of one such experience prepared me for any rough weather we might encounter ahead.

Continued later

Today the sun has been shining gloriously, turning the exposed skin of many lads bright red. I try to keep out of the sun as much as possible. I am sure we shall see lots more of it; too much no doubt. Walking along a ship's passageway I recognized someone I knew, it was Tom Walton, his home is in Rhyddings Street and he was employed at the Co-op. How surprised we both were. He has been asking about everyone. I am sure I shall see a lot more of him during the time we expect to spend on board confined within the limits of the ship. I know you will be wondering where I am and what I am doing, don't worry, I am OK and thinking of you all. Give my very best wishes to all relatives; tell grandma she is not forgotten, I shall write to her soon.

We anchored at Freetown, West Africa, and stood off shore for a few hours taking on water and fresh supplies.

April   *AT SEA*

Again writing to you knowing we shall eventually reach another port where there will be an opportunity to post more news about my exploits. The letter handed to the censor at our first port of call will be on the way to you, calming your worst fears when you read I am in good health and telling briefly the first part of my sea journey went well. In this letter too, I can say everything so far has passed OK, except for the blazing heat of a tropical sun. I now know what it is like to sweat from morn till night. Travelling further on our way, the temperature each day becomes a little more bearable.

We have been told we will be allowed shore leave at the next stop, I shall be extremely happy to put my feet on dry land to enjoy a pleasant break. A great deal of my time has been spent sketching portraits of the lads, without any need to look around for orders. I have drawn many portraits on this ship, maybe more than during the whole of my life, bringing in a fair amount of cash. There are orders in hand from lads begging me to copy photographs of girl friends. Copying photographs is not the type of drawing I like to do, but I comply, carrying on the good work to please them.

Since my first accidental meeting with Tom Walton I have seen him several times.

After disembarking, the Battery was given the task of searching Italian prisoners of war captured in North Africa. The prisoners were waiting to board the ship on which we had arrived. A number of men in my unit were regularly spaced at intervals in a long straight line inside a loading shed on the docks. A group of Italian prisoners were brought in and ordered to stand facing a soldier. Every prisoner, and the small amount of belongings each was allowed to carry, was thoroughly searched for matches, knives, dangerous or suspicious objects. If any were found they were confiscated. When the line had been checked and cleared, a new group would march into the shed to undergo the same procedure. Hundreds of prisoners were quickly dealt with in this way. Many Italians appeared joyful to be out of the war. When we found family photographs in their belongings, they became excited trying to explain with signs and gestures whom the relatives were. We had been warned not to fraternize, but treat them with respect. There was never any hostility towards us and we carried out the job successfully without incident. This fascinating event dealing with captured enemy prisoners would have made a great story in a letter, but censorship regulations forbid any mention of the occurrence.

The Regiment was billeted in a transit camp, on a sandy plain at Pollsmoor, 9 miles from Cape Town. Trains from a nearby station at Retreat provided a regular service with connections to travel around Cape Peninsular. A Jewish family that escaped persecution by the Nazis and settled in Muizenberg offered me open house. I often spent a whole day enjoying their hospitality and excellent meals. The younger of their two daughters was an exceptional dancer and we spent many evenings together dancing. Life was idyllic; no black-out restrictions, food plentiful, delicious fresh fruit and jams, shops displaying all manner of goods for sale. It was an experience none of us had enjoyed for almost two years. However, we were fully aware the present lifestyle was very different from the obligations we were to face in the future.

21 April *AIRGRAPH microfilm printout*
I am very much thinking of you today as I know you will be thinking of me, everything is fine; my 21st birthday is being spent visiting Cape Town. I don't know how long we expect to stay in South Africa; I shall try to write to you whenever I can. I hope Harry spends his birthday well, give him my best wishes and also the rest of the family.

An airgraph was a letter form 10 x 8 inches in size, specially printed to expedite and ease the flow of correspondence with people overseas during the Second World War. The letters were copied onto microfilm and forwarded in bulk to be printed 5 x 4 inches, and then folded and sealed in a window envelope with the recipients address visible. The message had to be clearly written within the confined borders on a single sheet of paper, with the address legibly printed in a rectangular box at the top of the form. One airgraph was issued each week to personnel serving overseas. The service began in 1941 and was discontinued on 31 July 1945.

25 April   *AMERICAN CLUB For Service Men – headed notepaper*
In England you may be thinking of taking Major out for a walk unless you are having the usual April showers, that is the sort of weather here today, similar to an English spring and not the least bit cold. I am living like a king. We enjoy almost anything you can not get, and I could fill you with envy telling the amount of fruit I have eaten. Four pence for a bunch of grapes, by the time you have got through eating half the bunch you can not manage to eat the rest. We were allowed out of camp this morning; I went to Cape Town and had a meal in one of the many canteens. For the price of 9d I got two fried eggs, sausages, chips, bacon, bread, butter and coffee. The sweet was a treat you have forgotten ever existed, a bowl of fruit salad.

Far away from home during the past weeks my biggest disappointment is the same for all, not a single word from anyone since leaving England. I could spend time writing every day, receiving in return answers to my letters in one large bundle to confuse my mind.

My 21st birthday was spent like any other day, each minute my thoughts were for everybody at home. I know you would have been thinking of me. Harry was not forgotten on his birthday, the 23rd. I hope he will be able to spend his 21st birthday in style, the war over and him wearing civvies. I treated myself to a wrist watch, something I very much longed to own, never finding one to my satisfaction at home. The watch I bought is manufactured by a famous Swiss firm, has a rolled gold case, stainless steel back and 15 jewels movement. With it comes a 20 years guarantee, for what use that could prove to be. I paid £4-10 shillings with money earned sketching portraits on board ship, and consider the rewards well spent.

Has grandma joined the land army yet? If not, tell her the service claims to improve the figure. If she found there was a marked change it could be used to attract many more women to enrol than they could cope with! Give her my love. Cheerio and God bless you all.

28 April   *AIRGRAPH microfilm printout*
After writing my letter last Sunday, a local resident invited a friend and me to supper at their home, a visit we both thoroughly enjoyed. We were

told we would be welcome at any time to call and see them again. The people of Cape Town are very friendly and hospitable; trying hard to do all they can to make our stay a pleasant one.

5 May *AIRGRAPH microfilm printout*
I have received no mail to which I might reply, fully aware no one is to blame for the predicament, I shall find something to tell you in a longer letter later. The season in South Africa is moving slowly towards winter, in England you will be looking forward to summer weather approaching steadily.

May
I do not expect to get much of this letter written tonight, I am in the camp canteen waiting for a picture show to begin. I came early to get a good seat and brought along my writing pad. Life is as enjoyable as ever in Cape Town except for receiving not a word from anyone since we sailed from England.

We are getting plenty of exercise walking on the hills surrounding the camp. A couple of days ago we set out to climb a mountain about the same height as Table Mountain and what a magnificent sight we saw before us when we reached the top. I only wish I could have sat there painting the whole scene. It was a beautiful view in brilliant colours, the entire Cape Peninsular visible, below my eye line there was a long trail of white cloud above the sea on the distant horizon.

I promised you this letter some time ago, never getting a chance to write until now. Most of my spare time has been spent visiting a family living not far from the camp. I was with them the whole day last Sunday, from a little after eleven in the morning until 9.30 at night. It was an unusual feeling sitting comfortably in a private house away from army routine, almost like being at home. I was offered tea immediately I arrived and enjoyed an excellent lunch, tea and supper. The family told me to visit them any time I wish. I heard the news broadcast over the radio from London while I was there. Half day free tomorrow, if I am not chosen for duty I shall once more call on my new friends as soon as I am handed my pass. I make no arrangements and go there whenever I please. I am afraid if I carry on writing I shall find myself in darkness with the picture showing on the screen. Cheerio for now.

We embarked on the troop ship SS *Orbita*, built by Harland and Wolff, Belfast. The ship was launched in July 1914, converted to a troop ship in 1941, and broken up at Newport, Monmouthshire, in 1950.

Continued at sea

A fair amount of distance and time separates the full stop placed at the end of the first part of my letter and the beginning of this sentence. Every reason I can provide for this happening is in my favour. A couple of days after starting this letter, before I could finish and post it, came news we were to be ready to move immediately. I am on board a different ship somewhere at sea. Everyone took advantage of the wonderful days spent in Cape Town free from the war, waiting to embark on the next stage of our journey. It will bring gladness when we finally reach our destination. Every moment in South Africa was like a holiday amid pleasant surroundings and wonderful people. Almost everything one could wish for except an opportunity to wear civilian clothes. I made many friends in Cape Town, talking for hours to the family I was friendly with about everyone at home and how much I longed to be there.

It is very warm down here on the mess deck; the deterioration in my writing is due to the rolling of the ship and clammy hands sticking to the paper. I am missing your letters, hoping I shall receive news from you as soon as we get to the end of our journey. Many times my thoughts wander as I try to imagine what each of you is doing at that moment, I am sure there are times I could not be very wrong. I must not write more, I see hammocks being strung up all around me it is time for shut eye and snore. The watch I bought is going well and keeping good time.

CHAPTER 5

Arrival in India

The following story of the interesting sights and customs that greeted me on my arrival into Bombay was written over the course of the next year and finally sent home on 2 April 1944.

My First Day in India – Bombay

It was midday when we sailed into the calmer waters of an Indian harbour, the sun at its zenith shedding full rays of heat as we crowded in the shade peering over the hand rail at this foreign land. What was in store for us, what mysteries, pleasures, and eventually what devils of war would we meet? This we would know and perhaps all too soon. We had been told many stories about India by lascars on the troop ship, happily alarming us boasting about what we might be expected to endure. We put all these tales aside knowing we would comprehend the truth, seeking for ourselves the experience and knowledge of all that is embraced by the crest of India, her Star.

Our voyage was quite different from any cruise expected of luxury liners, and we were sailing on board luxury liners, famous vessels requisitioned for the duration of the war and refitted to transport troops. It would not be fitting to describe the downhearted feelings felt by everyone during our sea journey, the discomforts we suffered, or to say we were at any time happy or joyful. We were confined to cramped quarters in a hulk of steel for weeks on end, completely isolated from the outside world with sparse news about the progress of the war. The horizon was always the sea, with vessels in convoy for neighbours. We could not reach port soon enough, anxiously wondering would we arrive safely without interference from the enemy. Sleeping in a hammock was a new and strange experience. I took to it with hardly any difficulty and found it comforting and soothing as it gently swings with the rolling of the ship. The knack of getting in, and out, of the perilous suspended canvas sheet that cocoons you is soon mastered, changing position when sleeping required delicate manoeuvres. Each person has their hammock to sling above tables on the mess deck at night, and stow away before breakfast in the morning. Walking about in semi-darkness dodging a mass of swinging bodies on a rolling ship is practiced with dexterity. Sea water was on tap for ablutions at limited times during the day, essential for hygiene, but not a habit I could recommend. Special sea water soap was issued for washing and taking a shower, no amount of scrubbing would ever produce lather. Attempts to wash the hair were futile; the salt water left hair feeling more sticky and grubby than it ever was before. No lights were allowed on the outside deck after sunset; serious consequences befell anyone striking a match to light a cigarette. Discharging scraps of rubbish overboard during daylight hours was strictly forbidden, an act of folly leaving a trail of flotsam confirming a ship's progress, alerting enemy submarines prowling the seas. Opportunities for sleeping on the open deck during hot tropical nights were a rare occurrence, a pleasant experience shared by the vast numbers of troops on board.

To suffer the full effects of sea-sickness for the first time is an unforgettable sensation. The mind is devoid of sanity, certain you will go mad if the horizon persists performing an unpredictable rhythmic dance. Eyes can no longer focus on the green turbulent waves and the ears are bombarded by the sound of angry waves beating against the sides of the ship. Sickening hallucinations harass one's imagination with fantasy, and a raging headache is assurance you are alive with no means to escape the horrific sensation. Human awareness slowly returns to normality as the waves abate their violent attack on the heaving vessel, and prayers of hope are uttered never again to suffer such a distressing battle. A few hours passed before I fully recovered. From then until the ship finally docked I was never again sea-sick. Later we experienced waters equally unfriendly as those we had earlier faced.

Ropes began to lash and curl through the air made fast to tug boats hooting signals as the ship was manoeuvred alongside the quay at Bombay. A European veteran of the sea wearing white tropical dress and flamboyant peaked cap, shouted orders from the cobbled dockside to Indian coolies rushing here and there, obeying instantly every command to bring the ship safely into port. I cannot chronicle here the details and vast extent of the panorama bustling with activity, or the peculiarities I saw before me in this strange foreign land. I was fascinated by the modes of dress and different types of castes easily distinguished, but not yet acquainted with their individual characteristics. Their strange apparel added splashes of brilliant colour, dotted about in clusters in contrast to the grey stone landing stage where groups of workers rested after completing their tasks. Yards of gaudy cloth wound about their bodies may seem more fitting for a jester as I tried to imagine what sensation an Englishman might cause walking along The Strand, in London, wearing a suit as colourful. Perhaps the world would appear more cheerful if people chose brighter apparel to wear.

The fantasy I gazed upon made my future more mysterious and I had a longing to immediately step ashore, to wander and explore this part of the world where the sun bestows its whole hearted attention. We had heard about the wet monsoon which was at no great distance away, and the Indian summer had almost reached its full lease of life. The heat at that stage was unbearable, and impossible to imagine the high temperatures that had prevailed a month earlier.

Disappointing news was quick to reach everyone's ears; we would not be allowed to go ashore that day. Having witnessed the activity, confusion, and endless energy among the dockside workers to port, my gaze turned starboard towards a group of idle ships moored in the docks before moving below to the mess deck to write an Airgraph home, and laze away the rest of the day like it was any other during our voyage.

Long after the sun had set, lascars and native labourers pattered bare foot along the wooden decks in darkness, unloading cargo from the hold. Large brilliant lamps cast lengthy shadows about the ship. Periodically a great iron hook suspended from a crane dangled in beams of light, hovering for a second before plunging out of sight into the depths of the hold. A moment later it would reappear with a perilous swinging load ascending into the cylinders of light. How long the bustle and noise continued into the night, I can not tell. Below decks everyone was resting and settling down to sleep in the clammy stuffy air of the mess deck. At last it was a little comforting to have the port holes open, never before had this been allowed during the whole time at sea.

As the new day dawned, we learned we were to be allowed to set foot in India, but some hours of the morning passed before the promised news proved to be fact. Passes were made out for 2 o'clock, and we dressed in tropical uniform for the occasion. A pay parade was arranged, the first of many to receive local currency from a foreign mint. We were warned to take extra care, to learn the different coins and notes, and the value of the rupee. The Indian merchant is flattered with craftiness and guile, knowing several ways to raise his wealth at the expense of newly arrived troops spending a strange currency.

I joined streams of K.D.[9] clad figures hastening down gangways, the moment I trod on the foreign shore I felt an inexplicable sensation, where I should go I had no idea, and resolved to let my feet be my guide.

I followed the crowd past anchored ships, striding over a railway line, and noticing a vessel in dry dock, I carried on walking towards large gates which I knew I would not pass through again until some of the sights of India had been seen.

Strolling along a spacious roadway, I was met with natives of all ages engaged in every sort of trade. The most numerous were filthily clad urchins running at my side, tugging my sleeve crying "Shoe shine sahib?" It took some time to shake them off, but a technique was soon mastered with abundant opportunities to practice. A strip of cloth with many tails was thrown around their dark skinned waist. Bare feet, and matted hair were clearly noted at a glance, and an instant awareness of how destitute and primitive these youngsters were. The most likely cause is poverty, never having sought to improve their status in life. For whatever reason they endured this wretched situation, their future path was an easy guess.

To see for the first time a turban being wound about the head of an Indian is a complex process, and I was intrigued watching the deft and expert manipulation of yards of cloth. It offers lightweight protection from the sun, and the Indian name for this type of headgear is puggree. Boys learn the technique at an early age, I dare not try to express in words the method how it was done, and I would find myself tangled more than if I was to carry out the task. I must have been fortunate to witness the occurrence at an early stage on my first visit. Never again did I see a turban being wound about the head until several weeks later.

Many bodies lay fast asleep on the pavement, taking advantage of the shade in porticos and doorways of buildings, three and four stories high, that lined one side of the road. It was impossible to dodge the full rays of the sun shining directly from above, frequently using a handkerchief to wipe sweat from my brow. In a narrow side street I saw a bullock cart approaching and hesitated in my step, this indeed was an object to observe. Moving steadily towards me, the lumbering open cart with two large wooden wheels dwarfed a native driver who appeared to be dozing. A beast was straining at the yoke making slow progress, accompanied by an irritable squeaking of the hubs for want of attention by a little grease as they turned on well worn axels. I found it to be a common sight almost everywhere I went.

The lack of wealth and primitive existence were apparent when I reached the heart of the native quarters of the city. Pictures we know of the narrow filthy London streets before the Great Fire, hold pride to the confined hovels and bazaars I found here. My nose detected a number of vile smells, others quite unusual, some pleasant and alluring without similarity to any known that I could compare. People and animals were everywhere wandering this way and that, cows, hens, goats. Stray dogs were feeding on wasted scraps of food found in alleyways. Women were carrying glistening brass and copper gourds balanced on the head, without any support to steady them, walking with ease and confident the burden was secure. They must be one of the most appealing gaited races in the world by the upright manner they transport many of their goods on the head. Men were wearing the dhoti, a length of white cloth that could be straight off the loom, wound about the waist the end drawn up between the legs and tucked into the waistband. The sari is traditional dress for women, similar to the dhoti, more usually a bright colourful fabric with decorative border worn over a short sleeve bodice. The sari too, is wound about the waist leaving material free to drape over the head, or across a shoulder. The loose folds of the garment have a delightful habit fluttering with the slightest movement, adding grace and charm to feminine deportment when walking.

Squatting on a shelf, the proprietor of a stall sits next to goods fully exposed to flies, dirt and dust. If you approach the stall for a closer look at what he has to offer, he hands to you the object he thought had caught your eye, asking at first a fabulous price which he never expects you will pay. The moment you turn and walk away, an expression of utter disappointment is registered on his face if you do not accept a challenge to bargain. On a nearby stall bundles of fresh bright green leaves arrayed on shining brass pots surrounded a sleepy owner sitting cross legged on what could hardly be described as a counter. It was difficult to comprehend his trade; I guessed it was peculiar to a personal taste or local diet. My curiosity was soon satisfied when an aged bearded man stepped into the shade of the overhanging canopy, instantly arousing the drowsy owner to attend his customer. An exchange of Urdu between both men prompted the owner to select a juicy looking green leaf from a tray, dip the end of a stick into a pot of chocolate coloured mixture and spread it thickly over the leaf. Dipping a stick into another pot, he added what might have been flour paste, but I guessed it was not. Folding the leaf to seal inside the mixture, the proprietor exchanged it for a coin with a pleasing glance from the old man's eyes. Gently, and slowly, a wrinkled bony hand raised the purchase to the old man's lips, and as I pondered whether it was food, or luxury, he turned and disappeared into the throng with a faint expression of satisfaction on his face. I felt sure the concoction was not fitting for a white man's health, and was intrigued to know more. Some time later, I discovered it was commonly called betel-nut. Chewing the mixture is the pleasure of many of the poorer natives. It produces copious amounts of crimson saliva, and provided an answer for numerous dark red splashes like blobs of blood, dotted everywhere on cobbled streets and pavements, that had puzzled me. The noxious waste is spat upon the ground by passing addicts and the cause of reddened lips and teeth I had observed on a number of men.

Dodging bullock carts and children uttering perpetual cries, "Baksheesh. sahib?" I turned away from the dirty smelly passageways to explore a more comforting and tolerable view of foreign life. The noise of traffic became louder as I moved towards the direction of the affluent part of the city. Two wheeled garrys[10] were dashing about in all directions, carelessly impeding cars, disregarding maddened drivers hooting and shouting abuse, challenging their contempt for other vehicles on the road. Shops, banks, cinemas and cafés had a similar appearance to what I knew, inside the constant whirring of fans hanging from ceilings gave refreshing comfort from the humidity outside. Many itinerant dealers and hawkers were displaying goods on pavements, offering worthless charms and trinkets to the passer by.

As night fell it was pleasing to continue my tour amidst a blaze of brightly coloured lights, in contrast to the black-out conditions in cities and towns left behind at home. Everywhere beggars were as numerous as in other parts around the town. I had to tread with care lest I should set my foot on a homeless person sleeping on the floor. Men, women and children laid claim to any dark corner of the pavement to settle themselves down for the night; often there was barely room for me to get by.

The final stage of my shore leave came almost unnoticed; so many interesting and unusual experiences had occupied my time. Passing again through the old dock gates, stepping over mooring ropes and chains, I made my way towards the gangway of the ship. My feet felt weary the moment they trod on deck, having taken me as far as time allowed, on a journey I could never have imagined. The greatest feeling of happiness, and climax to the day came when a pile of mail was thrust into my hand, astounded to receive the first news from home for twelve whole weeks. I need not say how I spent the next hour before slinging my hammock, to find comforting sleep at the end of my first day in India.

Having disembarked at Bombay on 10 June, we travelled by troop train to a tented camp at Bangalore, southern India.

27 June   *To my brother Harry, AIRGRAPH microfilm printout*
Congratulations gaining a stripe, I hope you are keeping well and not continuing to enlarge since I last saw you. We arrived at this camp a

1. Home Guard
1942 (L to R): my brother Harry; Fred Clark (cousin), RAF Catalina pilot; me; John Clark (cousin);
Major, my German shepherd dog.

2. New Arrivals

3, Inoculation

4. Reading the Army Act

5. Dental Treatment

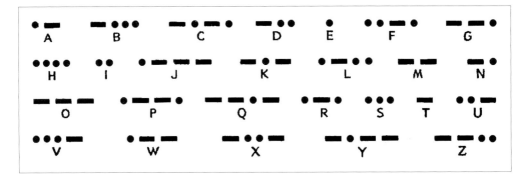

6. Morse Code

Samuel F. B. Morse, an American portrait painter fascinated by the new electric telegraph, invented a system to transmit messages using a series of dots and dashes. The Morse code was universally used from the 1840s until the latter part of the twentieth century, when it was superseded by faster telecommunication. The complete code includes numbers, punctuation, and transmission procedures.

7. Gun Drill

8. B Troop, 366 Field Battery, R.A., Felixstowe, Suffolk, February 1943

9. Self Portrait on Letter Paper

10. Studio Photograph, Poona

Overleaf: 11. Relaxing in a Dugout (Maurice)

J. FENTON 1944

12. Chico Dressed in a Fez

13. Boy Wearing a Turban

14. Gusamba

15. Burmese Chico

Above Left: 16. Young Girl, India

Above: 17. Young Boy, India

Left: 18. Boy with a Basket

19. A Letter Home

20. Indian Troops Preparing Khana
After the Capture of Myitson

Above Left: 21. Pagoda Chinthes, Mogok

Above: 22. Guardians of the Monastery, Mogok

Left: 23. A Pipe Dream

Right: 24. The Temple of Buddha, Bahe

25. Peasant Toilers

26. Economy Wash

27. Thatch Weavers, Hlaingdet

28. Making Thatch, Hlaingdet

29. Young Rascal

30. "Me Next!"

31. The Brahmaputra River at Pandu

Left: 32. Pagoda at Yamethin

Below Left: 33. Mama's Boy, Hlaingdet

Below: 34. Friendship, Burma

few days ago and are marooned here, there is a good reason for the predicament, the Regiment has no transport. You can imagine we are looking forward to vehicles being supplied very soon to take us the few miles into town. I found time to paint watercolour portraits of natives around the camp; these you will get to see when I send them home, if they can be kept well protected and undamaged.

12 July *BLUE AIR LETTER CARD*

Last week I paid my first visit to the nearby town and found it was not much of a place, I doubt I shall make any effort to get there again. A truck is going into town tonight, the standard of entertainment to be found there holds little interest; I prefer to stay in camp. We are living on eggs; we get an average of two eggs each day and are browned off with them.

Charwallahs[2] can be seen everywhere about the place, squatting by urns of hot tea. Nothing is better than to shout "Charwallah!" at half past six in the morning to enjoy a cup of tea while dressing. Preparations for sleeping at night has taken on a completely different course of action in India, putting up a mosquito net above my bed is a ritual to safeguard against nasty bites by those tiny obnoxious insects carrying the deadly malaria disease.

We moved north by troop train to Poona, and were stationed a few miles outside the town in a tented training camp at Kharakawasla.

27 July

I have returned from a swim in a nearby lake, a daily routine I thoroughly enjoy. Following a short rest after a meal in the evening, I join a few friends for a swim. Tonight I stayed in the water rather longer than I intended, the time is 8 o'clock and it will be dark very soon. If I do not finish writing this letter within the next half hour I shall have to put it aside, dusk is almost here, if you can call it dusk. Once the sun has set, daylight fades quickly and darkness is all around before you are aware of the change. This is the monsoon season; heavy black clouds hasten the failing light and intermittent bursts of rain over the past week have turned the ground muddy underfoot. Now is the time to beware of our hated friends the mosquitoes. During the rainy season the parasites are highly active. They have not yet troubled me, touch wood. Last night on guard I heard them buzzing around, the anti-mosquito cream spread on exposed skin effectively keeps the little devils at bay. I wish you could have seen the pretty fireflies as I saw them flickering in the darkness.

28 July

Once again, back to my tent following a swim in the dam as usual. You may have guessed I am in a different camp, telling you I am swimming every day. We have been here about a week and everyone is beginning to get accustomed to our new surroundings, which are much more comfortable than the rough and ready situation at our previous camp. We are busily engaged during free moments doing a wonderful job of work, decorating around the tents. We were complimented by the sergeant-major on the appearance surrounding the area to our tent, making it look cheerful and bright. A path to the entrance is laid in crazy paving, close to the entrance the title of our sub-section and Star of India is set in white stones. In the centre of the star, and each side of the title, we planted a cactus. Designing the decorative layout landed me a job tomorrow, marking out a piece of ground in the centre of the camp to display a large facsimile of the Royal Artillery badge in coloured stones. Drawing portraits captures the fascination of an audience standing around watching me, and the Battery captain has asked me to sketch his portrait on an Airgraph. He would also like a portrait in watercolours.

I am sorry if you find my writing is beginning to deteriorate, the blame lies with failing daylight as darkness approaches. Fortunately, I am able to continue writing this letter inside the tent aided by light from an oil lamp. The night time charwallah has timed his call at the door perfectly. You would be surprised at the amount of tea I drink; there is little opportunity to find water safe to drink. Our cooks do the cooking at this camp and the food we are getting is far better, an improvement attributed to catering supplied from a different source. We have never been served eggs since leaving our last camp, for this everyone is satisfied. When I saw there was jam roll for dinner today, I said to the fellow sitting next to me at the dinner table, "I must write home about this."

The rest of the lads in the tent are putting up mosquito nets making beds ready for the night. I can boast about the luxury of sleeping on a bed, a charpoy; a unique design common throughout the whole of India. The base consists of a rectangular frame of wood supported at each corner on stout legs. The frame is interlaced with rope in a diamond pattern, fashioning a strong flexible surface. Overlaid first with a ground sheet, spare clothing or blankets for padding makes a comfortable mattress. The base gradually begins to stretch and sag after continuous use, a problem easily rectified by readjusting and tightening the ropes. During the monsoon season, a mesh of fine netting fixed above to upright bamboo canes at the corners of the bed offers protection at night from mosquitoes, if you quickly nip inside before the little blighters seize the chance to follow close behind. More I have to say must wait until tomorrow.

30 July

I am sorry; I did not keep my promise and finish this letter yesterday. I came back from my swim calling immediately at the canteen to have supper. Chatting with a group of friends, the evening passed unnoticed until it was time to return to the tent, put up my mosquito net, and slip into bed.

The work I am doing on the R.A. badge design is coming along fine, and many comments of praise and admiration have been expressed about the progress. I must close this letter, not to begin another page which might make it above the weight for air mail. Don't ever let anyone say to you that Lancashire is a place where you can find lots of rain, they should come here!

1 August   *To my brother Harry*

The monsoon season has begun and all I ever see is rain, never a day passes without rain. One minute the weather may look nice and bright, suddenly the rain can be heard beating against the roof and sides of the tent. At the moment the sun is shining faintly through dark clouds, but a rainy appearance is for ever present.

A faithful charwallah has paid us a visit asking if we wanted char and cake, almost everyone got out a mug and told him their requirements. He squats on the ground with an urn of hot tea, nearby him a tin trunk filled with rock cakes, and cigarettes, his chicos[3] continuously running around serving customers. When a chico returns delivering an order he anxiously expects a reward, prostrating with a delicate salaam immediately he receives a buckshee. Any time of day the charwallah's chicos are at your beck and call, particularly faithful when it is raining. They dash around in bare feet sloshing in mud; even for this they are happy to receive only one anna for the service.

Mail is arriving regularly; air letter cards and Airgraphs take about nineteen days, ordinary sea mail about three months. I have abandoned sending letters ordinary mail because of the long delays getting news to you. We are allowed up to ½oz airmail rate for eight annas postage, anything above this weight will be sent ordinary mail.

I am looking forward to being granted leave, but have no idea when that may be. I hope to spend it with Mr. and Mrs. Carrington at Jhansi. It is a few years since we met the family in England, it would be a wonderful opportunity to see them again. I have already written a letter saying there is half a chance I might soon get leave and would love to visit them.

Our usual ration of 60 cigarettes is no longer issued in this camp, it is no great loss to us, cigarettes are cheap to buy, Woodbines cost two and a half annas for ten, equal value is less than three pence English money.

The lowest currency in paper money is the rupee, worth one shilling and sixpence. You may feel rich with ten one rupee notes stuffed into your pocket, in reality this amounts to a mere fifteen shillings.

The flying dhobi[4] is here collecting dirty washing. Underwear and shirts for washing are handed in to the quartermaster's stores, and regularly sent away to be laundered. If you are in urgent need of items to be washed, the camp dhobi will take care of it for a small charge. Washed clean, nicely ironed, and returned in less time than it takes to tell.

Keep your chin up Harry, also your *cherry ripe*, perhaps you will win another to go with it.

CHAPTER 6

The Regiment is Given a New Role

The camp at Kharakwasla was sited nearby a deep water lake contained by a large dam, with ideal facilities to practice assault landings from small boats. The 25-pdr field guns were replaced with 3.7-inch Howitzers; lighter guns, more adaptable for use in assault landings and close jungle warfare. The regiment was reorganized to undertake an entirely different role, and a new rigorous training programme was adopted. It was a major change to be reclassified as a Light Battery and Assault Field Regiment, in preparation for sea-borne attacks against Japanese forces in Burma.

366 Light Battery R.A.
178 Assault Field Regiment R.A.
India Command

3 August   *AIRGRAPH microfilm printout*
Along with yours and other letters there came one from Mrs. Carrington at Jhansi, wishing me most welcome to stay when I get leave. Please note my new address

8 August
You will already have found enclosed, the photograph I had taken in town last Monday. I collected three prints yesterday that cost four chips, a common expression for the rupee. My next portrait I hope to have taken full length wearing K.D. shorts. That reminds me, very soon I shall have to change into slacks, anyone found wandering around with sleeves rolled up and wearing shorts after 7.30 in the evening is liable for the office next morning. You should guess this is added protection against mosquito bites.

I spent time walking around the town yesterday with a pal; we were fascinated with colourful silks of all kinds displayed in the bazaars. I shall buy some nice pieces I think you may like, and post home in a parcel taking a few months to reach you by sea mail.

Today is warmer in spite of regular showers; pleasant enough for my daily dip which I missed yesterday visiting town. Another portrait I sketched on an Airgraph, a request for one of the boys. An Indian woman wearing a sari draping her head and shoulders is a portrait I have in mind to sketch, this I am aware will prove difficult to achieve. Women are timid, and shy away if you attempt to approach them, in particular any soldier wearing a uniform.

16 August   *BLUE AIR LETTER CARD*

You will no doubt notice another change when addressing letters. I am no longer a signaller since being newly employed as a clerk in the Battery office, once again classed as a gunner (Gnr), moving from B Battery to B.H.Q. (Battery Headquarters). I work in the office each day doing a responsible job dealing with army routine and official matters.

Recently we have not had quite so much rain to which we are accustomed. Sitting outside the tent at night, spending moments of peace under a brilliant moon, the mind is flooded with memories of home without any encouragement whatsoever.

I can make no complaints about the *grub*, it is pretty decent. We enjoy many fruits young children in England have never seen due to rationing and the war. Bananas, oranges and mangoes are favourite fruits we buy anywhere. It is impossible to find famous brands of toffee. An alternative, almost part of one's daily diet, are sweet coated sticky peanut bars.

I am getting a little short of water colour paints. I hope I shall find some in the town without depending on you to post some to me. If, and when, we are granted leave, I most certainly expect to spend it with Mr. and Mrs. Carrington since receiving the invitation to stay.

4 September   *BLUE AIR LETTER CARD*

Air mail letters take longer to reach you than air letters posted from England to me. Parcels are getting through. If you could manage to send one there is every chance it would arrive safely. The time is 8 o'clock and light is failing fast to end my day, only half your day has passed; dad will have walked with Major to his allotment to attend the garden. You mention war news in Europe is good; I hope and pray it continues favourably and may surprise us all.

5 September

The rain has decided to give us a turn, it will be short lived. The sun's appearance over long intervals during the day has increased the temperature. The intense heat of the climate we have yet to face, arriving as we did in India when the hot season had moved on. The leaves will be falling in England about now, and the summer months of 1943 fading fast. Dad will be working on a marvellous plan for his vegetables, and plants in the garden. Do not attempt to grow cactus, you will never achieve the size they reach out here. I shall have seen far too many interesting tropical varieties compared to specimens I might find on my arrival home.

I have just noticed the Q.M. wearing the new type bush hat we are to be issued with. Some are being distributed tomorrow; the style is much like the wide brimmed Australian hat. Everyone will be rushing into town to have their photograph taken when we get the new headgear, me included. We have no love for the old fashioned regulation issue hard military topee we wear at present.

The paints in my paint box are dry and have been for a while; the pleasure of drawing is limited to requests for portraits and designs for special greetings on Airgraphs.

I was on Church Parade this morning for the National Day of Prayer, also a last tribute to one of the lads who last week lost his life. He got into difficulties learning to swim in the nearby lake and was drowned. It came as a shock to everyone. He was a very good friend I knew quite well and I was talking to him about an hour before the news went through the camp like fire. Everyone who could swim was at the lake side in no time. One of our officers, an Australian competition swimmer dived into the deep water to get him out and tried to revive him, but to no avail. My friend was given a great funeral.

The time is half past four and soon I will be at the cookhouse looking for my tea. Tonight I shall visit the camp cinema; there are a range of prices for seats, annas 6, 12, and one rupee; equal to about 7 pence, 1 shilling and 1½ pence, and 1 shilling and 6 pence, respectively.

6 September   *To my brother Harry, AIRGRAPH microfilm printout*
Thank you for your letter card received yesterday, I note your remark winter is coming round and from my experience of the Scottish weather, I know what you can expect. I saw the film, *Sergeant York*, last night and enjoyed the full length version, not cut to pieces as they sometimes are. Tomorrow night the film, *In Which We Serve*, is to be shown, and I would not like to miss that.

8 September
In both your letters received today dated 24 August, you say you did not light a fire yesterday, what a thoughtful subject to write about when I am doing my best to keep cool. The final rays of the setting sun are casting

a red tinted veil on everything around. I wonder if the moon tonight will follow faithfully as it did last night.

I can understand why you ask if flies are one of the many troubles out here, the answer, emphatically, is Yes! There is not the slightest chance to take a nap half naked on your bed at any time without inviting the pests. Before you can doze off, a fly finds good live meat inviting all his friends. The arms emulate slow revolving sails of a wind mill discouraging them to settle, or better described as a game of tiddlywinks with flies. The answer is to rest wearing slacks and the shirt sleeves rolled down, alternatively, make a hastily retreat inside the confines of the mosquito net for protection.

Cheerio, and my regards to everyone, if I were to mention by name each of my relatives in turn it would require a whole page.

14 September   AIRGRAPH microfilm printout
Your holiday, dad, will have drawn to a close and you perhaps will be wondering how many more years must you attend the office, please note I did not allude to work. I am sure that during the break you took pleasure turning the earth and planting seeds, tending your allotment. Harry will be home with you when you receive this and I hope he enjoys his leave.

14 September   BLUE AIR LETTER CARD
I am writing to you for the second time today. I have been working on designs for Christmas cards and very soon hope to make a start on them. I could sell many cards, the amount of time each one takes would not be appreciated and I could never ask what I should for producing them. I may make a special effort painting one or two cards for the lads; my paint box is looking rather sad and finding a shop to replenish the colours will not be easy.

16 September
My financial situation is good. I collect a regular amount of cash each week, and seven shillings a week is credited to my army account, amounting to more than £5 at the moment. If I wish to withdraw extra money on pay day, I make sure it never exceeds my weekly income.

The pencil portrait sketch on the last page of the letter will give you a glimpse of my appearance wearing the new issue bush hat.

19 September   To my brother Harry, BLUE AIR LETTER CARD
The weather is getting warmer as the monsoon season draws to a close. Showers of rain can occasionally drench you to the skin, catching you unawares with more than a hundred yards to reach shelter. When rain comes there are no half measures in its violence.

Thank you for the many letters you have written, your news keeps me well informed how you are getting along in this dreadful war. You could never imagine the mad scramble in camp gathering around the person handing out newly arrived mail. Everyone gets excited, swapping interesting snippets of news with friends, or sharing it with others who are willing to listen. Dad is thinking ahead saying, when we are once again wearing civvies, we shall look back many times on the good and the bad days spent serving in the army.

I hope this letter finds you on top of the world.

27 September

Forgive me for recent breaks in my mail; it has not been convenient to write letters, we have been moving around doing special training exercises in preparation for the responsibilities ahead. I was the only person on duty in the Battery office yesterday to type out Orders for the Day. I was not given full instructions for parade times, all were printed ten minutes late, it had little effect, and one worried or cared about it.

Each week we are issued with one free blue Air Mail Letter Card, and one Green envelope, this should explain the problems I have dealing with correspondence to relatives, planning to whom I should send which, and when. Green envelopes have preference and go through army base headquarters. If two Green envelopes are sent by one person the same week, only one of the letters will go air mail. The same rule applies to blue Air Mail Letter Cards.

The letters to which you affix a blue Air Mail label do not always travel by air, some are sent surface mail. The P.O. in the U.K. has been cheating customers not announcing this fact. People in the U.K. have been sending air mail letters with 1/6d, and 2 shillings or more stamps to India, thinking news was reaching its destination in record time by air. This is a warning to rely only on the standard blue Air Mail Letter Card, or the regular Airgraph service.

When there are spare moments, I shall put down on paper the customs, mode of dress and life as I see it in India, I am sure you would find it interesting. Two days ago I took out my paints to sketch the portrait of an Indian woman, abandoning the attempt when I found it very difficult to make her understand I wished to make a painting of her. Unfortunate as I was on that occasion, my patience will never be exhausted.

3 October   *BLUE AIR LETTER CARD*

I went into town yesterday with one idea in mind, to paint a scene in watercolour. I was limited to making a sketch in pencil, I could find nothing to hand that would hold water to use my paints. From all sides came a constant chatter, presumably flattering remarks in a language I was unable to comprehend. A policeman on point duty in the centre of the road frequently left his post to chase away an abundance of children and spectators surrounding my throne, who were impeding the flow of traffic.

I would like to create a series of cartoons caricaturing a soldier's experiences of life in India.

12 October   *POST CARD Air mail*

The situation of some paints in my box has caused me to change my mind, requesting you to send me colours I desperately need. There is little chance I shall find what I want here. In my next letter I will give you a list of the paints, and a sketching pad would be handy.

Please acknowledge receipt of the cartoon P.C. posted yesterday as soon as it arrives, I should like to know it has reached you safely, before sending any others by air mail.

14 October   *BLUE AIR LETTER CARD*

I found a newspaper on my bed when I returned to my tent after tea tonight; it had been left by one of the fellows in the Battery who lives in Haslngden. Local papers are sent to him and he promised to pass them to me when he has read them. I was able to know about the news in your part of the country from a different source.

I shall enclose in this letter a list of paints I hope you can obtain and post to me. The paints must be in tubes, to easily refill the pans in my paint box. Students will be OK, Artists quality will be too dear nowadays, even if you can buy them. I would like Chrome yellow; Yellow ochre; French ultramarine; Cobalt blue; Prussian blue; Emerald green; Vermilion; Crimson; Scarlet lake and Sepia. These are the important colours; please include other colours you think I may like to have. I also need a watercolour sketching block 9x12in, Whatman not pressed surface. My paint brushes are in reasonable condition giving good service.

19 October   *BLUE AIR LETTER CARD*

Yesterday I posted cartoon No.2. When I think of new ideas, I will continue to draw them. Give my regards to grandma. I have not written to her lately, she will soon be putting another candle on her birthday cake.

21 October

I still enjoy my new job in the office, there are both good and bad points going for it. There is for instance no chance of promotion, we are allowed one P/A clerk in the Battery office and that position is already filled. I have no guard duties or chores to bother me, except I do my bit when, along with the whole Battery, I am outside the camp on training exercises. At present I feel more content in the army than ever before.

Many Happy Returns on your birthday mother, and grandma also, you will find two birthday cards enclosed one for each of you.

25 October   *BLUE AIR LETTER CARD*

Items such as toothpaste, razor blades, and black shoe polish are sold at inflated prices, neither are they easy to find in the shops. Six shillings the value in English money is asked for a good brand of toothpaste. Soap is not a problem, and plentiful at a reasonable price.

In a recent competition to design a Christmas Airgraph for the Regiment, my entry was chosen along with one other; I will send to you a print as soon as it has been reproduced.

27 October

As there in not much possibility of getting leave in the near future, or finding any attractive material on sale in town, I may decide to send home some of my credits to be put aside until I am once again wearing civvies. I shall give you ample warning when I do decide to transfer some cash. We can send home four Duty Free parcels each year, providing each parcel does not exceed 5lbs in weight, is valued no more than 30 shillings, and observes rules applying to exporting foodstuffs and cigarettes. The cost of postage is about 2Rs (three shillings). There is no charge on receipt. The parcels are automatically sent registered mail and must be signed for on delivery. They require special labels marked in red ink, 'Duty Free Troops Parcel'. Sometimes it is my job in the office to deal with these parcels. If you require more details I will look up the book of rules which is at my disposal.

28 October

Another day has passed since I began writing this letter and I shall be unable to conclude all that I have to say, the film show at the camp cinema will gain my attention tonight.

29 October

I am alone in the Battery office; almost everyone is away on a training exercise, leaving me to do office work. I am pleased Harry enjoyed his leave and was able to take Major out walking.

This morning I was in town attending to official business for the Battery, able also to look around doing a few jobs for myself. I bought a drawing block for 3Rs, and a few watercolour paints not of good quality, don't let that put you off sending the list of colours I requested. The block is drawing paper, not an ideal surface for use with watercolours. There was an opportunity for me to have my photograph taken and I hope to collect prints in about a week.

The film I saw last night was *Flight from Destiny*, other films seen recently were, *Kings Row*, and *Between us Girls*.

Your remark in a letter about hair combs is timely; you would be ashamed of my comb with less than half a row of teeth I was using until last week. One lad noticed me using the comb, grabbed it from my hand throwing it away, kindly offering me one of his spare combs.

3 November

What a pleasant surprise on Saturday sorting mail for distribution when I found a parcel of 200 State Express 555 cigarettes you sent me, and yesterday a parcel of 200 State Express 333 cigarettes from the Observer Cigarette Fund. I smoked some of the cigarettes from your package; you need only to be within hearing distance when I ask if anyone would like a cigarette. Today has been an unusual free half day in the middle of the week, and the chance to finish a watercolour portrait of one of the young Indian bearers who serves in the camp canteen. I began the painting some days ago spending a great deal of time working on the portrait, I believe it to be one of my best I have done recently.

All air mail letters for Christmas must be handed in by the 5th, I am enclosing my greetings cards within the stipulated date. Please forward to Harry the card made for him, and the other card to grandma; I am not wealthy enough to find stamps to post them separately.

At the moment I am up to my eyebrows with a cold; if there is no improvement tomorrow I shall report to the M.O. on sick parade.

6 November   *BLUE AIR LETTER CARD*

Night is moving on and I am ready to visit 'ye olde' camp cinema, the title of the film seems familiar; I could already have seen it before. For a couple of hours it is a perfectly good reason to sit and relax in the evening. Thankfully my cold is much better, and a sore throat that followed has deserted me. Give grandma my love, and say I hope she enjoys Christmas dinner, if as usual she gets a leg off the chicken, I am sure she will. A Happy Christmas to all.

8 November   *AIRGRAPH microfilm printout*

Only one of two winners of the Christmas Greetings Airgraph designs has been reproduced to limit costs, unfortunately you will not see my winning design, it has not been printed.

10 November

I found myself with time to spare in town and visited a photographer's studio to let you see the type of tropical dress we wear outside the camp. Not always do we dress in shorts you see in the photograph, slacks must be worn in the evening. The style of dress worn during working hours in the camp is exactly the same, a regular lightweight cotton uniform, often stripped to the waist during the daytime when the heat is unbearable.

14 November

Friday last I received an Airgraph from Auntie Molly which pleased me. Answering letters to all the persons writing to me can be a handicap. It is only right they should be answered, hoping it is clearly understood I try my best to reply. I shall visit the camp cinema tonight, often never knowing the title of the film until the programme is almost ready to begin.

Last week, I was asked by 2 I/C of the Regiment, to design an altar cloth to be used by the padre during religious services. I submitted a couple of rough sketches to the colonel, and prepared a finished working drawing to scale from the sketch he approved. The alter cloth is being fashioned to my design, but I do not know to what stage it has so far reached. I was told the next time I bought paints, or materials, I was to present the bill to the office for payment. In the past I have carried out a fair number of jobs using my own paints and materials for the Battery, and I most certainly will send in the bill for the next batch I buy.

My mosquito net has been fixed up after taking a shower and changing into slacks before the 7 o'clock deadline, the light of the sun's rays can no longer be seen and the approaching darkness is heralded by the noise of crickets coming to life. They are as a large orchestra striking up the opening bars of an overture to a musical score, constantly repeating the same notes with utter disregard for melody. Whilst writing, I glance up at the clouds unperceivable change from grey blue to the darker shades of evening, lacking signs of movement like the minute hand of a clock making an hourly revolution of the face. Occasionally the mood changes as night approaches from all sides, until the darkness is threatened by a faint glow, steadily growing in strength, lighting the earth by the manifestation of a brilliant moon.

One of the lads has called at the tent after a failed mission to the picture show, reporting the machine has broken down and cannot be repaired for the first performance, there is no guarantee it will be working in time for the second show tonight.

19 November   *BLUE AIR LETTER CARD*

Thank you very much for all the mail I received this past week, I most certainly have not been neglected, and a day never passes without getting a letter from someone.

21 November

I let some of the lads see my photograph in the local newspaper you sent to me. This is what my lance bombardier work mate said, "You look quite fourteen in that picture, Jimmy." He also added jokingly, "I can imagine the old darlings in the Oswaldtwistle knitting class saying what a shame for a boy of his age to be in the army." Don't you think he was rather rude? If you have enclosed money in your parcel as were your intentions, I hope it is neither coins, or notes, Postal Orders are the only acceptable way to exchange English money into Indian currency. I know fellows who have been struggling for ages to exchange pound notes, and ten shilling notes, without success. They bring notes into the office to see what we can do to help. I am OK for money, for the last two weeks I have drawn none of my pay, I am holding 20Rs spending money to use in town. In addition, I was given 5Rs for painting a portrait and have an order from the same person for another next week.

22 November

This morning I posted cartoon No7, which you should receive before this letter, and the next cartoon has been completed. I may vary the style using India ink, or colour, for the next batch. They will need to be posted inside an envelope to ensure they arrive in good condition. The incidents so far portrayed are actual events, not all of them from my own personal experience. The cartoon of a soldier leaving the cookhouse carrying his dinner, assaulted by a cheeky vulture swooping to snatch a sausage in its claws, taught me a lesson to be more careful and to avoid any similar occurrence in the future.

Big changes are taking place in my office; the sergeant in charge is going on a course leaving Johnny (the L/bdr) and me to carry on the good work. I have been learning how the army pay system works, finding myself in a tangle sometimes. I shall pretty soon get the hang of it with a little practice. Johnny is not so hot on pay procedures. His job is taking dictation in shorthand notes, typing letters or documents, and each day printing the Battery Orders.

A snake was seen in camp today and killed by the lads before taking it to the M.I. room to be identified. It was yellow and black, a young krait, a little larger than a fountain pen, but one of India's deadliest snakes. Two snakes have been seen when we have been out in the country on training schemes. One was delivered alive in a tin to the Battery captain. The chap got a telling off for carrying a snake in that manner without first killing it. I saw the second snake after it had met its doom with a blow from a spade. This was definitely a cobra with a lengthy body. I stretched out the hood on the snake's head and the distinct 'V' marking made it clearly identifiable. On a night away from camp during an exercise, wandering through paddy fields, I was full of apprehension, foolishly not wearing gaiters to protect my legs. In the darkness I had a strange sense of danger knowing I might disturb a poisonous snake to suddenly make a deadly strike, feeling relieved when I returned safely to my bed. You may imagine we are constantly threatened by these reptiles; that is not the case. Snakes are not numerous and choose to avoid confrontation with humans. But, shaking hands with one of the many deadly species is almost certain to be fatal without immediate medical attention.

25 November   *To my brother Harry*

Thank you for your letters, you mention the loathsome chores of spit and polish you are showered with, cleaning brasses and blancoing equipment. In our training camp we have a much better solution to deal with the task, a smart set of white washed webbing is kept solely for sentries to wear on duty. I confess to know little about standing on guard, one of the perks of my job, except I am expected to do my bit when away from camp on assault training exercises at night.

I like your photograph you sent to me, Harry, and I shall make a protective case to keep it safe. Every spare moment is spent writing letters, or sketching designs on Airgraphs for the lads celebrating birthdays and anniversaries. Tonight, before writing this letter I made a fourth wedding anniversary greeting for one of our officers. On Saturday during my free time I sketched a chico in the canteen. He is about six years old with lovely modelled features and wears on his head a hat like an upturned plant pot with tassel. I first met him last week. After much ado with help from an English speaking bearer, I managed to make him understand I wished to draw his features. One of my best watercolour portraits recently is a study of a young Indian bearer about 18 years old called Sawa. I made two sketches and signed one for him to send home to his family. Last week I earned 15Rs making several sketches of the lads, who like to enclose them in letters to wives and girl friends.

1 December

Thank you for a couple of air letter cards dated 6th, and 16th November, a letter is mentioned that has not yet arrived. Mail can reach us out of sequence, turning up eventually. I have been to the dam for a swim, it was grand. I am not able to enjoy a daily dip as I did before taking on the new job; work keeps me tied to the office until it is time for tea. Saturday afternoon I usually spend writing or drawing. I finished painting a Christmas card to send to the Carrington family in Jhansi.

My bed will not have the preference of a hot water bottle you tell me you are enjoying, and I am most certainly glad about that. Having become accustomed to extreme heat and pleasantly warm evenings, some mornings can feel cold. Cheerio, and good night.

2 December

The missing letter turned up today. Airgraphs arrive more quickly from England than the time it takes for those we send to you, blue Air Letter Cards take a little longer. I should not expect you to grumble at the meat ration you buy. I am pretty sure we get goat's meat, or cuts from a bullock regarded too old to work. If you were here and could see the animals and conditions under which they exist, you would never touch meat unless you were certain of its origin. Leave uncooked meat around for a day and you would be able to conduct arms and foot drill with the writhing regiment of life around it.

My weather is very different from your present situation, it makes me inwardly smile when I read how you are feeling the cold and expecting snow. Right now I am sweating profusely and will very soon be going for a swim to cool off. The Battery is away on a training exercise and I am one of the few remaining in camp, able to find time enough to take a dip.

I am enclosing my cartoon for this week. The first series of cartoon Post Cards I produced was sketched in sepia wash. You will be aware I have changed the medium for this new batch, drawing the cartoons in black line India ink. After drawing about eight of this type I shall again change the style.

5 December

Yesterday and today have been air letter days, the total catch of nine letters bringing a lot of news. I am sorry you have not received one letter in the space of a fortnight; no blame can be attributed to me, this length of silence recently has never been allowed to elapse. The conditions for writing letters are difficult, no place to write is comfortable except in the tent at night by the light of an oil lamp, or sometimes I may go to the office and write there. You need to be near the light to follow the words you are writing and insects attracted to the light persistently knock themselves silly against the lamp glass or white paper.

It is comforting to know you received four cartoons portraying 'A soldier's life in India,' two days ago I posted cartoon No.9. Please excuse me a friend has called to join him for a swim.

Later the same day

I have had a swim, and teatime meal, the food was not very inviting, spuds with gravy, a slice of bread, tea and an orange. We are very rarely served a decent meal at the weekend, the food is far better during the week.

Offering to help sort a large amount of mail that arrived in the office, delayed a 2 o'clock meeting to sketch an Indian chico during my free afternoon yesterday. It was past 3 o'clock before I got to the canteen and found the young fellow waiting patiently for me to turn up. I did pretty well producing three quick pencil sketches. Quite a few of my sketches have been given away to friends as souvenirs.

The Battery is absent on a training exercise affording peace and quiet for the few remaining behind, and a rare opportunity to spruce up the camp. Headley, the medical orderly who sleeps in my tent, suggested I should decorate the plain whitewashed walls of the M.I. room. Searching around I found some large linen backed sheets of stout white paper, used for plotting maps, ideal material for wall panels. About 9.30 at night, with no one of importance in camp to disturb me, I spread a large sheet of paper onto the floor and began painting in the tranquil surroundings of a deserted room. My friend Headley occupied his time writing letters while I was busy painting. I was getting along nicely, concentrating on the design when suddenly I heard a squeak from a dark corner and a grey streak flashed straight across the paper with a sound like rapid machine gunfire. The intrusion was a mouse, its feet making a noise 'rat-a-tat-tat' running across the freshly painted wet surface transferring a line of coloured footprints over a clean white area. Kneeling on the floor, my head close to the paper, the mouse passed the end of my nose by barely six inches. I finished painting the first panel about midnight, by then it was time to take to our beds. A second design I completed the next day. The panels may not be comforting to soldiers reporting sick, and I am not sure what the M.O. will say when he returns to find them adorning his walls. One design has a skull and skeleton shoulders staring at a gloved hand holding an inoculation syringe, around it a stethoscope, test tubes and a group of measuring glasses. The other panel shows an eye at the eyepiece of a microscope, an ear, a hand holding a thermometer, forceps and medicine bottles. The designs went straight onto the paper without previous ideas or thoughts. Cans of household paints left lying around from other jobs, limited the choice of colours, and an old paint brush thrown out as useless were the only materials I was able to use. All of us remaining behind in camp this week have had a leisurely life, it will cease tomorrow when the Battery gets back to business as usual. I shall certainly miss rising late from my bed in the mornings!

7 December

Except for the cold mornings, the heat in the afternoon and the insects that plague us at night, I am getting along fine in this country where only white men with ambitions to explore its mysteries and delights should endure. A holiday tour in peace time would be a wonderful experience crammed with history and intrigue. Serving with the army engaged in a war has not this pleasure. Our happiness would be profound given an idea of the number of sheets yet to be plucked from the calendar before England is no longer a mental vision.

Today, I posted a parcel by sea mail which will take eight weeks to reach you. Enclosed are four yards of nice material compared to what you can buy. To overcome restrictions on the value of goods posted at one time, I shall be later sending a similar length of white silk.

12 December

Yesterday evening in town I saw the film, *Hitler's Children*, an interesting story with a great deal of propaganda to digest. I advise you to see it if you get the chance.

Having relished sandwiches and a cup of char in the canteen during the evening, it is time for letter writing inside my tent. Outside the Indian moon is progressing slowly across the night sky, in a few hours it will emerge above another horizon shining on a place I recall only too well. Waking insects are everywhere doing their utmost to annoy the serenity of the night. The oil lamp has been lit, casting a frieze of irregular shadows around the draped mosquito nets in the eerie light. Where the shadows strike the angled roof of the tent they are distorted, bearing no resemblance to the objects that fashion them. Their fate is inevitable. 'Lights Out,' the final act, blowing out the light by the last person to get into bed predicts their death. That same instant a moonlight glow seeps faintly perceptible through the canvas covering overhead, human interruptions are less frequent and the subconscious mind is soon overcome with restful sleep. I shall reach the bottom of this page before the light is put out and I disappear inside my mosquito net. You will already have found cartoon No.10 enclosed with this letter to meet the limited maximum weight of air mail postage.

19 December   *To my brother Harry, BLUE AIR LETTER CARD*

You complain in your letter about the cold weather you are having, we suffer extreme heat during the day and sleeping at night I wear an army pullover to combat the severe cold.

22 December *BLUE AIR LETTER CARD*

Yesterday brought one of the most welcome letters posted directly to me from Uncle Fred in Sweden. He says I may write direct, replying to him, this I know would involve too many censorship restrictions and I shall continue to correspond with him through you as usual.

Tonight my thoughts run in one direction only, the annual Christmas Art Ball in Accrington, organized by the art school. A letter from Lilian, a friend at art school, tells me it is being held tonight and the students have been making final preparations. When it is in full swing I shall be fast asleep. As the dance draws to a close and the ballroom empties of revellers, I will have emerged from the folds of my mosquito net to a new day well past dawn.

23 December

The time for Christmas festivities is almost upon us, which will not be fully appreciated until the fun begins. There are no special attractions publicized in India as there are with you, no colourful festoons or Christmas decorations in the shops. Christmas dinner should provide jollity for the Battery, and a concert on Boxing Day in the camp cinema should capture the mood to round off the celebrations. I have produced a large poster advertising the show.

25 December

You should have noticed the date, Christmas Day, it has almost passed and I have arranged my bed for the night, at home you may be at ease digesting Christmas dinner.

I can honestly say the enjoyment throughout this day has been one of the best for a long time. The cooks put on a good spread served by officers and sergeants, sharing good will and happiness between all ranks. For the first course we had potatoes, peas and chicken, afterwards came Christmas pudding with white sauce. Drinks were also handed out. Nuts, raisins, dates, biscuits, cheese and mince pies were served continuously. Meanwhile the Battery band played music as food was consumed. During the second course, Chopper, alias Major Hackett (Battery commander), was requested to give us a turn. To follow this, the officers were called forward to speak, everyone shouting, "We want -------- !" in one voice and stamping feet until the officer named stepped up onto the forum to say a few words. The dining hall was filled with laughter throughout the whole performance. This was the most jovial gathering the Battery has witnessed since leaving England, and continued for quite some time, long after other Batteries in the Regiment had dispersed.

We found our way back to our tents as the major and other officers strolled around the Battery lines very much worse for the bottle. The major came into our tent, sat down on my bed and immediately turned to Johnny saying, "Take a letter." Johnny picked up an army pamphlet lying nearby, and using his knife, proceeded with the pretence to take down a letter in shorthand dictated by the major. I never saw anything so spontaneous as the two acting out the part, entertaining everyone inside the tent for quite a while.

Strains of voices singing Christmas hymns and carols are reaching my ears; a sign community singing has begun around a camp fire to finish off the day. I must get along there to join in the fun. Cheerio until tomorrow.

Boxing Day

There was very little happening at the camp fire gathering last night, I did not stay. I visited a few tents here and there singing with the lads before making my way to bed. Some of the boys were merry and quite obviously suffering from the effects of alcohol. There was not much liquor to be had, restraining any signs of rowdiness. Most of the beer was brought into camp by the lads a couple of days ago and had been consumed.

After tea one of my pals said he was taking a truck into town and only two other guys had chosen to go with him. I agreed to join them, and was fortunate to see a marvellous film, Cary Grant in *Mr. Lucky*.

I collected a ticket for the concert tonight and was reminded I had promised to produce three posters to be used on stage as props for a bar scene in the finale.

- 1944 -

1 January

The start of a new year and an enormous bundle of parcels and papers arrived; straight away I discovered three packages for me. Two were cigarettes, 200 in each package; one a gift from Harry with Craven A plain, the other Piccadilly cigarettes. A third package the size of a sketching block gave me to know what it was before opening. Sorting through more mail I uncovered a fourth with the greatest of joy, it contained a horde of paints – they were as nuggets of gold. Everything arrived in good condition; they had been so well packed it took quite a while unwrapping them before carefully replenishing the paints in my paint box.

I have news to surprise you, I shall be going on leave in the next two or three days paying Mr. and Mrs. Carrington a visit. Immediately the information was made official I wrote a letter requesting proof of an invitation to stay at their home. After posting the letter I realized conformation from Jhansi may not reach me quickly, and right away dispatched a cable. Two days later, yesterday, an answer came back, 'Welcome spend leave.' All has been arranged for ten days with extra days travelling. I should be leaving on the 3rd of January; the train reservations will be booked today. I hope the Carrington's do not judge me too harshly it has happened so quickly, some of the boys are going on leave tonight. Scribbling away at this letter I have failed to finish it before the daylight faded, I must now light the oil lamp.

Details about the leave have been pressing on my mind since we got the news. There is a great deal of office business to be completed. I managed to get through a fair amount working overtime. If I get away on the 3rd, I shall to be back about the 16th, by which time my leave will be over when you receive this letter. I have been hurriedly making preparations and I bought a pair of new shoes hand made by the mochi⁵.

Last night I was in bed by eleven o'clock and slept the New Year in. Our Scottish section sergeant, far from sober, expressed his devotion to this special day when he brought into the tent a couple of bottles. He insisted each of us should choose one of the bottles and taste a dram, rum or gin. Both bottles had before been held many times at an angle and not being well acquainted with either, I chose rum, there was slightly more in the bottle of rum than there was in the gin bottle.

I hope you are all well and managing to get through the cold weather without suffering winter ills. We have seen no rain for about two weeks.

Ten days leave at Jhansi, 3 – 16 January (including four days travel).

5 January

No doubt you were surprised to receive my previous letter telling you I was hoping to visit the Carrington's, let me surprise you more, I am writing this letter in their home. Yesterday, Mr. Carrington with grandson Keith met me at the station to drive me to their house, and standing on the front porch to greet me were Mrs. Carrington with her daughter Norma. I shall be staying ten days with extra days allowed travelling for the long journey. Last night it was quite a change sleeping in a comfortable homely bed in my own room, never having the pleasure of such luxury for a long time. This morning I was handed a cup of tea in bed by the house servant. When the sun goes down I find it cooler at Jhansi than where I am stationed in the training camp. Fortunately, as I was leaving I grabbed my overcoat to bring with me and it has come in very handy at night.

A shikaree[6] called at the house this morning with a bunch of geese bagged on a shoot, offering Mrs. Carrington to take her pick. She chose three of them which I expect we shall enjoy eating before long. We talked about their visit to England when they stayed with us, and asked me to send their best wishes to you, neither was grandma forgotten.

11 January   *BLUE AIR LETTER CARD*

I am enjoying myself to the full, aware these exciting few days of freedom will end all too soon. I consider myself lucky, having dreamed about meeting our friends in India.... In the evening after writing my last letter, Mr. Carrington took me out in the car showing me around Jhansi, he had with him his gun but we saw nothing by way of game to shoot. I was given the chance to drive the car home and in many ways found it quite strange in comparison to the heavy army vehicles I have been driving.

At 6.30 the next morning while it was dark, Mr. Carrington, myself and three friends piled into a car and set off for a hunting ground about 16 miles distant. As the sun rose we settled down in the mist of the morning in separate groups, with loaded guns hoping to see a buck, wild pig, or game to shoot that came our way. Half an hour of utter silence and stillness passed as we waited and watched. Suddenly our luck changed; there before us were the makings of a good shot, unfortunately it was a magnificent doe, no prey for a sportsman's bullet. The buck then appeared followed closely by five young, but we could not pick out a buck from among them which would have given ample reason for a shot. The group of young deer moved slowly out of sight to our left; as they disappeared from view we suddenly heard a shot fired from the direction of the other party. Scrambling out of the scrub George appeared, followed by a shikaree, knowing full well all the game round about would have fled with the noise of the gun. The rest of us emerged from our positions collecting at the car for a cup of hot coffee. We teased Mr. Major about the incident, for it was his gun fired the shot. He had seen the young deer pass within ten yards of his position, thinking just one from the group would not trouble his conscience he let fly. But He Missed!

12 January   *To my brother Harry*

You may think that you rank among the forgotten during this past week; nothing is further from the truth. You have been very much talked about by the Carrington family. I expect mother has already told you I am spending ten days leave here and I arrived a week ago yesterday. If your mathematical brain has not been denuded by army life, and capable of functioning normally, you will realize there is very little of my leave remaining. It has been a pleasant relaxing experience, travelling around with Mr. Carrington seeing Jhansi and visiting a hunting area on safari. At Agra, about 40 miles from Jhansi, stands the most exceptional and renowned edifice of Indian architecture, the Taj Mahal. I considered making an over-night journey by train to see this magnificent tomb, returning the next night. Unfortunately it was impossible to arrange. I hope there may be another opportunity to visit Jhansi when I shall have more time to see the tomb. A couple of days after arriving, I made a quick watercolour sketch of the local market which I gave to the family, along with a pencil portrait of an Indian sketched earlier at my camp. I asked one of Mrs. Carrington's young servants if he would sit for me, he agreed and promised to let me know when he was free from working.

14 January

I made a sketch of the chico, and the same day visited friends with Mr. Carrington and Norma. After dinner in the evening, Norma and I went to a picture show to see the film, *Tonight We Raid Calais*, a war film with lots of action. Next morning I was out of bed early to go on safari with a shooting party and returned with my first grouse. I am looking forward to tasting its nutritious qualities at lunch time. For dinner last night everyone enjoyed a cut of meat from a deer shot by Mr. Carrington on the same hunt.

The sketch of the young chico employed to sweep around the house delighted Mrs. Carrington so much I was happy for her to accept it as a souvenir of my visit. In the afternoon of the day on safari we visited close friends of the family, Mrs. Major and her two daughters. I had been approached to paint one of the girls dressed in Indian dance costume. The model posed perfectly still and I was able to produce a colourful portrait of the girl for the mother, who was more than delighted with the result.

This marks a sad day for me; I shall be leaving this afternoon to return to army life. Everyone I met has been so good to me. I can not thank the family enough for the generosity they have shown and the happiness I found far away from home, visiting old friends I have not seen for many years.

18 January

Back once more to the usual routine. I have yet to thank everyone for the bundle of fourteen letters awaiting my attention on returning to base. The camp cinema is an ideal place to make a start on replies to letters before tonight's show begins. A friend is queuing to get my ticket and I shall soon put aside this letter to enjoy the film, *They Shall Have Music*.

The time I spent on leave with the Carrington family can only be described as home from home. They would accept no money for the generosity lavished upon me, the only item I was allowed to pay for amounted to 4ans, to the dhobi for washing my clothes. Luxury food served at every meal, teal, grouse and venison, game we shot on safari in the bush, and more that was brought to the house shot by friends. Several different traditional Indian dishes were prepared by the cook, and many of the meals were quite new to me I found to my liking.

27 January

This morning I went through the usual channels reporting on sick parade when I suspected a front tooth needed filling. Sitting in an uncomfortable dentist's chair at peace with the world the dentist told me the tooth had already been filled. His observation confused me; to get an urgent appointment with the dentist, the M.O. took it upon himself to write on my report I was suffering from tooth ache. However, a thorough inspection by the dentist revealed a bad tooth and he decided it must be the cause of my trouble, and would be better if it came out. The surgery is far from camp and a visit takes a whole day travelling in the body wagon (hospital truck), returning when all patients have been treated. Not everyone required dental treatment; one chap was attending hospital for an x-ray. Last week I had a jab for cholera that left me with a nasty headache and my arm felt sore for quite a while.

I posted a parcel of sketches recently and I will give you details of what you can expect to find. Five watercolour portraits of canteen bearers. A drawing in pencil of a chico. A watercolour portrait of Sawa, a young bearer wearing a turban with headband in R.A. colours. Also a pencil sketch of the same person which I am sure you will recognize from the likeness. A pencil portrait of a good friend in the Battery wearing an old style topee, and this I would like you to forward to his family. Finally, a still life study of a group of items painted on board the troop ship; a life jacket, sun helmet, water bottle and tin of hard rations. These were to be carried at all times on board for survival at sea if we were attacked and the call came "Abandon ship!"

29 January   *BLUE AIR LETTER CARD*

Thank you for the long awaited sea mail letter with snaps enclosed, everyone looks well and it is a good photograph of Major. What sort of mob is Harry serving with? I notice he is wearing uniform with a clothes line on his shoulder. The R.A. discarded wearing the lanyard[11] out here; normally it is standard dress to be worn at all times. There are five lanyards stored in my kit at base, issued to me at various times; none have been worn since we left Cape Town.

Yesterday I received a letter from the Carrington's and I quote – 'I must treat them as foster parents and will always be welcome in their home.'

31 January

Here are two new cartoons to make up for the lapse of progress while I was enjoying my leave. I shall keep sending them as long as I can think of humorous ideas to record. I found inspiration to sketch in watercolour a few of my friends spending a quiet evening together in the canteen, a common sight in the camp when not on a night exercise. I was able to work on it for about an hour; tonight will find me there once again adding the finishing touches.

I hope everyone is in good health and the weather is not too cold, I recollect you made some mention of snow and frost. I am doing fine eating and sleeping well, sweating throughout most of the day and almost freezing at night.

2 February

Last night I began a watercolour sketch of the charwallah touting for business crouched inside a crudely fashioned make-shift shelter. A nighttime study in late evening, he is filling a mug with hot tea from a large urn bathed in the light of a simple oil lamp casting deep shadows. By his side is a tin trunk containing cakes, and packets of cigarettes, ready to serve a needy customer.

Next Saturday I plan to make a start on yet another portrait of the young canteen bearer Sawa, this time using pastels. I have no means to fix this medium, presenting a problem I shall have to deal with. It is 10.15pm, only fifteen minutes remaining before the regulation lights out placing the tent in darkness, ending the day with me and my companions in bed.

8 February

Thank you for the timely arrival of 200 State Express 555 cigarettes and the old rag, Accrington Observer newspaper. I was completely out of cigarettes and about to purchase a packet from the charwallah when I recognized the parcel of cigarettes addressed to me. I began to open the package without delay.

Returning from leave I spent a day in Bombay hoping I might visit Thelma, the oldest daughter of Mr. and Mrs. Carrington. On previous occasions when visiting this large city I had no knowledge of her address, and I did not find an opportunity to call on her this time. Many lads in the Battery chose to spend their leave at Bombay, and were allowed to inform the folks at home. Neither am I breaking censorship regulations telling you Lord Louis Mountbatten paid the Regiment a visit two weeks ago. He was greeted with cheers as he mounted his soap box; I was close to him when he gave a friendly chat about the progress of the war to a large crowd of soldiers.

Four yards of plain white material I bought is in the post on its way to you, also included are four ties and embroidery silks, all of which had to be within the value of 30 shillings. Take little notice of the prices I valued the contents on the export form. Cloth is not as cheap as you might think it would be. Pick any of the ties you like dad, and Harry too, it will be a small present for Harry ahead of his 21st birthday. You are quite correct reminding me the 25th of February will be one year ago I was with you at home on leave.

The packing of four more drawings is completed and ready to be posted, one in particular I do not want hanging around it is quite the largest of all the sketches. It is a portrait in pastels of Sawa, wearing canteen bearer garb winding the last length of turban about his head, with an obvious title – The Turban. I have no means of fixing the delicate pastel colours to prevent the surface smudging; it is rolled carefully around a cardboard tube for protection. This should warn you to please take care when opening the package.

Another letter must end abruptly like many others.

CHAPTER 7

Into Action Against the Japanese

We, the 36 Division,[12] took a troop train from Poona to Calcutta Docks, and from there sailed to Chittagong on board the SS *Jalagopal* (launched 1911 SS *Edavana*). We then travelled from Chittagong to Cox's Bazar by paddle steamer, and from Cox's Bazar to Arakan by road.

Extract from 36 Division War History:

> The formation of the 36th Division came at a time when our strategy against Japan was beginning to change from the defensive to the offensive, after the enemy had been brought to a halt at the very frontiers of India. It was organized as an assault formation and consisted of 29 and 72 Brigade Groups.
>
> In January 1944 Lord Louis Mountbatten, the Supreme Allied Commander, South East Asia, who visited both brigades in the Poona area, told the troops that they were to take part in an amphibious operation that was to be mounted against the Japs in the immediate future.
>
> The division was equipped in a matter of weeks and advance parties moved off to Chittagong. The object of the operation was to assault and capture Akyab, the small port on the Arakan coast. But events then taking place in the Arakan were to change the destiny of the Division.

Booklet outlining a brief history of 36 Division printed on active service by Division HQ press (1945), and distributed to soldiers serving in the Division.

23 February   *BLUE AIR LETTER CARD*

It is two weeks since I last wrote to you and I can assure you my silence has not been due to neglect in any way. You may have guessed it is because I have been on the move and unable to write. We are with the 14th Army living a solitary life, no opportunity to go to a town, or to see

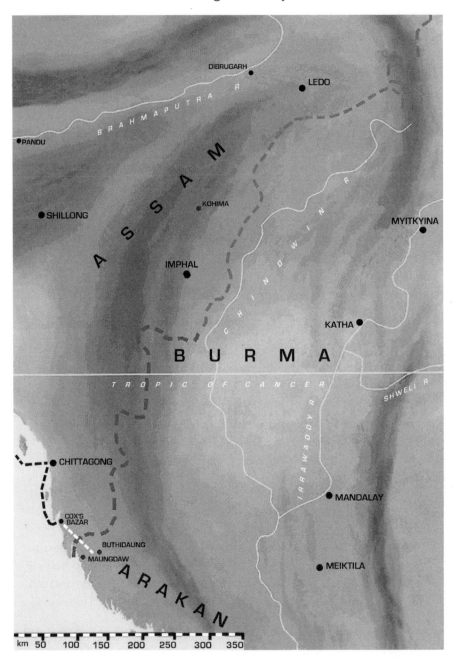

Arakan Campaign, February – May 1944

The Regiment moved by troop train from Poona into Calcutta docks and boarded the SS *Jalagopal* to Chittagong. At Chittagong, the journey continued by paddle steamer along the coast to Cox's Bazar. From Cox's Bazar the unit travelled overland by road to Arakan, and here completed successfully the first encounter with Japanese forces.

a film show. In spite of the lack of amenities I am living a life that is never boring. No mail has come through for some time; goodness knows when any will turn up. I had the good fortune to paint a couple of portraits in watercolour I had in mind for some time, native soldiers serving with my unit, a Gurkha and a Sikh.

The day before I moved out of the training camp your photograph arrived, how splendid you both look, it will be with me wherever I go.

26 February

Yesterday my luck was great enough to let me have some mail which was never expected to find us for at least another few days. I have developed a nasty cold and right now my head feels like it is filled with sawdust, yet I am sitting writing to you wearing neither a shirt nor a vest; it is very warm here within the Burma border. Aircraft are droning overhead leaving no space in time when their engines can not be heard. We are in the middle of a jungle into which your eyes penetrate no more than a couple of yards, and some places ankle deep in dust. My home is the Battery office tent where I sleep on bedding arranged over a ground sheet placed on the hard earth, no longer the cosy comforts of a charpoy. I may not be able to write frequently because of the remote postal service, the censoring of letters, or the availability of postage stamps, formalities liable to interrupt the steady flow of mail.

26 February   *To my brother Harry*

It is hot; we are miles from nowhere, in dense jungle shrouded in dust where all wild life has fled to escape the chaos of war. In this hostile environment I devote my free moments to writing and drawing. How much of this letter I shall write I can not say, the time is 6.15pm, any moment the B.C. may turn up at the office to give me tomorrow's Battery Orders to type.

2 March

The sun is beginning to descend towards evening lowering the oppressive temperature. I appreciate your statement about wearing an overcoat in England if I should arrive home in summer. I believed vanity was in the hearts of lads I met returning from the tropics in this situation; personal experience has changed my mind. If during the hours of sleep I become uncovered I am soon aware how cold it gets at night. Each day we swallow a yellow pill about the size of an aspirin, the taste is awful, but I accept it for my own good. The pill is a substitute for quinine; it does not prevent malaria but it has the ability to suppress the sickness if you are infected. Continually taking the pill turns the skin yellow and claims not to have the unpleasant effects attributed to quinine. We are eating tinned bully-beef for breakfast, bully-beef for lunch and bully-beef for dinner; I shall be putting a ring in my nose very soon. "I have received a smashing parcel from home!" was a recent remark made by one of the lads. "What was in it?" he was asked. "A tin of bully-beef!" came back the reply. The censors have recently declassified some outdated information, I am allowed to tell you Bangalore, and Poona, were two places in India where we were stationed, you may pass this news to mother and dad.

2 March

I am immobile on a medical stretcher, crippled, lying beneath a lattice canopy of bamboo leaves, and a gas cape protecting me from the heat of the sun. Returning from a patrol in darkness the night before last, I badly damaged my ankle jumping off the back of a truck. My feet landed awkwardly on uneven ground. Fortunately, Headley the medical orderly was with us and immediately treated my injury, assisted by Maurice, a friend who works with me in the Battery office. The two lads arranged my bed, settled me into it for the night doing their utmost to festoon the mosquito net above me for protection. My first thoughts were the ankle was broken; it was extremely painful and badly swollen. Next morning I was carried to the M.O. who made a careful examination of my foot diagnosing a severely sprained ankle. Unable to walk a step, I am laying on the medical stretcher getting constant attention from all my friends, and a life free of hard work and duties for a few days.

Spend no time worrying about me; I am being well treated except for irritant flies.

4 March *To my father BLUE AIR LETTER CARD*

This is a poorly prepared birthday greeting to wish you Many Happy Returns of the Day, I shall be thinking of you on the 26th. My ankle is much better, I am able to hobble about once again with the aid of a pair of make-shift crutches, and I expect to make a full recovery in a few days.

Birthday card design in colour painted on the Air Letter Card.

10 March

This letter is dated the 10th only a half an hour of the day has gone by, I am on duty for one and a half hours more before I am relieved. Your last letter brought good news that the first parcel had arrived and I trust the others I posted will get there too. April showers will be falling encouraging flowers to bloom making changes to a winter scene about the time you receive this. All I can see are palm trees, dense jungle, sun baked earth, and scorched grass everywhere.

I painted two watercolours, one at dusk and the other a portrait of a friend on guard by moonlight; both sketches I trusted to skill and good management so poor was the light. Not until I could carefully examine them in daylight a while later was I able to complete them. I am recovering gradually from the injury to my ankle, taking great care moving about. It can be painful if I place the slightest pressure on my foot. It is time to give Maurice a shake to take over my post, soon to crawl into the confines of my mosquito net and snatch a little sleep at the end of a night (morning) on duty.

19 March

Time means nothing, each day is a repetition of the previous and ceases to be named, lesser still ever knowing the date if it was not for managing my work in the office. This tropical sun is shedding brilliant rays onto the paper as I write, causing me to squint, and my bare back is receiving full sunray treatment. My pen is behaving badly, the heat is evaporating the ink on the nib making it difficult to write, and the splurges of dirt on the paper are caused by my sweating body. In the middle of lunch a stack of mail arrived, all work ceased and the cooks stopped serving the meal. Do not trouble your conscience writing to me, I get as much mail as anyone in the Battery, and it is indeed something to be proud of. You can not fail to notice my writing is a little better after removing a load of sand from the nib.

Water is our main beverage continually drunk from morn till night to counteract the copious amount of sweat we lose in this infernal heat. I would love to sample a nice cool drink of water instead of the chemically purified stuff we drink. Once each week we are issued a ration of rum, strong enough to rot your guts; perhaps offered as consolation for the horrid water.

20 March

It is my pleasure to sit as comfortable as I can to write, taking things easy this afternoon after bathing in a nearby river and having a short swim. Headley and Maurice salvaged an empty butter tin to make a brew of tea – I hear someone hollering, "Char Up!"

An art exhibition is being held in Delhi from the 15th to the 16th of April, and I propose sending two of my sketches if I can get can get hold of them in time. They are back at base and a fellow is expected to arrive soon who is bringing them here for me. Entries must pass scrutiny to be accepted, and can be unframed. Perhaps I shall submit the portrait of a Sikh, and a contemporary design for a wall panel. An Indian woman returning from a well carrying a gourd of water on her head with a chokree[7] on her hip, a common sight in India.

The Christmas card you sent to me must surely be lost and also the first parcel. We have been most fortunate for the successful arrival of letters in both directions. Last night I made a birthday card for Harry and I am sending it early for you to keep, and forward near his birthday. I composed the verse printed inside the card to evince the design on the cover.

COMING OF AGE

Time and tide moves on
And through this changing year
The life of youth be gone,
The life of man appear.

As the hour wanes
Of one and one score years,
The spear of manhood aims
To murder without fears.

Speeding on its course
The heart of youth its mark,
Propelled by man's brute force
That flings it in its arc.

Witches magic brew
Can not destroy the score,
The shaft now red tipped hue
For youth will reign no more.

Man is free to lead
And plough through future strife,
All sin to keep unbound
Within the bonds of life.

21st Birthday card to my brother Harry

One year ago today we were on the high seas, almost everyone on board ship was sea-sick. A week earlier we sailed from England in a large convoy of ships protected by escort vessels, a heartfelt moment leaning on the ship's rail counting every turn of the propeller taking us farther away from home. On the Sunday, workmen and sailors gave us a hearty send off as we pulled away from the dock to anchor overnight in the

35. Home Guard, Before a Night Patrol, Oswaldtwistle Moors
Exhibited – City of Manchester Art Gallery Civil Defence Exhibition, May 1942.

36. Gas Alert
Modelled at Accrington School of Art.

37. 3.7 Howitzer, 'Screw Gun'

Affectionately immortalised in a poem by Rudyard Kipling. Reputed to be the best type of mountain gun ever produced, it could be dismantled and carried by pack mules over difficult terrain. The barrel was constructed in two parts; breech and muzzle screwed together, hence its legendary name. Shells were loaded separately and a series of explosive charges ranged the gun (supercharge) to a maximum distance of 7,000 yards. Working in close support with the infantry made it ideally suitable for jungle warfare in Burma.

38. Training Camp, Kharakwasla, Poona

39. Sawa
Canteen bearer, Kharakwasla camp,
Poona, November 1943.

40. A Tamil Canteen Bearer

Above: 41. Survival Kit
Life jacket, sun helmet, water bottle, and
tin of hard rations; items to be with you
at all times on board the troop ship.

Left: 42. The Turban
Sawa, canteen bearer.

Right: 43. Babu
Canteen manager, Bangalore.

Above: 44. Joe's Canteen, Kharakwasla Camp, Poona

Left: 45. Charwallah

Right: 46. Sikh Warrior

1944   'SIKH W...

47. Abandoned in Defeat
Japanese military equipment.

48. Assam Hillman

Overleaf Left: 49. Self Portrait
Pen and ink wash.

50. The Gamblers

51. Listening Watch

Overleaf Right: 52. Gurkha, 72 Brigade

'GURKHA'   J.FENTON 1944

53. Plantations in Assam

54. Arakan

55. A Gathering Storm

56. Monsoon Sunset

Overleaf: 57. 'Stand To'

open waters of Liverpool bay. On the Monday morning the engines were restarted never to be still until we reached the port of Freetown, West Africa. Standing off shore loading stores near the equator, we suffered the full tropical heat of the sun. Once again under way never knowing our next port of call would be Cape Town, and six wonderful weeks relaxing far away from the reminders of war.

Dinner will be ready at 5 o'clock; beforehand I must abide by the anti-malaria precautions and spread an unattractive smelly cream on my hands and face. I have been fairly fortunate with good health except for a serious bout of dysentery immediately after my arrival in India at Bangalore. I made no mention of the sickness that might have caused you to worry. For days I suffered the effects of the weakening disease. At one stage, the M.O. considered sending me to hospital, just as I began to shown signs of recovery. A badly sprained ankle and a few colds is the extent of other ailments. Many lads are troubled with tropical sores, small scratches or cuts that become infected, developing into tropical ulcers, sinister lesions refusing to heal.

Every day we notice a cloudy atmosphere that will continue promising rain until the monsoon breaks next month. I am allowed to tell you that we have been in 'action' against Japanese forces. Don't ever worry about me I am fine. If at any time you wonder what I am doing at that particular moment I can tell you – I shall be digging a slit trench. 'A portrait of me, I am on the other end of the spade!'

A cartoon in pencil at the end of the letter – the blade of a spade ejecting earth from a deep hole in the ground.

22 March   *To my brother Harry*

Life is very different in *action* compared to regular army routine, there are no silly inspections or red tape, every bit of energy is spent digging and preparing a defensive position. The roads, if I may call jungle tracks roads, are dry and covered six inches deep in the finest dust. When a lorry rolls along it stirs up an opaque cloud thicker than any Lancashire fog. We are getting acclimatized to the excessive heat, sweat runs down the forehead into your eyes and causes a tickling sensation dripping from the tip of your nose and chin, a discomfort forcefully endured. Digging into the hard earth disturbs a film of dust that sticks to your skin, and ribbons of sweat trace snaking lines in abstract patterns collecting more debris as they wriggle over your body. I am afraid I must leave my letter at this stage Harry, it is getting dark and you must know in my situation I can not light a lamp to continue to write, vigilance and absolute silence must be observed everywhere throughout night.

Continued 23 March

Things have happened since last night regarding the weather. We naturally are sleeping out in the open on the ground, in the early hours of this morning spots of water started dripping through my mosquito net onto my face; I knew immediately it was rain. I grabbed my gas cape from underneath the blankets and slung it over the top of the net. It did not cover me wholly but I was too tired to care and slept on. During the last two hours the rain has stopped, this is the first phase of the chota[8] monsoon. Rain is a welcome aspect reducing the profusion of flies and dust. It is said the constant firing of heavy guns, which I hear booming at this moment, contributes to rain arriving earlier than usual.

I want to make mention for mother who will read this letter, I am transferring £8 from my credits to the paymaster in England, he will issue a money order that can be exchanged at the G.P.O. The transaction is posted sea mail taking several weeks to process.

25 March   *BLUE AIR LETTER CARD*

Today I packed a sketch for the exhibition in Delhi, a painting done recently by moonlight of a sentry on duty with bayonet glinting in the half light, and gave it the title, Dangerous Moonlight – Arakan. I shall have it censored tonight and get it in the post. The sketches I am waiting for that were left behind at base camp have not yet arrived.

We mainly exist on bully-beef served in a hundred and one different ways, in spite of the monotony, the cook's resourcefulness is keeping us alive and I enjoy my *grub*.

27 March

I received a reply to my letter of thanks sent to the family in South Africa who overwhelmed me with generosity and friendship. Many soldiers passing through Cape Town before me have been shown the same hospitality. I could turn up at their home whenever I was free arriving in time for dinner in the evening, afterwards very often dancing with one of their daughters. Their mother, an expert dressmaker was forever sewing, making a garment or a dress. They are a Jewish family; father, mother and two daughters fled their home in Lithuania a few years ago. The father speaks Yiddish, his command of English is very poor and I found his accent difficult to understand. The girl I often took to dances asked for my home address saying she would write, knowing how pleased you would be to have news from someone who had recently been in contact with your son.

28 March

I started a drawing for Harry copying his photograph as he asked in his last letter. To acquaint you with the comforts I endure, his birthday card was painted under extremely difficult conditions sitting in the confines of a slit trench. We can buy a few luxuries when supplies arrive in the canteen. For a special treat I bought a bar of chocolate, a bottle of cordial, tomato sauce and some sweets. There is nothing other than a few odd items on which to spend money except cigarettes. Each week we get an issue of 50, not of good quality but acceptable.

29 March

Before dinner today I began painting a watercolour still life group of captured Japanese army equipment. I do not feel unsatisfied with the result and may start afresh tomorrow, if I can find the time. Please let me know if any cartoons are missing, number 15 was the last one I sent?

2 April   *BLUE AIR LETTER CARD*

I made another attempt to sketch the group of Japanese equipment and I feel more content the way this has turned out. With the enemy in retreat there is a lot of discarded equipment scattered around, almost everyone has picked up a Japanese war trophy.

The long promised story relating interesting sights and customs that greeted me on my arrival in India has at last been written [see page 59]. I can not send it as a single package because of limitations imposed on the weight of air letters, I shall post it in two separate parts. I hope they arrive together, you will note there is a sequence in the order they should be read.

6 April

Thank you for the parcel, everything was most welcome especially in this part of the world, I feel sure you never thought it was bound for Arakan when you packed it. My ankle still troubles me; it is sore and swollen needing more time to recover.

7 April

No mail came in today; I can imagine there will be a large batch when it does get here. Before beginning this letter I completed cartoon No16 and hope to post it soon.

Our passage across India to Calcutta was a pleasant but slow sight seeing trip taking several days by special troop train, sleeping at night on bunks, six to a compartment, stopping on branch lines for the cooks to prepare food and to eat our meals. We had been travelling for four days, when at night after dark about 8 o'clock, we halted on a double track waiting for an oncoming train on a single line ahead to pass. Maurice, Headley, a friend and me, stepped out of our carriage to exercise our legs, walking by the side of the line before turning in. Headley and the other fellow headed off towards the engine, noisily blowing off steam. Within moments they came rushing back, yelling at us not to look for them for the next hour, they had persuaded the driver to let them travel on the footplate. This was too good a chance to miss; we wasted no time asking the driver if there was room on the engine for two more. With immediate agreement, Maurice returned to tell mates in our carriage not to worry about our absence; we would be quite some time before getting to bed. Full of excitement we all climbed aboard. Our European driver gave us an account of the many different gauges, and controls inside the cab while we waited for the signal to proceed. The Indian stoker wearing overalls as black as himself, and a bundle of cotton waste in his fist, welcomed the extra company with a smile. His white teeth, contrasted strongly with his filthy garb making his teeth look whiter. We waited in the darkness for the red signal light to change to green and begin an extraordinary journey every boy can only dream about.

The stoker flung shovel after shovel of coal into a raging furnace dancing and dazzling with red heat; it is a skill you could not imagine. The opening into which the chunks of black coal were flung, seemed to be only a few inches wide. I was handed the narrow shovel to load more coal, and the stoker's noisy laughter at my futile attempt was overwhelmed by the raging roar from the open furnace, the rushing wind and hissing steam. The grinning white teeth betrayed his hilarity. It is a work of art getting every bit of coal from the shovel into the furnace doors, not all to be thrown into the same spot. The amused stoker began gathering by hand, lumps of coal dotted about the footplate that never reached the intended target due to my clumsy effort.

I never thought it possible for a railway engine to rock so alarmingly and stay on the rails. I learned this is quite normal, requiring a great deal of skill stoking the fire. Standing firm with legs astride, feet bouncing on the footplate, you are mesmerized by the small glowing hole wobbling from side to side as you try to feed the flames with coal. In a moment of decision to strike, the blade of the loaded shovel crashes against the side of the steel door spilling all its contents, the opening no longer where you anticipated it should be. The evening was cool with rain in the air, the heat on my trousers felt as if they might at any moment go up in flames. I turned my back towards the open side of the cab letting the slipstream cool me down, and tried to imagine the discomfort working in the full heat of the Indian sun at midday. The loud drumming of clanging metal pounding the rails was relentless as we sped along, showers of sparks spilling past creating a spectacular display in the darkness. Peering from the cab we could see ahead the lights of a station, and as we approached a red signal light warned the driver to slow down and stop. We waited opposite the danger sign, the driver and stoker bustling about making several checks around the engine before we were given the all clear to get on our way once again. As the red light changed to green, my hand gripped the whistle lever giving two warning hoots before the driving wheels began to turn, and we were once more on our way. Two hours had passed quickly by when Maurice and the other chap decided it was time for bed, leaving Headley and me to enjoy more thrills on the footplate.

Everyone aboard the train had been asleep for hours, never thinking one of their pals had taken charge driving the engine with a hand on the throttle, controlling the speed as we continued on our way. I learned to move the starting lever cautiously, and coax the engine to begin slowly to roll forward; ears alert for the sound of the large driving wheels skidding on the rails, warning the throttle is open too wide. After a few attempts, I mastered the knack of taming the giant beast. The driver told me the regular speed we achieved was about 30 to 40mph. The driver and fireman were to be relieved by a new crew when we reached the next station, 20 miles further along the track; Headley and I were happy to stay with them until then. It was almost midnight when we pulled into the station, offering the driver our greatest thanks for such a wonderful experience, bidding him, "Goodbye," and to us, "Good luck," as we parted after spending almost four hours on the footplate before getting back to our carriage, and our beds. The next day, the two of us joined a different crew on the engine, never to be invited to participate in any part driving the train. But, we enjoyed the adventure of heat, steam, speed, and wind, just the same as we had the day before.

8 April *BLUE AIR LETTER CARD*
I was almost ready for bed last night when I learned it was Good Friday. That is how much importance we attach to days and dates.

13 April
Since last I wrote we have had a very pleasant half hour entertained by Stainless Stephen standing on the bonnet of a Jeep, his voice was easily recognizable from his opening words, exactly as he sounds on the radio. He began with the famous, "Semi-colon, semi-conscious, full-stop." He was one continuous scream of laughter from beginning to end and came prepared with many jokes about Burma. He removed his bowler hat with a ribbon of tin around it displaying short ruffled *thatch*, saying a

Gurkha had cut his hair with a kukri, (Gurkha knife), and not knowing the Hindustani word 'buss', which means 'enough,' was almost bald before he could stop him. He was walking down a street in London and asked someone if they knew which side the War Office was on? They replied, "Well, judging by the way the war is going at present I should think they are on our side." The Battery was once stationed in his home town and some of the fellows knew him. He said when the Battery was there, everyone planted their garden flowers in concrete. He told us one of his shows had a cosmopolitan audience of Gurkha, Sikh, American, Chinese and Sun-worshippers from Manchester. He repeatedly told us we were doing a grand job, and getting so brown we would make Turner and Layton look pale in comparison.

14 April

The same night, Easter Sunday, directly before the entertainment by Stainless Stephen, there was a church service by the padre. A pile of ammo boxes was arranged as a make shift altar. The padre was half way into the service when he was suddenly interrupted by a group of dive bombers flying overhead, preparing to attack Japanese positions nearby. To watch them in action is a thrilling sight, fully aware it is real, not a scene in a newsreel film of war. In the far distance the planes break formation, turn and follow each in line, the first plane begins to make a vertical dive, the engine increasing to a screaming roar, quickly followed by another bomber on the same path. A series of loud explosions drown the noise of their engines, and volumes of dense black smoke rise from behind a nearby hill as the planes reappear from their dive to return to their base, the mission completed.

Not long ago, we were halted sitting in the back of a truck during a move, when about five young kids appeared from nowhere. They collected by the tailgate with the usual request, "Baksheesh sahib?" We began to talk with them in fractured conversation using what little of the language we had learned. It was a pleasant change meeting strangers when we had been looking on the same faces, day after day. They were amazed to hear the ticking of my watch, and when I began whistling a tune to tease them, the youngest fellow almost blew out his teeth trying to imitate the sound. It would be appealing to finding ourselves in a village encountering the villagers, in preference to total isolation in scrub and thick jungle.

Tonight I handed in a telegram to be censored and sent off for Harry's birthday. It is growing dark quickly and I must put this letter aside until I find a free moment to continue.

15 April

I have been unable to attempt any sort of work today, the heat has overwhelmed me, a strange feeling the like of which I can not truthfully explain. A sudden dizziness in the head threatens the stability of the whole body, finding it almost impossible to stand upright for fear of fainting. If the problem persists and develops a stage further, you are liable to go mad running around in small circles. The condition is caused by heat-stroke. Drinking salt water and resting in the shade is a simple remedy. I drank a cupful of the terrible stuff yesterday, and again today. It is not easy to swallow, sipping it slowly to prevent being sick.

16 April

There is time only to write a couple of lines before going on duty, to thank you for the mail received yesterday. I was unable to acknowledge your letter in my letter handed in yesterday before the arrival of the day's mail. Thank you for the birthday card and good wishes.

17 April

Sitting inside what might be called for the want of a better word, a tent, and smoking a Woodbine cigarette, one of fifty issued this morning, I am listening to familiar music coming to my ears over the Tanoy loud speakers. One of our blokes is playing the tune *If You Had Your Way* on an accordion. The prime task of the speakers is to relay 'fire orders' to the guns. I am adding more to my letter before putting it aside to begin digging, which will take up a good deal of the afternoon, and afterwards a bath in a nearby stream. I am in a disgusting state, wearing only blue P.T. shorts, boots and gaiters, my body covered in sweat and Arakan dirt creating patches of mud laying in the wrinkles of my skin. A perfectly good excuse for the condition you will receive this untidy letter and illegible scribble, written under duress.

About a week previous we were caught in a pucka[13] storm, continuous lightning and thunder that lasted quite a while. It was moonlight when I went on duty. As the night wore on and everyone in bed, approaching black clouds gradually blotted out the moon. Without warning a strong storm wind began to whistle about our ears, and large drops of rain started falling fast. Everyone was up and out of bed in a moment, holding down tents and objects caught by the force of the strong wind. Efforts to secure some of the tents were futile as they sailed briskly away. Rain, rain, and more rain fell in half an hour than you expect in a week. Beds were swimming in water, and tins for making char floated away like model boats on a pond. I was fortunate to retrieve my towel and a pair of socks left outside, before they could disappear out of reach. Headley and Maurice saved our tent firmly holding it down, the corner on my side caved in water cascading from the roof onto the foot of the bed soaking my bedding. When at last I came off duty to get into bed, I lay down awkwardly and uncomfortable trying my best to get a little sleep, avoiding the part of my bedding that was soaked by the rain.

16 April   *To my brother Harry BLUE AIR LETTR CARD*
After dinner tonight I got stuck into a bottle of beer, it must not be drunk while the sun is in the sky. I think I have drunk about four bottles since we came to Arakan, it helps to quench a constant thirst. I refuse to drink the regular ration of rum having no liking for the taste; I did drink the stuff when it was first dished out.

21 April
You can see it is my birthday, and I must be the luckiest guy in the world. An entire day free to do whatever we like from sunrise to sunset, the first of its kind since we left India. I can hear jovial voices ringing out somewhere close by, way out of tune filled with happiness, typical pub songs; there is NO pub, and NO beer. I am in the best of health; the heat-stroke has not troubled me since I last told you how it had affected me. You must well remember the words of the song, *Mad Dogs And Englishmen* – a habit I swear to you in truth is absolute fact.

What good news, you have received the first parcel of drawings, I now await confirmation the second parcel posted on the 10th of April has arrived. I am writing within the confines of Maurice's and my abode. It is a rectangular hovel about 5 feet by 6 feet, dug down 4 feet into the ground with a narrow channel cut about 18 inches deeper end to end lengthways, deep enough for us to stand. A narrow shelf each side of the dug-out provides a couple of sleeping bunks, where I sit writing with my feet on the floor in the centre well. Steps at one end lead down into the dug-out, at the opposite end a narrow passage gives access to a slit trench, a defence position occupied quickly if we should come under attack. A camouflaged roof with a slight apex makes good cover, and I am as comfy as one can be. A similar defence position is immediately constructed each time we move forward. Empty sandbags lining the side walls stop dry earth crumbling and falling on me while sleeping. Maurice has pinned up two photographs of girls, and a drawing of a girl's head by Vargo, purely for decoration. None of the pictures are his acquaintance; they have been cut from magazines.

23 April   *To my brother Harry BLUE AIR LETTER CARD*
Let me begin by wishing you Many Happy Returns; you can see I am writing on your 21st birthday. You are probably fast asleep at 2.30 in

the morning, unaware your special day has dawned. The time here it is 7 o'clock, I have had neither a wash, nor breakfast, both will be taken care of within a short while.

You would not know me if you could see me at this moment wearing only a pair of slacks, the sun has been working full time on my skin turning it brown. You could never imagine how hot it reaches during the day, just now there is a slight breeze kicking up dust as fine as tobacco smoke. One or two solitary puffs of white clouds against a background of blue sky. Nothing is green anywhere, the sun has scorched the bush and trees to a sombre colour; this, after all, is Arakan. Cheerio, I sincerely hope you have a very good birthday.

24 April

I have just been informed I am on duty tonight, 'One For The King,' a colloquial remark we often use, no spit and polish, "Eyes right!" or parading to mount guard; very different from the rigours of discipline exercised in the barracks or training camp.

News was circulated yesterday that a noted band was coming to our forward position to entertain, and everyone was asked to welcome the group. I was busy making up my bed when I heard shouting, and a melodious din approaching amidst loud peals of laughter. Intrigued to know what was happening I hurried to meet a dozen fellows from the Battery, parading smartly to a well known marching tune. It was quite a BAND! The musicians were playing a collection of weird instruments, paper and comb, a couple of bamboo sticks drumming a petrol tin, and an ammo box being thumped with a lump of wood the end wrapped with sacking. A piano accordionist was loudly bolstering the tune. The conductor leading the mischievous mob held aloft a bamboo pole, fastened to it was a bicycle bell he was ringing erratically. I can honestly say the whole Battery joined the spirit of fun, laughing at the way everyone had their leg pulled. A hoax dreamed of secretly by a group of the boys.

Two cartoons are enclosed, No16 and 17, to put with the rest of the collection.

27 April

I received a telegram for my birthday that was a bit late, nevertheless welcome. It was an E.F.M., a similar communication I sent to Harry. A piece of wit was uttered by one fellow in the office today when he saw the E.F.M. cable list. Three separate phrases selected from a printed list are combined to construct a single message; each phrase has a code number for easy transmission. This guy asked if we were aware of a new phrase added to the list, "I am expecting a baby," he said. "Who would want to use that at this end?" piped up another voice.

Night is drawing on and time to go on duty, keeping my eyes open and ears alert, silent vigil in the darkness. Not throughout all those weary hours, long enough to strain the nerves. Finally, when it is over I crawl into bed to grab what little time is left for sleeping. My heart is happier when I see the dawn; thankful another night on duty has been completed, hoping the next few nights will be free until I am called upon to repeat the assignment.

30 April

I am sorry I did not finish this letter yesterday, I was too optimistic thinking I would be able to answer mail that came in. There was one item for me, my drawings returned from the exhibition at Delhi. I sent off the parcel uncertain of the full postal address, it has returned with more flashy labels than a holiday tourist's suit case. It never found the exhibition, travelling all around Delhi, gathering a label for this place, and one for that. The post office made every effort to deliver it, eventually abandoning their attempts marking it, 'Return to Sender.'

If you would like new shoes, dad, I can order a pair hand made for you by the mochi, when we come out of *action*. I need a range of measurements, and say if you want black or brown.

1 May

It was good news to know the birthday card for Harry and the copy of his photograph I made has arrived, also the second parcel of drawings. There seems to be confusion regarding the pastel drawing. The portrait is not a Sikh, he is a young bearer from Rajputana, serving at tables in the canteen. The Sikh is easily distinguished by his prominent features, bushy black beard and uncut hair.

I have been asked to offer you the greatest thanks on behalf of Headley, he got a letter today from his wife telling him she has received his portrait you forwarded, and said it is a remarkable likeness. The drawing of the other fellow you posted will in all probability have reached his folks in the Isle of Man; unfortunately, he is in hospital with dysentery. I expect to get to know it has arrived, when he is back with us.

2 May

Having had breakfast, and before getting down to work in the office, I must tell you I am OK. None of those nasty tropical diseases touch wood, instead a great deal of discomfort with prickly heat (medical term – miliaria). A rash of red pimples around pores on the skin; it is itchy, irritating, and a prickly sensation as the ailment implies. My trunk and arms are most affected. The problem is caused by continuously sweating profusely in this monstrous heat. Any attempt to relive the suffering by scratching, exacerbates the problem. Bathing the skin with water and cooler temperatures are the only means to alleviate the symptoms.

7 May

I can only write a short note when including a cartoon; this is No18 of the series. The heading 'R.A. Terms in Lighter Vein,' was chosen to convey activities about the Royal Artillery. One or two captions and phrases may be difficult for you to comprehend, they are commands, or terms, applying directly to orders in *gun drill*, when *laying* a gun, or *firing* a gun.

It is getting much too dark to see, I must abandon my letter writing. Cheerio, and Good Night.

CHAPTER 8

A Well-Earned Rest

The 36 Division was moved out of action from Arakan on 10 May 1944, and travelled by road convoy to a rest camp at Shillong, Assam.

Extract from 36 Division War History:

> The main route across the Mayu ridge, the road which linked Maungdaw and Buthidaung, still remained in enemy hands. It traversed two tunnels held by the Japs in strength, and to the 36th Division fell the task of capturing these positions. After extensive artillery preparations an attack on the western tunnel was put in by 72 Brigade on March 26th, and two days later the South Wales Borderers and the Royal Sussex entered it. The following week the Royal Welch Fusiliers successfully attacked the eastern tunnel, after the Glosters had captured a vital controlling feature known as 'Hambone.' The Japs had lost the greater part of their task force, whose strength was originally estimated at 8,000. By the end of April advance parties had already left for India and in May the whole Division moved up to the Assam hill station for a rest and refit.

> *Booklet printed by 36 Div HQ, on active service (1945)*

21 May *Continuation*

Just look at the date!! It is two weeks since I began this letter and much has happened in that time, so much that I can not hope to tell you everything. Let me explain saying we are in Assam, well out of reach of the Japs. The last two weeks have been spent moving by road to a rest camp and getting organized after arriving. We have been here two whole days, this is the first opportunity to pen you a letter. There was a flood of mail for us after a period of silence for almost three weeks. Tonight when I took out my bundle of mail that came in, "You've a lot of mail to catch up on, Jim," remarked one of the lads. So I have, and all I can say is

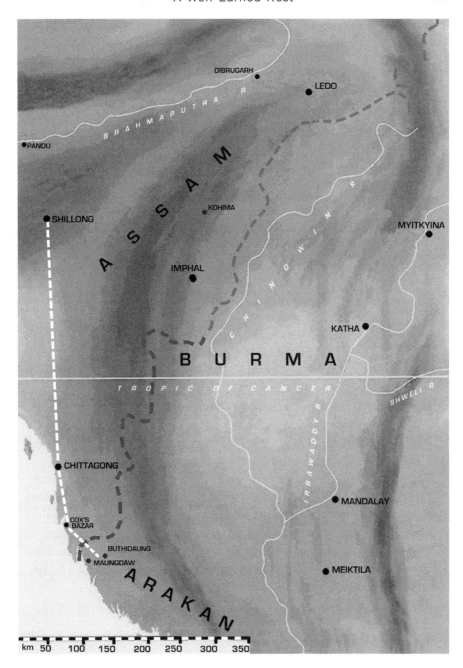

Shillong, Assam, May 1944
36 Division moved out of Arakan by road convoy to a Rest Camp near Shillong.

thanks to everyone. Often during the past weeks I was aware you would be constantly worrying about the long silence, never at anytime was it possible to post a letter to anyone. You will have felt uneasy thinking we were busy fighting the Japanese in Arakan, wondering why there was no news turning up from me.

My greatest thanks to Harry for the birthday gift, I was deeply touched the moment I read about his thoughtfulness and immediately wrote down these few words. I wish I could thank you personally Harry, but that is not possible under the situation I find myself in at this present time.

> There's just three words that I can say,
> A brother's kindness to repay,
> But this is like a an ear of corn
> Set in a yellow field.
> No matter what I scribe by hand
> Is love that shines in this far land.
> A loving brother you are true,
> And these three words I say to you,
> **'Thanks a million'**

This letter has been interrupted by spoons scraping on enamel plates. One fellow rolled into the tent with a can of peaches to share between four of us, it was very tasty.

I have more paintings to add to my stack, a couple of portraits I did on the journey here at places where we halted overnight. At last we are back in the civilized world once again, trying to put aside those past months engaged in hostile combat, suffering tropical heat, and unfriendly jungle. For the moment we are out of the war zone, thank goodness, and a little happier having in some degree played a small part in this horrible conflict. The watch is going fine except a couple of straps rotted in the harsh tropical conditions and had to be replaced.

25 May

It now seems obvious that somebody at the Field P.O. has lost the telegram I sent to Harry. This is not the first time it has happened, other chaps have sent cables that have never been received. *It is no good crying over spilt milk.* I am sat on my charpoy, the first signs of luxurious living for months. My rifle is unloaded, leaning against the tent wall and that too is unusual. All live grenades have been handed back to the stores and my ammunition pouches are empty, and very much lighter. A wonderful feeling of satisfaction to once again enjoy civilisation. Rain has been beating down since the first light of morning. Today I ate dinner with two parts rain water. The ground is deep in mud, the like of it never seen in Alice Street during the wettest days. Twice I visited the nearby town[14]. Entering a Y.M.C.A. and seeing white women helpers serving troops in the canteen was like a dream. It was a strange feeling, fresh in the mind are encounters fighting an enemy in the wild jungle of Arakan.

I do not know how long we will spend in Assam; we are recuperating on a well deserved rest cure, taking life easy, no training parades or drill. After about two weeks, we begin a period of *blanket treatment* (resting on a charpoy), ten days of leisure with nothing to do but dream away time. The regular daily dose of mepacrine[15] tablets we have been taking to suppress malaria, and are still taking, will cease abruptly. Mepacrine is a substitute for quinine; it does not prevent malaria, it stabilizes the disease to keep it under control. It is obvious, when we stop the treatment some of us may find ourselves with signs of this unpleasant tropical sickness. It takes an average of ten days to surface, hence this joyous period of relaxation. I have tried to keep fit and healthy, but malaria is not associated with cleanliness or good health, it is attributed to those impudent mosquitoes that have a nasty habit of gorging blood.

The short piece of prose is an appreciation for the care and attention you have shown me over the past years.

Man's home like a star in the heavens
Glows with radiant brilliance,
Trusted to guide his path throughout the night.
On the awakening day when golden rays appear
The grey of the morning fades, he ventures forth in joy
The road ahead is clear.
What human soul needs perils to prove his shelter?
Or separating seas and countless time?
Those who know these hazards and the loneliness,
Appreciate the priceless gem – **HOME.**

Major is fine from the accounts you have been giving me about his health. I often think of him, hoping one day I shall get the chance to see him again.

30 May

I began a letter four days ago but scrapped it, the reason you may note is my new address, S.E.A.C., initials for South East Asia Command. Once again we are classed as a Field Battery. It is no great change; my days in the office, however, may be numbered. The complement of a Field

Battery makes provision for two clerks only in the office. If the lance bombardier returns, and the sergeant also after completing his course, I shall once again be signalling, and Maurice back to his job on the guns. We shall see how things turn out.

Since I last wrote I have bought an end of plain white silk, 5 yards in length, at a shop in the town. I shall pack it carefully and send it off to you as soon as I can.

You recently asked, Why all the digging in the R.A.? I might have asked the same question if it were not for my experiences in the jungle, in *action*. Fighting step by step and gaining control of villages, important towns, access routes through dense jungle and mountainous slopes difficult to penetrate, we had to be securely protected at every advanced move. There is no continuous front line of defence identifying limits of conflict by opposing forces in Burma. Strategic positions are plotted for gun positions, and trenches dug for protection should those yellow devils decide to pop round for supper, or breakfast, the preferred time the enemy often chooses to attack.

Throughout the campaign, 'Stand To' was observed at dusk and dawn each day, over a period of half or three quarters of an hour, in preparation for a surprise attack. Nobody was allowed to move, talk, or smoke, absolute silence maintained to conceal our position. Everyone had their allotted place in a two man slit trench, grenades at hand, and weapons loaded poking out above the top of the trench recalling the scout's motto by Lord Baden Powell, 'Be Prepared.' Each time the guns were moved forward, establishing a new defence position was the first priority. Individual trenches and recesses for sleeping were dug, two men sharing a slit trench within the compound. A ring of trenches surrounding the perimeter, covering every angle of fire, were manned during darkness by pairs of sentries in contact with the command post on an open telephone line.

During those many weeks we were thankful Japanese patrols never made direct contact. Once or twice the enemy got pretty close to our gun position. One night, a Japanese infantry patrol creeping along a chaung[16], passed within yards of the guns, unaware of our position, and were surprised by an alert infantry unit guarding our rear, killing the whole Japanese patrol. Signallers, and gunners in forward positions alongside the infantry at observation posts, had scary stories to tell. A group of guys lost in the jungle came near to their fate. Signallers laying lines of communication, and gunners bringing up ammunition were vulnerable to ambush. Two fellows driving along a road in a Jeep were suddenly confronted by a Jap, crashing out of the bushes firing a weapon furiously. The driver's guard raised his Sten gun emptying a magazine on his target.

Of the shots fired from the Sten gun, seventeen hits were counted on the Jap's body. The gun position was frequently under enemy shell-fire. An incident, funny and fraught with dangers occurred when a group of lads were lining up for dinner. I had opened my paint box to put finishing touches to a colour design. The familiar sound of an incoming Japanese shell and the loud roar as it burst nearby proved decisively this was no time to be painting. I pushed my sketch pad and paint box beneath my bedding to protect them, and dived straight into a slit trench. Again there came the whistling sound, this time the bursting shell was closer. The fellows queuing to get dinner thought more seriously about the dangers than their stomachs, taking the longest strides possible to the nearest cover. This was one of many accurate bombardments ranged on our gun position, more often occurring regularly throughout the night. On this occasion there were no direct hits within the gun position, the barrage of shells straggled a small hillock close by.

It was prudent not to write home about two incidents that occurred during the campaign, knowing that all letters were read by officers on censoring duty. The first account might have caused me to answer some very awkward questions, and the second could have been brought to the attention of the officer concerned, although there was no discredit to his capability, or leadership.

The first incident was related to the checking of hand grenades. The gun position is defended by a ring of slit trenches around the perimeter, occupied during the hours of darkness by sentries in pairs, with loaded weapons and hand grenades. The defence positions are each identified by a number, linked to field telephones on an open line connecting neighbouring trenches with the central command post.

One night, well into my watch, I noticed the box of hand grenades had suffered corrosion exposed to the humid conditions. The night was dark, but I could distinguish rust on the outer casings, split pins, and ring pulls that prime the grenades.

The split pin is a device locking the firing mechanism in a safe mode. The moment the grenade is thrown after withdrawing the pin, a spring lever is ejected, activating a time fuse detonating the grenade. I was doubtful the pins might not be easily removed because of corrosion, delaying immediate counter measures when under attack. I tried pulling the pin from one of the grenades, which at first did not easily move, but withdrew using much greater force. With my left hand grasping the grenade holding down the firing lever, and the ring pull in my right hand, I prepared to reinsert the pin to hold down the firing lever. Normally a simple task, in the darkness the rusty split pin was difficult to relocate in the tiny hole. Trying desperately to coax the pin back into place, every attempt was futile. Redoubling my efforts, time, and time again, the pin refused to slip into the hole. Nerves and sweaty hands complicated the task, and tired fingers griping tightly to the firing lever began to feel the strain. Fully aware I must not loosen my grip, I needed to quickly find a solution to render it safe. It was not wise to ask my friend to insert the pin; he could dislodge the grenade from my hand. To fling it outside the perimeter would alert the Battery to suppose we were being attacked. I asked my companion to remove both my long leather bootlaces, which I wound tightly around the grenade tying down the firing lever. But I was aware the bindings might easily become loose, and the perilous situation was by no means averted. Speaking on the telephone to the guard posts on each side of our position, I warned the sentries about the situation, telling them I was about to crawl outside the perimeter, not to fire on me thinking I was the enemy. I selected a spot at a safe distance from our position I would again recognize, leaving the grenade where I could retrieve it the next morning and refit the pin. Dangerous as it was, the facts never came to light except for my few friends on guard duty that night.

The second incident occurred when a fatal accident was closely averted. During a lull in engagements with the enemy, everyone was taking things easy; Maurice and I were sitting by our slit trench, relaxing in conversation under a blazing hot sun. The gun position was well established, all defences prepared, and everyone had completed their hole in the ground to make it as comfortable as possible. All was quiet and peaceful. Suddenly, a half naked figure wearing only shorts and boots, leapt out from a nearby dug-out followed immediately by a loud muffled explosion, clouds of smoke, dirt and dust. The figure was barely recognizable as my squad lieutenant. Glancing towards Maurice and me, his bronzed features registered a whimsical grin as he hesitated for a moment to steady himself, before disappeared into his hole in the ground. Maurice and I were the only persons to witness the drama, and no mention of the incident was disclosed to us, or explanation offered by the officer. The devastation inside the dug-out could only be imagined. I assumed, like me, perhaps, he had been checking a hand grenade and let it slip from his grasp after pulling out the pin. It is fortunate he found time to make a quick escape leaving the confines of his dug-out to contain the full force of the explosion.

He was a likeable fellow. One afternoon before we left England, the Battery was returning to base towards the end of a gruelling route march with full kit and rifle. With some way still to go, he grabbed my rifle from me by the sling, and carried it hooked on his shoulder back to camp. He must have thought I looked weary and exhausted being a little guy, and could use some help.

1 June

I noted the PS in your letter informing me Harry had received my cable a little late for his birthday. There is something I should like to have in spite of telling you there was nothing I wanted; you may think it is a tall order and quite a surprise. I would like you to send me my camera; I could take some interesting photographs to look upon in later years. You could post it to Mrs. Carrington for safe keeping. I could ask her to send it on to me when I find it would be convenient and when I am allowed to use it.

It was a free half day yesterday, and I left camp with five other lads to pay a visit to a theatre in town that doubles as a roller skating rink at certain times during the week. We stood at the edge of the rink watching the people flying around, waiting to hire skates as they became available. I was lucky, a chap handed me his pair of skates as he left the floor. For the very first time in my life I set out on a rolling experience, suffering hardships and hard knocks. As a first time learner, determination and perseverance foremost, I made a pretty decent show spending the whole afternoon there. I got around the floor two or three times before a fall, admittedly, not when I first began skating. There was a Yank on the rink that left no doubt he had played this game before. He could skate!

Inspired by your praise for my poetic work, here is one more.

THE FORGOTTEN ARMY
36 Division – Burma 1944

The maddened sun beats down on sunburnt skins
That sweat, and toil, to save this evil world;
All spent to better what is held within
This sphere, around which earthly man is curled.
No days, no dates, no time, is known to those
Who fight to free the universe from bonds,
And Nations' flags on standards fly unfurled,
While humans take up sides with armour donned.

As Burma's tropic heat retards the gain
And all the devils of disease that be,
Avow the warrior's progress seems in vain,
To once more set the Far East free.
No cowardice, no fame, is sought by those
Who fight against the foe without a fear,
And pinnacle a Star from poles to see
Because, they fight for that which they hold dear.

We learn of battles fought for which they pay
With sightless eyes, prone on the field.
Those men have fought for us and won their day,
And sown the seeds, but know not what they yield.
So strong prevailing in the mind
Lost friends in Burma's green morass,
In hearts, and thoughts, forever sealed,
Brave deeds no greater concepts can surpass.

Men hold their ground and pray the time is near
For Europe's war to meet a peaceful close,
When these men too can hold a spear,
Together banishing the Eastern foe.
The 14th Army's men have won great praise,
But, many lay at peace in jungle graves.
What towering heights of fame have those men rose?
In history, is marked another phase.

I have written the whole of this letter amidst a joyous uproar, some of the chaps have turned up that have been in hospital. Johnny, the L/bdr, clerk in the Battery office, is here, and has told me my sketches packed in the office boxes at base should be arriving shortly.

3 June Y.M.C.A. *headed note paper*
I have just had tea at the Y.M.C.A. in town, tonight I hope to see the film, *Gay Sisters*. The length of silk I bought has not yet been sent off; maybe tomorrow I can have it censored, and post it. Take no notice of the price declared on the label, it must be below a certain value, the actual cost was 44Rs, £3-2s English money.

On Monday I return to my old job as signaller, the B.C. said I had put up a good show doing the office work in Arakan, he did not want me to think that I had been 'kicked out'. It was simply a matter of changes to the unit, reassigning Battery strength. I shall be sorry to leave the job. A great deal of responsibility was attached to the work, with no chance of promotion.

4 June
I can not get the parcel away today, Sunday, it is impossible to find officers around the lines to have it censored. Yesterday in town, I handed a local tailor an old canvas ground sheet to make a waterproof case that would be suitable to protect sketches and drawings when moving around. I picked up three sketches that had been stored safely in the office boxes at

base camp. Please excuse me, one of the boys wants me to make a sketch of him in ink on an Airgraph he wishes to send home.

10 June

Spending half a day in town today with some of the lads, and writing this letter before we have some *grub*; then, across the way to the cinema to see the film, *The Invisible Agent*. The length of silk has been posted. If you do not wish to have it for yourself, you might make Harry a shirt. Harry has been constantly in my thoughts since Tuesday, 6th June, lunch time. We were taking things pretty easy over lunch, when suddenly came news that the Second Front had opened. A breathless guy, rushed into the tent to relate reports of the landings in France. A crowd collected in quick time around a nearby wireless set, and from out of the tumult a cheery voice was heard to say, "Pack your kit bags lads!" For hours after learning the startling news, it was the only subject everyone could talk about.

My sketches and drawings are on show in the Information Room, a tent prepared specially to display the latest news from all fronts, and numerous articles of interest. I have been allotted a large wall space where anyone can view the pictures, showing scenes at the training camp in India, and in *action* in Arakan. There are eleven sketches on display, including two watercolour portraits, one a Gurkha, the other a Sikh. Another much admired, is a painting of a sentry on guard a night in the moonlight, wearing a fixed ear piece, and holding a field telephone ready to report an attack on our position by Japanese infantry.

I can hear faintly someone playing on the piano – *You'll Never Know*, a song Alice Faye sang so well in the film *Hello Frisco Hello*, and shown here recently. I have again been roller skating with a bunch of skating pals; they were surprised at my progress. I picked up the skill without much trouble, while here I shall spend every opportunity I can on *wheels*.

I received about three quarters of an air letter card from Harry. The censor had cut out a whole paragraph. Harry at the end of the letter made apologies for being unable to tell me very much on account of censorship. (Some joke!)

10 June   *To my brother Harry*

Thank you for three quarters of your air letter card, the censor probably wanted scrap paper to make paper dolls. Good work, you are putting up a grand show on the Second Front, I follow the news the best I can. You may hear folks say it is no good ducking, believe me that observation is nonsense. Saturday today, you will soon have been going at it for a week. While you are in the thick of it, I am out of it; dressed in K.D., sat in a writing room in a town, later I shall see a film show. Tomorrow marks the first anniversary I set foot in India.

17 June   *BLUE AIR LETTER CARD*

All this week my leisure time has centered on making a cigarette case, the idea came to mind when I picked up a spent Japanese brass shell case. My original plan was to design and engrave a memento onto a sheet of brass, hammered flat; imagination took me one step further to make something useful. Every spare minute, even at lunch break too, I have been bending and shaping two pieces of brass, trying to get the cigarette case finished before our lazy days end, and the *fun* begins once again.

Interruptions during the progress of this letter are coming from either side, a couple of guys are asking for instructions about drawings they are doing. I am beginning classes on Monday, after being asked by one of the officers if I would teach art to any lads who may be interested. I was in town today buying materials with money I was given for the purpose. I hope those wishing to take up this opportunity will make worthwhile progress learning to draw, and find satisfaction in their achievements. I shall let you know how the scheme is getting along.

18 June

Again, I have been working on the cigarette case; it has been much admired now it is taking shape. I am a step nearer to engraving a design on the front. When searching for materials for the art class I found a shop selling watercolour paints, mostly in pans, but one or two tubes. I dived straight into my wallet and 'spurred the horses,' so to speak. The paints were student's quality, many colours I already have, but finding any art materials here is so rare.

What a day it has been today, rain and more rain, the evening is beginning to brighten and for the past hour no rain has fallen. I'll say cheerio, and light myself a State Express cigarette.

21 June

Those thunder storms I reported have been repeated once only since we almost lost the tent and my bedding was soaked with rain water. A more recent storm occurred as we were making our journey out of *action* from Arakan to Assam; an incident as traumatic as it was amusing, and hope you can picture the scene from the story I tell.

After a long day's journey the trucks halted in an open clearing for the night, everyone set about arranging a place to sleep. I laid down my ground sheet and bedding on lush green turf before putting up my mosquito net as usual. The evening looked pretty black, and doubtful we would have a dry night. An old groundsheet fastened to the top of the four bamboo canes supporting my mosquito net made a protective canopy above my bed. The night was so hot I stripped off lying naked on my bed, sweating all the more because of the ground sheet canopy restricting any movement of air, but there to shield me if it should rain. Having endured the oppressive heat for half an hour, I said 'boo' to the thought of rain, and took away the ground sheet, eventually falling into a peaceful slumber. Unaware how long I had been asleep, I was awakened suddenly by a howling wind of great strength, warning the weather would very quickly turn much worse. I jumped out of bed ripping away the strings holding up the mosquito net, this was not a time to spend unfastening knots. I rolled everything together into one conglomerate mass as the first large drops of rain began to hit the ground. A few seconds later, rain was lashing down furiously. Scrambling barefoot for cover I made straight to the nearest wagon, dumping inside what I had carried and rushed back to gather the rest of my gear. In the half light, I found time to look at my watch and saw it was near to 5 o'clock, feeling relieved only one hour of sleep had been denied me. The officers were not so quick; they took the easy option scampering for cover inside a nearby temple, leaving the wind, and rain, to play havoc with their bedding and kit. Everyone else sought shelter in the wagons talking and joking, but before long, torrential rain beat through the canvas cover as we crowded inside. Luckily I managed to find my trousers in the jumble of clothes, and put them on. The B.C. began strolling around the wagons in the pouring rain, the wind whipping the palm trees in all directions, their leaves making a swishing sound as they thrashed against each other. The B.C. wore a dripping wet grey blanket about his shoulders, white underpants, and a pair of sandals. He reached the end of our wagon and peered inside enquiring if everyone was OK. As he turned to walk away, a loud cry "Charwallah!" came from inside the back of the wagon. The B.C. halted when he heard the call, stood for a second before moving casually along to the next party, the setting so real and hilarious. Anyone familiar with the appearance of a charwallah would recognize the similarity the B.C. presented, ambling along in pouring rain, legs bare beneath an improvised grey shawl, and wearing sandals that sunk out of sight in water with every step. Breakfast was most certainly late that morning; the cooks struggling to prepare a meal wading in three or four inches of water.

Every night I watch brilliant white streaks of sheet lightning flashing across the sky, with no thunder to follow. One evening recently, I might easily have read a newspaper during the continuous display, a lightning flash stabbing the night sky immediately followed by another. A chap manning the signal exchange during a severe storm received a nasty shock when lightning travelled along the telephone cable to the switchboard.

22 June

I am pleased with the interest shown in my second art class held tonight, and getting better organized as we progress. The officer who suggested the idea was keen to attend; unfortunately, he was admitted to hospital the day before my first class. The colonel was full of admiration for my paintings displayed in the Information Room, and wished to buy some of them. You know I would never be willing to sell; I shall keep them as a pictorial record of my experiences serving in the army.

Two weeks since I lost my job working in the office, now I am signalling again I shall probably have closer encounters with the enemy next time we go into *action*. Everyone was expected to take their turn doing guard duty during the period we were in Arakan, sergeants, sergeant major, all had to do their bit. There were about a dozen listening posts around the perimeter of the gun position. Throughout the night, eight men in pairs took turns on watch for two hours at each post. Officers manned the central command post to coordinate counter measures during an attack by the enemy, and issue fire orders to the guns.

25 June

I am indeed sorry to learn that Harry was wounded the moment he landed in France, fighting on the Second Front, but pleased he is back in England in hospital with nurses looking after him. By the time you receive this letter you will know I sent him a cable to wish him well.

27 June

The latest parcel of drawings has been censored, perhaps it will be in the post tomorrow and I shall outline what is included: – A landscape of a pass sketched from memory, a view I saw twice, first going one way and then returning, a place that witnessed a tale of war. The contemporary design for a wall panel of an Indian mother and chokree. Portraits of a Sikh, and a Gurkha. A portrait of a bearded old Hillman holding a bamboo staff. A painting of the boys playing cards in my tent at night. A moonlight study on guard at a listening post. These nights we would hear rifle fire, bumps of exploding grenades, or the awkward rattle of a Japanese machine gun, a noise distinct from a British machine gun. You can not fail to see the pen and ink self portrait. A portrait of a young girl wearing a red sari. A pencil study of Maurice reading in our dugout. A landscape in Assam, blue sky and clouds above brown fields. A landscape of a gathering storm, dark clouds and yellow sky. A monsoon sunset. A design for a tie. A rough embroidery design for the back of a shirt. There are also a few pencil portrait studies, simple ten minute sketches where we halted at various places on our journey to Assam. I have done about as much work on the cigarette case as intended, you will find this in the parcel. The design on the front was engraved by the pointed tip of a penknife. If you do not see me again, it is to be given to Harry.

29 June   *BLUE AIR LETTER CARD*

About four hours ago I had a cold needle pushed into my arm, an inoculation that has left it feeling sore. The bit I like is 48 hours excused duty. I am so pleased you are hopeful Harry will recover from his injuries caused by the blast from the German bomb, and his loss of hearing will improve with medical treatment and plenty of rest. I wish you had given me his address; I should like to write to him before he is moved from the hospital.

The parcel went off yesterday, there is another drawing included I did not mention, a portrait of a friend on *stand to* in a slit trench, with rifle poised ready to repulse an attack.

I may have got the wrong impression about this place, it was first claimed to be a 'rest camp,' but there has not been much rest. We have been undergoing lots more training for another crack at the Japanese. Our spirits are high, but will be much higher when we again get down to the real business in this war.

CHAPTER 9

Preparing for Action

In early July 1944, we were moved to a holding camp at Dibrugarh, close to the Burmese border, preparing to go into 'action' in Burma.

7 July   *BLUE AIR LETTER CARD*

This is the first chance I have had to write since we moved to a new position on the XXXX XXXXX[17] Burma border, and should explain the absence of letters. I have your letter telling me Harry is making fair progress; his recovery does not want to be too rapid, he may find himself once again in the midst of this war. He must feel pretty rotten about his loss of hearing knowing how much he enjoys movie films, and music.

I am almost as brown as I ever was sat in the hot sun without shirt and wearing only shorts, but suffering with a pretty bad cold which may be due to a change of location and climate.

13 July

It has taken me about three minutes to find the date, and the day is Thursday. Dusk is approaching and any moment I shall begin to hear the zoom of mosquitoes buzzing around. What a joint this is, it usually rains once a day, – All Day! Another pest has begun to trouble us at our new camp, silent leeches with sneaky tactics stealing blood. As yet, I have caught only one beginning to nibble, but thwarted him before he could cause trouble. The lighted end of a cigarette does the trick quickly, and efficiently. Pulling leeches off is not a good idea; it ruptures the skin causing it to bleed profusely. My cold has not left me but is much better.

I should like to have the camera with me, would you please post it to the Carrington's, it would be convenient to have it forwarded to me here when I know I would be allowed to use it. A competition is being held in South East Asia Command for a Christmas Airgraph design, all entries must be sent to Delhi by the end of this month. If we do not get settled somewhere soon I shall have no chance to submit any ideas.

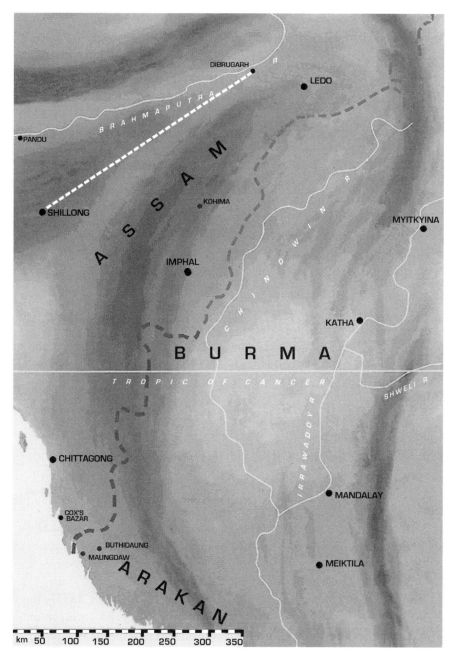

Shillong to Dibrugarh, July 1944
Regrouping, and undergoing preparations to engage the Japanese in North Burma.

19 July   *BLUE AIR LETTER CARD*

I have not yet had breakfast and will scribble a few lines before beginning my daily work. There has been no mail since I last wrote; I am at a loss to know how long ago that was. Days, or dates, mean nothing; it was not until I made enquiries and realized the date is the 19th and the beginning of my third year in this darn army. I get no spare moments until after dinner in the evening, which leaves me with about one and a half hours to write, or sketch, before the daylight vanishes. Some of the chaps coming away from the cookhouse after eating breakfast praise the porridge, I must get along there and check this for myself.

26 July

My first night here I made a quick sketch before dark of an Indian temple. I was determined to go there again and choose another view, spending more time on the second attempt. On three separate evenings after dinner, I was painting until the light faded at dusk. One of the lads has bought a cigarette case having seen the design on the cigarette case I made and asked me to engrave on it a souvenir inscription. Every morning, often before breakfast and between working hours I spend a little time designing a Christmas Airgraph for the S.E.A.C. competition.

This is a miserable camp; if there is no mud underfoot, there is a blazing hot sun above, and we have had to endure some of the hottest days yet. Our working times changed at the beginning of this week in harmony with the climate. Reveille is 5.30, at 6 o'clock a cup of char, *gun-fire*; parade at 6.15 to begin working until 8.30. One hour for breakfast, then more work from 9.30 until 1 o'clock, with a half hour break between. The full heat of the afternoon is free until we begin work again at 4 o'clock for one hour until 5 o'clock.

There are one or two open air camp cinemas nearby; a film called *The Uninvited* is showing tonight which I shall make an effort to see.

1 August   *BLUE AIR LETTER CARD*

Mail has been following us about for the past three weeks, finding us at last at our new location. I recently painted a couple of watercolour sketches, a scene of a local bazaar, and the monsoon weather, which is set to continue a few more weeks before coming to an end.

2 August

A welcome Air Letter Card arrived today, the first for quite a while and I could not fully understand one bit of it; two weeks mail seems to be missing. I expect when the jumble of letters find where we are, all the details you mention will be made much clearer. I have just finished another Airgraph cartoon in the series, R.A. Terms in Lighter Vein, and found a space to add a few lines telling you about the receipt of today's letter.

The time is 8.30pm; I am sat on my bed in my tent, writing with the aid of a simple light from a wireless set battery connected to a spare car headlamp. In about three quarters of an hour we shall be lighting a fire to prepare our bedtime coffee, and take to my bed early. I was on guard last night. Looking outside I can see the moonlight playing on the white roofs of the tents, and to my ears comes the night life of India, bullfrogs, crickets, mosquitoes, and occasionally a monsoon beetle making a monotonous drone like the buzz of a circular saw.

We have a make-shift canteen where we can buy sauces, soap, razor blades, tinned milk, coffee, sugar and sometimes fruit. I bought a packet of Post Toasties recently to eat with tinned milk for supper. A mug of coffee has been handed to me, and while drinking it the boys were busy with the flit gun and caught the weirdest thing you ever saw!

5 August

Yesterday I was overjoyed to find four letters for me. I am glad that Harry is improving, and before long hope to hear he has made a good recovery. I did not like to read that his nerves were not very good, responding erratically to sudden noises and strange sounds.

Last night there was a heavy downpour of rain with thunder and lightning thrown in, and during breakfast this morning there came a sudden lightning flash that struck the scrub about twenty yards from the tent, producing volumes of smoke rising from the spot. I have a full day off today; I was on the signal telephone exchange for the past 24 hours. It proves to be quite a good number; two signallers take over the duty every three days. I should like to know if you have received my cartoons, the ones sent recently are, The R.A; Director Method; Action Rear; and Angle of Sight.

My stomach was upset the whole of yesterday. I can not say if the cause was something I ate. I lived only on water until evening when I ate cornflakes with chocolate sauce and a cup of tea. I bought a tin of Andrews Liver Salts recently at a third the normal price from a native wallah, it had been affected slightly by dampness. I swallowed a couple of doses of the stuff this morning and feel more myself again.

I miss eating juicy pineapples we were able to buy until recently. Cutting away the outer skin is not easy, but they are so delicious it was well worth the trouble. Apples I have never seen since we were in Cape Town, and the best oranges also. At the training camp in India we could buy a large variety of fruit sold by native fruit wallahs. I preferred to buy limes which are very nice; there is no fruit to be seen at this dump.

6 August

Today is a red-letter day, an unusual amount of mail, six bags in total has turned up and among them for me were eight Air Letter Cards, 200 State Express cigarettes and two Observer newspapers. After leaving the first part of this letter yesterday, I took my paints to the local bazaar not far from here to enjoy myself. The usual crowd of chicos and curious natives gathered around to witness my efforts as I sat painting the scene.

6 August

Not more than a minute has elapsed since I finished the last letter, now I will fill this sheet. First I must mention the camera. I sometimes thought you might never be able to post it to me, that has all been cleared up and I know it will be OK. I think you have done really well to get three dozen photographic plates. I have no doubt I can overcome any problems I may encounter developing negatives. Photography could be used to capture rural life, customs and habits of the native population wherever I may be, in addition to the portraits, and scenes my drawings and paintings portray.

A voice from inside the next tent has just blurted out, "Jimmy, what are you drawing now?" I replied, "I am not drawing – I am writing." My itching feet are driving me crazy and I have removed my socks, the skin between the toes is cracked, a problem troubling everyone caused by sweat. The flies round about are in paradise exploiting a playground of pure enjoyment, very much to my annoyance.

I can imagine Harry on leave in *Ossy* might cause a stir when walking in the street, any person knowing him whispering to a friend, "He's back from the Second Front."

I am fine, but longing to be home. It is surprising how easy it is to settle down to army life, familiar with the people living around you, sleeping anywhere and everywhere, using whatever is to hand for a pillow, usually folded trousers, lying naked under a mosquito net taking life as it comes and thinking only of the days when I shall be home.

6 August *To my brother Harry BLUE AIR LETTER CARD*

I began to write you a letter (8ans postage), only to discovered I have but a 4ans stamp, therefore, you must be content with this shorter Air Letter Card. It is good news to learn you are recovering slowly after your front line experience and I hope you continue to improve. You have certainly done your bit towards the war. The inner white lining of the tent roof is reflecting a dim electric light making it just possible to write this letter on the comfort of my charpoi. Through the doorway I see pin points of light flickering and dancing as fireflies revel in a tropical night. Towards the east a creamy moon is striving to wax, teased by monsoon clouds suppressing its effort to survive. Much will happen before that mellow light bows to the superior sun. Men will die, babies will be born, battles will be lost and battles will be won, hopes will wilt, others will prevail, but evolution will stride on. We will build ourselves a new life after this job, so long big boy.

13 August

Mail is now coming in regularly, three letters I received dated around July 24, I cannot keep the same check on your letters as I did in the past. The letters informed me about Major's relapse, I hope the next will bring better news. I received a second box of 200 State Express cigarettes and comparing the date with the first package, it has taken quite a time to get here.

You say the censor has erased the name of our location mentioned in my first letter from here. When we move we are given orders about what we can, and what we cannot write home about. We were informed it was permissible to mention where we were. However, after handing in my letter, and before the letter was passed by the censor, the order was cancelled and for this reason the details about our location were blocked out. I am doing exchange duty every other day now. As usual, I am *in the pink* (brown).

13 August   *To my brother Harry BLUE AIR LETTER CARD*

Thank you for your Air Letter Card. We too have convalescent depots out here, the regular routine will be the same, perhaps not so many nurses to run them you seem to have. We get to hear all about them from the fellows that have spent time there.

I am doing my best writing by the dwindling light of a 6 volt battery that has almost run down. I might do better catching a bundle of fireflies I see flittering around outside in the darkness, and bottling them. They may give me more adequate lighting than the poor system I am struggling with at this moment.

My roller skating lessons have been quashed, the reason should be obvious; I am once again suffering the rigours and hardships of army life in a remote corner of India. Don't be too keen to see this part of the world kid, you may regret it!

17 August

I have exchanged my canvas residence for a native basha, (a structure of bamboo and thatch). We moved a short distance to new quarters and I have chosen a neat comfortable corner for my bed in a large room. Most of the boys are out tonight at a field cinema.

My day has been spent painting a portrait of an officer I previously sketched on an Airgraph, soon after we arrived in India. He moved away to a new Battery when he was promoted major and I met him again when he turned up at this camp. He requested a large portrait approximately half imperial size; the only large paper I could find is drawing paper. It is not easy working in watercolour on a sheet of ordinary drawing paper so big.

We are getting Blighty papers with news of the advances being made on the Second Front, and Churchill saying he has not forgotten the 'Fighting Fourteenth.' Three bottles of beer were allowed each man when rations came in last week; I took only one bottle. Lemon cordial can be bought from canteen supplies and I have been drinking it frequently to your health, in preference to beer.

24 August

I would love to eat some home grown tomatoes, the ones we get are tinned but very welcome. Beetroot is another favourite that comes in tins, I never grumble when this is on the menu. We are served a fair amount of tinned fish, pilchards usually, one only for each person but I always beg a second; they are not relished by everyone.

About a half hour's work on the large portrait should see it completed, the major has not been in camp for the past few days; I am awaiting his return. When he last saw it, he was really pleased with the result. I have posted another Airgraph cartoon; this information should reach you before the cartoon, a warning to be looking out for it.

25 August

Outside the monsoon rain is pouring down, we get a dry day then a wet one, if there are a few fine days, a deluge of rain follows over as many days as the weather has been dry. Before the rains came the ground was sun dried baked hard, scarred with deep footprints, tell tale signs of previous heavy rains, before long everywhere will be slush and mud once more.

2 September

I do not know what is happening to the mail these days, there should be quite a batch somewhere; we have not had a decent bag of mail for ages. I am getting along fine, listening to the war news on our signal wireless sets, tuned in to broadcast by Delhi radio. I was surprised to read you had been hearing the sound of church bells, the order to ring only in the event of an invasion has obviously been lifted, relieving the anxiety that German troops may suddenly arrive knocking on the front door.

3 September

It is 5.30 and I have just had dinner, outside black clouds are forming and it looks like a great shower of rain is ready to arrive at any moment. Having described to you the large amount of slush underfoot at this *joint*, I was prompted to place my muddy boots on the basha floor, take out my paint box, and make a watercolour sketch to show what an awful mess they are, more often they are much, much worse. The portrait of the major was finished a few days ago, the likeness was fine and I asked only 30Rs for my effort. It is already on its way to England.

Much of the world is now in the 6th year of war, of course I do not need to tell you this. I remember attending Sunday school that morning looking at the face of the clock on the wall as it reached the hour of eleven. So much has happened to change the world since then. I must stop here to wash before the mosquitoes come out for the night to try to get me.

7 September   *BLUE AIR LETTER CARD*

We are receiving no mail; there are no letters to which I can write replies. Rain, Rain, and again Rain, has been falling constantly the past few days, you have never seen mud like it in England and we are stepping in it up to our ankles wherever we walk. Moving about is far worse than walking on ice; Sonja Henie[18] can not better my skating technique in this situation. Tramping in the muddiest parts offers every chance to stay upright; placing a foot on the top of a slippery mound rising above water could send you sliding in any direction, ending up knee deep in muddy water. Sinking your feet well into the mud with every step to gain firm support and a sure grip is a trick I was quick to learn.

An allowance of three bottles of beer per man will be handed out tonight; this is not a free issue, I usually take one bottle only.

9 September

Today, I had another parcel of drawings censored and they have probably already begun the long journey home. There are not so many in this package, I do not want to be carrying them around, their condition will suffer the longer I hold onto them. The earliest is the quick sketch of the temple, and one I painted a short while later taking more time and care. Every evening a little after seven o'clock, around sunset, the mullah began calling the faithful to prayers. The incantations came from inside the temple for a few moments, then silence. Another painting of a scene not far from the camp captures the monsoon weather, fortunately it did not rain and the clouds passed into the night. Two local scenes, one a study of the poorest quarter of the town that would have been improved with more figures, another is a local market in sunlight. Also, the watercolour painting of my muddy boots, and a sketch of a gun in the jungle, the latter is being printed on the centre fold of Christmas cards for an R.A. Battery, not mine.

There are three parcels I am sending to you; I wanted to spend all the money I am carrying around with me, it is easier to do this than send home money by postal order. Unfortunately, I was paid 50Rs when I was holding 20Rs spare cash, and I also have the money for the portrait. There is nothing worth spending money on here. This is a special scheme and I will not have seen the contents of the parcels, they are packed with a variety of contents selected from a list. Money is paid into the office; the whole transaction is done by voluntary aid workers at Calcutta. We are allowed to send three each year. Here is a suggestion of the sort of things you can expect to find inside a parcel, handkerchiefs, four yards of printed cotton, a table cloth, soap, towels and other items, prepared, packed, and posted by aid workers.

9 September   *To my brother Harry BLUE AIR LETTER CARD*

I hope that life is OK and you are not again in *action*. Why you want to get back to your unit to have another go at Gerry I do not understand. I can appreciate your wish to make matters even for what he did to you, but that excuse is not good enough. The news we are getting about the war in Europe is good these days, and hopes are high that you will very soon have seen the job through. My Morse is getting a little rusty not having the need to use it for quite a while. How is yours, what speed can you read these days?

14 September *BLUE AIR LETTER CARD*

Looking through a recent copy of the Accrington Observer I spotted the headline report about Harry – 'NOT SCARED OF GOING BACK,' and I was quite surprised when I read the article describing the event, and felt very proud of him.

There has not been quite so much rain the past three days; today has brought no rain at all. Mail is not coming in but we have a good idea where it is and know it is on the way here.

19 September

A last we have received a small batch of mail, there is more yet to come. The earliest is dated 9 August, and the most recent the 25th. I am glad my drawings and cigarette case have been delivered safely. There are two more Airgraph cartoons on their way to you; I sent them off this morning. Thank you for attending to my request for the camera, I hope by this time it is well on its journey to Mrs. Carrington.

We have been given surprising news, leave is likely, and the first batch on the list is to get away soon. Perhaps I will be lucky and my name placed on the next selection. It can be two weeks at a destination of choice, plus extra allowance for travelling. This suits me fine, with high hopes of once again spending a glorious time with Mr. and Mrs. Carrington at Jhansi.

As I lay asleep in bed one night recently, there was a storm so severe I wondered if it was the end of the world. Lightning continuously burned brightly and the thunder was as loud as any raging battle. Rain came down in torrents and the thatched roof sprang a leak, drip, by drip, my face was kissed regularly. I turned away my head to avoid a continuous irritating dribble, finally subsiding when after a while the storm moved away and I was able to sleep.

24 September *BLUE AIR LETTER CARD*

There was a chance to wash underclothes this afternoon; the day looked like clearing a little having previously rained since day break. I made a trip into town with the lance bombardier to collect mail, it was a wasted effort there was no mail whatsoever for us.

A forces film show has been set up for the troops tonight in a camp nearby, maybe I will take myself there even though I have no idea what the film title might be. My cold is at its peak, if I were suffering with it at home I would be advised to do this, and not to do that, but I shall leave it go its own way knowing it will disappear after the usual uncomfortable period it will take to clear. There is no further news about leave; we need to know exactly how our credits stand to avoid personal accounts being overdrawn. Until this information comes through to the Battery office from the official Army Paymaster, nobody can collect pay to spend on leave. We may choose anywhere in S.E.A.C. area, two main rest centres are Shillong, and Calcutta. I have no worries about where I might go if I get the OK from the Carrington's.

I am about ready to go wading through deep mud to see tonight's film show. Cheerio.

29 September

Two days ago acting as co driver, I went again with the lance bombardier to collect mail and I am able to thank you for quite a few letters, along with newspapers that came by sea mail. I was driving the Jeep returning with the mail when we were held up by a truck that had gone off the road. Unable to proceed until the blockage had been cleared, I opened my mail and got through reading it a second time before traffic began to move. I was happy to learn the camera is on its way to Jhansi. I hope the thermometer you packed will register high temperatures, otherwise the heat may burst the tube. I have heard tell of medical thermometers bursting out here. Nowhere will I find photographic printing paper obtainable, unless I try Kodak in Bombay. The studios in India have trouble getting enough supplies to meet their needs.

Looking back over this letter I find numerous mistakes, I don't think I have made so many for a long time. There are two good reasons. (1) A guy has just this second finished bashing out a few tunes on an accordion close to my ears. (2) Today I visited the dentist, and oh what a time I had with him, or he with me. Long ago I felt something odd was happening in my mouth behind a tooth at the back. It never bothered me until I felt a small uncomfortable lump appear on the side of my gum, and thought it was time to let the dentist see to the problem. The dentist gave me a few good doses with the needle before setting to work. The whole treatment was worse than having a tooth out, a job usually done in a matter of seconds. My mouth was stuffed with cotton wool before he had his first nibble at it with a thin knife blade. Next, he used scissors clipping away my gum, regularly flicking bits of flesh into the rinse dish. The knife again appeared in his hand and a fresh charge of cotton wool in my mouth, by which time I began to wonder if there would be any part of my gum left. Finally the tweezers fished out something from my gaping mouth, and after smothering the wound with antiseptic, I was told to rinse my mouth and the job was finished. I am feeling OK except for an aching jaw. I never got to see the object he found, I think it was the remains of a tooth I had extracted by the dentist in Poona.

Harry is back in France you tell me, hoping to join up with his mob. The guy must be crazy is all I can say, good luck to him and I hope he stays well away from the enemy from now on.

The cigarettes that turned up recently came in a slightly rusty tin and the newspapers all showing traces of severe dampness.

4 October

Two air letters reached me today after a long trip, they are dated the end of August, and beginning of September, having been delayed somewhat. I noted you packed a Burroughs Wellcome photographic exposure calculator with the camera, and I hope the photographic chemicals you obtained to develop plates are in tablet form.

The leave situation is well under control, my turn will come as soon as the first party that left a few days ago arrives back in about two weeks.

There was an opportunity to make two quick paintings the other night, one was a moonlight scene, and a sketch as supper was being prepared by the chaps frying bacon on a Primus stove in the basha. We pool resources, invariably finding something to eat for our last meal at night before turning in. If nothing else, the least we manage to enjoy is toast and char.

My cold has disappeared, and my mouth has almost healed after its severe treatment.

9 October

There are about eight air mail letters to answer that have reached me since I last wrote, the dates are jumbled, and confused, with others received. The best news was Harry is back again in England with his mob. I don't want him to worry about writing to me; I know how difficult it can sometimes be. If I get news regularly from you how he is getting along, I shall be satisfied.

10 October

I did not finish this letter yesterday and that was most fortunate, having since been handed two more letters that I can answer. They came in the middle of dinner tonight as I was picking at a small portion of chicken, – yes, I really mean chicken! I can not remember when we last had this for a meal. I excitedly accepted my letters with greasy fingers, immediately slitting the seals with a knife tainted with gravy. Harry's letter, the earlier of the two was the first one chosen to read. I overcame my impatience finishing my vegetables and wiping my fingers to give the letter my full attention. Holding the letter in one hand, I stuffed my mouth with the second course, chocolate pudding, as I read on.

I am OK for paints, but if you can get some please send them out to me. I have half a block of drawing paper and anxiously await the package of Whatman paper. I am forced to use drawing paper for some watercolour paintings, as you may well notice with some of my sketches. Whatman paper is the best by far to use with watercolours.

Leave has been cancelled temporarily; I do not know when I shall get to visit the Carrington's. I received a letter from them, and I quote, 'Look after yourself, keep fit and happy, and remember our house is your home while you are in India.'

I have been doing office work again for about the last six weeks to help out the clerk in another Battery, which I find difficult to explain more fully.

19 October *BLUE AIR LETTER CARD*

Tonight, before beginning this letter, I did a bit of painting and I have drawn one or two more portraits for the lads. Mail seems to have collapsed over the past few days, I hope tomorrow will change our luck and see some letters arriving.

The monsoon weather is gradually coming to an end, the heat from the sun is less overpowering during the day and the nights are beginning to turn cooler. There has been no rain for the past three days which is unusual.

22 October

I can at last answer five air mail letters, and with them came the two Whatman watercolour blocks you ordered from the makers. I shall send Winsor & Newton an Airgraph to verify the safe arrival of the blocks. I prefer drawing portraits of local natives; the guys have little patience sitting a few minutes only for a quick portrait, and most of the sketches are given away to them.

26 October

We are passed the rainy season; the sun is shining brightly as it has been all day. A ribbon of light is laid across my paper streaming through a hole in the basha, where there is the slightest gap in the interlaced bamboo walls, flecks of sunlight filter through like gold coins. The street lights at home must look pretty seeing them once again at night after such a long absence, and a relief the blackout regulations are more relaxed.

The lads have just made a brew of char for a nightcap, you know my preferred choice is tea without milk; it makes a welcome change from army char served always with milk added. A witty friend has asked me if I went to night school because I do so much of my writing during nighttime, little does he know how right he is.

31 October

On Sunday I made a start using the new Whatman block when I had a whole day free, paying a visit to the quarters housing the Indian M.P.s stationed here. I always had the ambition to paint a portrait of an Indian army Red Cap wearing colourful headdress, and finding a willing helper I was able to make a start. The model behaved impeccably, sitting perfectly still between a few short periods of rest. I was not able to complete the painting by the end of the session. Yesterday, I managed to get off work in the afternoon when he was able to again sit for me, giving time enough to add the finishing touches to the portrait. The white sergeant in charge of their unit made me an offer for the painting but I turned him down. Selling it will be nothing more to me than money. Sending it home will give you the pleasure of seeing some of the work I have been able to do during my time out here. I should like you to get me some paints, there is little need to give you a list, you know what I like, crimson, and Vandyke brown are two colours in short supply I require, and a good quality brush would be nice to have but not too small. Also, a carbon pencil if you can find one, and Wolff's Black 3B pencil.

The monsoon has moved on, the cold weather is beginning to appear which hits us pretty hard at night. All day I have been wearing my bush jacket, normally I wear nothing but shorts. Last night I was at a film show, Ginger Rogers in *Lady In The Dark*, good acting by the stars, excellent photography and a decent story. The night was very cold returning from the show. When I got into bed I put on my army pullover and was pleased to feel the benefit. During the afternoon a few drops of rain produced a radiant rainbow arched plainly across the sky. There is an advantage with the change in the weather, mosquitoes are less troublesome.

1 November

I finished another Airgraph cartoon that will be posted in the morning. Next to me one guy is attempting to draw a cartoon on an Airgraph inspired by watching me at work, and another fellow doing the same, awakening in them their artistic talents.

Not far from here is a club with an open air swimming pool for Europeans, and white troops have been given permission to use it during morning hours. A time-table has been organized to allow all the different units stationed nearby an opportunity to go there. The water is not heated, but it was wonderful to enjoy the luxury of a swimming pool for the second time only since coming to India. Diving off the spring board was good fun.

About 5 o'clock this evening a heavy downpour of rain was sufficient to excite the pleasure of nighttime mosquitoes.

CHAPTER 10

The Campaign in Central Burma

I was a co-driver of a 30-cwt Dodge, a six-wheel-drive truck, in a convoy of vehicles making the first journey on the newly opened Ledo Road into Burma, to join the Battery and guns that had earlier been flown into 'action'.

12 November

I have been showered with letters since the recent long silence from me. I am writing letters while on telephone exchange duty, unfortunately I do not have the letters by me to give direct answers to questions put to me. There were letters from quite a number of people. One from Mrs. Carrington dated 4 November saying two parcels, the camera, and the photographic materials have arrived in good condition and they have been stored away safely. It was good foresight to have them sent to Jhansi. Now is not a convenient time to be carrying the camera with me, it will be sensible to have the parcels forwarded when the future is more stable, or I may be lucky to get leave and collect them myself.

16 November

More mail came in today, it is absolutely impossible to reply to all that I have received during the past couple of weeks. I am on duty, and the pad on which I am writing has a flimsy cardboard back resting on my *patent* cigarette case, a rusty Elastoplast tin supported on my knee. Writing in pencil I have to constantly keep shifting the paper using the limited surface area of the small box. The tin is perfect for keeping cigarettes dry, and withstands a lot of hard knocks. I am very sorry, I notice I have burned a hole in the paper with my cigarette and blame it on the uncomfortable sitting position in which I find myself writing this letter.

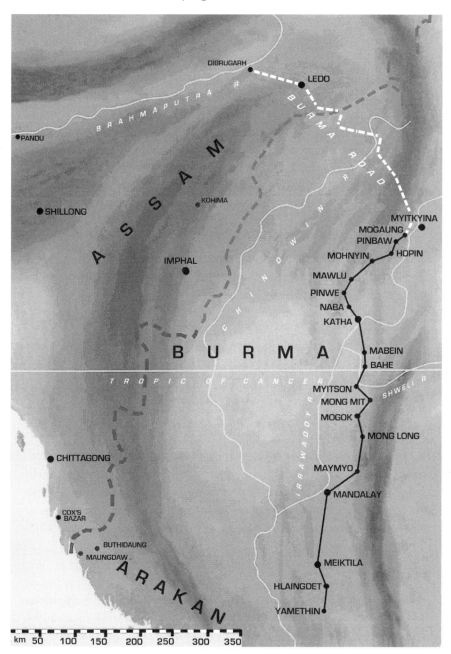

The Campaign in Burma, November 1944 – May 1945
A convoy of military transport vehicles left Dibrugarh at the close of the monsoon season to join the main Battery already attacking the Japanese in North Burma. The difficult journey took almost two weeks driving on the perilous newly opened Burma Road. The 36 Division was given the task of attacking and clearing the enemy from an area known as the 'Railway Corridor.' After the fall of Mandalay, the division was flown out of Burma to prepare for an assault landing on the Japanese mainland.

17 November

Now that you have late busses running again at night, it must be convenient, and a great relief, to get out and about after dark visiting relatives and friends.

20 November   *To my mother*

I made this birthday greetings card ages ago, knowing the future would hold little opportunity for drawing, and I am thankful I did. I am also enclosing a card I made for grandma, remembering it will very soon be her birthday. Two drawing pads have arrived from Auntie Molly, to which I replied thanking her and adding my best wishes for Christmas.

21 November

A short note to accompany this Christmas card, there is one for grandma too. I found spare moments to scribble Christmas cards in carbon pencil straight onto paper for many relatives.

28 November   *BLUE AIR LETTER CARD*

I am writing before having breakfast and early morning wash, the water in the bucket is cold, could it be wishful thinking the water will be warmer when I have finished this letter? Four Christmas cards made for relatives have been censored and posted.

30 November

Yesterday I received an old letter dated 21 September, no less treasured. It had been to a few places before finally reaching me. I am once again doing office work, one of the clerks is away in *dock* and I am on duty in the office. Very soon I shall be going to get my dinner from the cookhouse when my relief turns up. I am on duty again tonight when I hope to write more.

Later the same evening

Here I am back on duty at 10.0pm, how do you like the handwriting? Three Parker fountain pens came with the canteen supplies; wanted by so many, it was decided to organize a prize draw. One pen was given to HQ, and one each to the two Troops. I put forward my name, and got Maurice to do the same although he was not interested in having the pen. Maurice's name came out of the draw for our Troop and he handed the fountain pen to me. It cost 17Rs, has a stud filling reservoir with visible ink level.

The *grub* we are getting is pretty well OK, lunch today was bully-beef, beetroot, pickles and cheese, followed by bread and jam. Tonight for dinner we had stew with potatoes. Stew is not often on the menu I am glad to say. We had our usual beer issue two days ago, and last night we were given a ration of rum. The tot of rum, mixed with pineapple juice makes a warming nightcap. Nights are cold and I believe that is the reason for the rum. No lights are allowed after dark and we can not brew char. Often we gather together chatting in a dug-out about home and grand times in the past we like to remember, and there are many laughs.

2 December   *BLUE AIR LETTER CARD*

I am stealing office time in the shade after having lunch, sat at our work table which is like a summer picnic with a light breeze keeping down the temperature. In my last letter, there was no space to tell you about the earth tremor we had which was quite an alarming experience. The first phase occurred as I was busy digging, when I was overcome by dizziness and totally disorientated. My first thought was heat exhaustion was troubling me again, disturbing my balance. Suddenly, I heard a loud rumbling below ground and violent shaking of the trees, bringing down all our signalling lines, making me aware this obviously was an earthquake. I later learned other people had the same unsteady feeling and dizziness before there was any signs of the upheaval. A few seconds before the first tremor there was an uncanny silence and stillness everywhere. During the night, I was awakened from my sleep by a repetition of the ground shaking violently, the final act of the disturbance.

Thank you for the Ovaltine tablets, they are something new to enjoy, and the hair comb is by far the best I have used since leaving home.

You may be seeing me in the newsreels when I was caught on film in *action*. The cameraman was busy filming when I was helping the boys hook up the trail of a gun. He took another shot of a group of us sitting on top of a loaded truck, preparing to move forward.

· 5 December

Thank you for mail recently received, it is grand news another parcel of sketches has reached you. Last night we were talking together about how long it was since we last had heavy rain, and decided it was somewhere in the region of six weeks. It will feel strange to us at home before venturing out of doors wondering if the circumstances need taking along a mac. There are never days we are undecided during the monsoon to carry a waterproof cape, it is put away and forgotten when the rainy season ends.

Headley Cammack, a friend mentioned in many letters has been repatriated, and should be home about now. You may remember he is the person for whom you packed a sketch and forwarded to his wife. He was repatriated on compassionate grounds due to the death of his mother. Headley's wife has been running their hairdressing business since Headley joined the army, and looking after the family, and Headley's father too.

Some of the boys from the Regiment, but none from my Battery, are on their way home having been given 28 days leave in England. One of our chaps who saw them begin their journey said he had never seen a happier bunch of faces throughout the whole of India. Who would not believe this statement? Don't get ideas into your head you may see me rolling home very soon, completing two full years of service overseas is one of the conditions.

Enclosed are a few worthless currency notes of different values, printed by the Japanese for use during their occupation of Burma.

9 December   *To my mother BLUE AIR LETTER CARD*

Today, your birthday, you are more than ever in my thoughts, your time of day will be around one o'clock in the afternoon with half the day already passed, while here, the hours of daylight are disappearing fast. When the sun sets, our day comes to an end, no night life except official duties, or standing guard, and with luck a few hours sleep. I should have written earlier in the day, but I have been designing a poster to enter in a competition before the closing date on 31 December, promoting National Savings, for H.M. Forces.

11 December

Thank you for your letter dated 29 November, written at the time you said you had received no word from me for two weeks. This was a period when I was on the move, unable to write to you and no place to post a letter. I am now in a position to write regularly once again telling you as much as I am allowed about my activities. The poster for National Savings is finished; I shall soon see it is on the way to Simla where it is destined. I look forward to getting the watercolours you tell me Auntie Molly posted. I shall be well stocked with paints to keep me going for quite some time, however, I would like a decent rubber and a carbon pencil.

We are making preparations for Christmas, and the extra rations look good on paper, but we can not enjoy them in that way. The actions of 36 Division have been reported often at news time, on the radio in India, giving praise for our part in this war. I am getting along fine, in spite of a lot of effort turning over half the earth in this infernal country. The following remark made by one of the lads shows our spirit – "When I am back at home, if my wife asks – 'How about digging some of the garden my dear?' I shall simply say to her – 'I dug up half of Burma that's quite enough digging during my lifetime!'"

I am so pleased to be receiving good news about Major's health.

16 December *BLUE AIR LETTER CARD*

Today, butch[19] made a start on the Christmas puddings, and everyone is hoping they turn out OK. When this reaches you in the New Year you will have enjoyed Christmas celebrations.

20 December *BLUE AIR LETTER CARD*

I quite often see many different sizes and attitudes of Buddha everywhere, which we are forbidden to move, otherwise one would have been packed and posted long ago to Auntie Molly, knowing her keen interest in all things oriental.

I am writing this letter in a forward Toc H[20], with a quiz competition about to begin. Lately we have been having it much easier for a change, and looking forward to Christmas happily settled in one spot, instead of repeatedly advancing, forcing the Japs to move back which has been the tendency during the past weeks. Everywhere is much more peaceful, and we are halted near a decent size town. The past two nights I got undressed to get into bed, a pleasant change never possible for quite a while during the time we were in *action*. I shall have my clothes off again tonight.

28 December *BLUE AIR LETTER CARD*

Christmas went down very well indeed, the dinner was lovely and as much food as we could eat. I spent the day sketching instead of writing to you. Christmas night I stumbled on a group of Burmese wearing colourful native costumes, entertaining an audience with traditional dancing and stood enthralled throughout the whole performance.

A few ideas for humorous cartoons have come to mind, suitable for Men Only, or Lilliput magazine. I may soon get to work drawing them to a presentable standard for submitting.

29 December

There is a ground sheet rigged above my camp bed offering shade from a glaring sun, allowing me to write in comparative comfort.

A U.S. army-issue folding camp bed was given to me by a Yank soldier with whom I became very friendly, often visiting him and his pal, and watching film shows at their camp cinema. We were stationed on the border of Burma, not far distant from their unit where the Battery spent a few weeks making preparations to go into 'action' at the end of the monsoon. The change of company was as fresh to me as it was to them, and I enjoyed their hospitality standing in line at the cookhouse for 'grub', and sitting with them in their tent eating meals. I sketched a portrait of one of my new friends to send home to his wife. Out of respect I was given a US Army folding camp bed and military shirts. Sleeping on the camp bed was preferable to lying on the ground in the jungle, but I could only take advantage of the luxury when we were safe from attack or shell-fire by Japanese guns. Carrying it around was never a problem; there was always space available on a vehicle for a little extra kit.

The mid morning tea will soon be ready at the cookhouse and some kind guy will holler the words, "Char up!" Educating ourselves in Urdu has relapsed for a while. It was great fun testing our knowledge of the language on Indian tradesmen, chatting away like old women picking up more of the vocabulary. With expressive gestures, and a little of the language I learned, I manage to get along reasonably well. Many of the lads were unconcerned and had little sympathy or curiosity trying to talk to them or to learn their language.

I am sure you would be interested to know more about the dancing I saw on Christmas Day. I was on my way to a canteen at night, when my ears faintly heard a jarring din and strange rhythmic music. Away in the distance the brilliant headlights of an army truck illuminated an improvised platform, surrounded by an audience. I joined the crowd, leaned on my rifle and gazed at a troupe of professional Burmese dancers performing on the stage. A small group of natives squatting at one end of the stage were beating three different barrel like drums, and a musician was playing the melody on a type of flute, which chased all thoughts of *Elmer's Tune* and *Pistol Packin' Mama* from my mind. Surrounded by a semicircle of cymbals, another member of the band held a stick in each hand, tapping the cymbals in time with the rhythm. Walking about on the stage directing the performers were two men who would best be described as M.C.s, and sitting behind were more entertainers waiting to take part. The audience watched in silence, charmed by two young Burmese girls about thirteen years of age dancing gracefully in time with the music. They did not prance about the stage, but confined their movements to a small area. Each dancer was dressed in the most elegant costume, their jet black hair parted in the middle, drawn tightly together at the back of the head, ornamented with a tiara and adorned with a flower. One girl had dusted her face with white powder accentuated with heavy make-up. The dancing girls were all similarly dressed in a white and cream coloured bolero style jacket, decorated with embroidery and lace. The jacket was unbuttoned with pointed ends below the waist at the front and back, curled upwards and stiffened to keep their shape. Underneath the jacket was a fitted blouse. On their wrists they wore many thin silver bangles, glistening and sliding about their arms with all the different expressive movements. A skirt wound around the waist reached to the floor covering the feet, while full attention was directed to the charming movements of the arms and body. One girl wore a white skirt dotted with sequins; the other had on a plain red colour. The performers were gaily dressed and tidy, quite different to the normal attire usually worn by people seen walking about the towns and villages. The same two girls began a different song and dance, kneeling at the front of the stage chanting, stretching out their arms, swaying to one side of the body, turning and repeating the moves in the opposite direction; actions full of expression and flowing with grace in time with the music.

A small girl about six years of age constantly flittered about the stage singing and dancing. An M.C. announcing the sequence of dances kept her busy until it became obvious she was tired and exhausted. Throughout the whole show it was fascinating to observe the variety in the style and rhythm of the different dances. Some performances began with a person standing to the side of the stage, singing to the audience what I imagined to be a prelude to a story, the dancers acting out the sequence of events with gestures of the hands and arms, and movements of the body. The two M.C.s wore casual native dress but were distinguished by a yellow skirt, a dark waistcoat over a white shirt and turban on the head. I stayed enthralled until the end of the show when everyone slowly drifted away from the area where it had been staged.

The second event was also discovered by accident in the middle of the uproar at Christmas, while taking a stroll on a dark night to get away from the lads raucously singing carols. I picked up my rifle (we were not allowed to move without a loaded weapon) to wander away and as the merriment grew fainter, I once again heard music similar to the night before, coming from a dimly lit bamboo bungalow built on piles. I walked towards the front porch intrigued to discover the source. Making my way up the steps to the door, a group of Indian soldiers looking on showed the greatest respect parting for me to pass. More soldiers standing in the doorway blocked my view, but the moment I was noticed they too gave way and I peered inside the room to find a reason for the music, and satisfy my curiosity. Inside, I noticed a man in native dress and turban, dancing by the side of a young girl to music played by native musicians. The entertainment was different to what I enjoyed the night before, and by no means as colourful, or professional.

The only white persons present were four British officers and half a dozen Yank officers; the large audience was composed entirely of Indian soldiers wearing jungle green and army boots, from one infantry unit. It obviously was a privately arranged party for the soldiers, and I kept myself pretty well hidden, uncertain if the area was *out of bounds* to me. I stayed a short while watching the erratic capers, returning to our gun position before my intrusion could be discovered.

Arriving back at the gun position, I related what I had seen to a couple of pals who immediately wanted to witness for themselves all I described happening in the bungalow, but I warned them, we might get slung out of what appeared to be a very private affair. Taking care not to attract attention, we crawled inside the bungalow through a damaged wall at the back covered by a piece of cloth, and squat on the floor in the dim light to watch. Everyone was shouting and singing taking turns to dance, the Indian troops wearing battle dress, pounded about the floor in army boots. They had not the faintest touch of elegance, or style, and their clumsiness raised roars of laughter from all their friends. The moment we were noticed, they called on me insisting I should join them, but I flatly refused. Two British officers got onto the floor to dance; one had wound a piece of red material about his waist and was jigging around frantically in bare feet. We enjoyed the fun for almost a couple of hours before the party broke up. Seeing the band leader accept payment for the musicians from the officers, I knew it was not a customary celebration. The officers must have arranged the revelry for the infantry unit under their command, to banish for a brief moment the perils of fighting the Japanese. We had gate crashed their party, but nobody had shown objection to three strange British gunners in their midst. The least I could say about the affair – I did after all, have the privileged to attend a dance at Christmas!

A Church of England midnight mass was held on Christmas Eve, this was the first church service I have attended for quite a while.

29 December   *BLUE AIR LETTER CARD*
I have already written a letter to you today, since then I have received three air mail letters, two from you and one other. This may reach you before the one already written. I hope you will please send me my chromatic mouth organ, you should have no difficulty finding it, but I can not tell you where it may be. I have been asked to support B.H.Q. and take part in a quiz competing against A Troop. It is to be held tonight in the moonlight, on the *village green*, an area at the centre of our gun perimeter. At this moment aeroplanes above my head are lining up, dropping our supplies by parachute directly behind me – *I can scarcely hear myself writing!*

Parachutes manufactured from two different materials were used to bring in supplies by air, one type made of white cotton, and others of rayon in three very distinct bright colours, crimson red, turquoise blue and chrome yellow. They were dropped from Dakota aircraft, pushed out from the side of the plane flying over a designated area. It was a glorious sight watching the chutes open after leaving the aeroplanes and flutter gently to the ground. The bright colours identified different types of supplies each parachute carried. Red parachutes for ammunition and weapons, blue for certain foodstuff, and yellow medical supplies. White cotton parachutes brought in serviceable goods and general stores. More supplies were delivered by 'free drop', non perishable goods, clothing, socks, sandbags and lesser important hardy goods. These bundles were large and heavy, thickly padded wrapped in sacking pushed out of the planes at a lower altitude to obey the laws of gravity, and woe betide anyone not paying full attention skywards when they came crashing down. The instant they hit the ground momentum carried the heavy bundles forward bumping and bouncing over uneven ground in a drunken fashion for quite a long distance.

Because it was sometimes difficult to identify the drop zone in mountainous terrain and large areas of dense jungle, the Japanese soldiers benefited when mistakes were made, but fortunately this was a rare occurrence.

31 December   *BLUE AIR LETTER CARD*
Here is the last letter I shall be writing to you this year, nothing is happening to celebrate the dawn of a New Year; many of us had forgotten this moment has arrived. My watch tells me it is 2120 hours and all is quiet, except for jungle noises. No one is drunk – there is a very good reason, we have no intoxicating liquor to drink; it was all consumed during the Christmas festivities. I was given a touch of whisky from the sergeants' mess and was in full control of my senses, which is contrary to many unsteady souls I saw.

– 1945 –

2 January
My first letter of the year and looking forward to next year when I am due for repatriation, that sounds OK but my time will not be up until November 1946. I want to devote this letter to details that have kept you guessing during the past months. I am sure it will make you feel easier to

know about my mysterious activities. Some bans have been removed on censorship which until now was strictly applied.

I am serving with 36 Division and have seen almost a year of *action* except for a short rest period spent at Shillong, the capital of Assam. The climate in the hilly country at Shillong was cool compared to Arakan, and our greatest joy was sleeping at night without a mosquito net. There I painted only two sketches, one of the boys' playing cards in the tent at night, the other a landscape in the cool evening with mist on the distant hills and rough scrub in the foreground. Oh yes, the self portrait in ink was sketched here and the brass cigarette case made and engraved in the Battery workshop.

From Shillong we moved to Dibrugarh with the knowledge we were preparing to join the fighting once again. The monsoon was ever present, and we spent some wet and muddy weeks in camp waiting for better weather. As the monsoon period was coming to an end the Battery made preparations to be flown into *action* in North Burma. Flying in by plane presented many difficulties, not least of all the limited weight of personal kit we were allowed to carry. Hearing this news I told myself I would take with me my paints and paper at all costs. However, when the time drew near to leave I considered it my good fortune to be selected to remain behind with our transport and equipment to act as a co-driver taking our vehicles into Burma by road. During this period I painted the watercolour portrait of the major; Monsoon Mud (my boots); Dibrugarh; Dibrugarh Market; and The Bridge at Dibrugarh. The few of us ordered to stay behind as the rear party found ourselves taking life easy, meanwhile the main section of the Battery and the guns had been flown into *action* fighting the Japanese in Northern Burma. We could do very little as we waited for the end of the wet monsoon weather, our only relaxation was visiting a nearby cinema at a large Yank military camp where I saw many good films. They included *Lifeboat*; *Lady in the Dark*; *Jane Eyre*; *Two Girls and a Sailor*; *Broadway Rhythm*; and many more. During this time our thoughts were with our pals struggling through the jungle and mud around Myitkyina, pushing back the Japanese.

More than once I was told to get together my kit to fly into Burma, each time the final order was rescinded. Leave began and some of the rear party spent fourteen days of peace at Bombay, others went even further to the state of Hyderabad. I was to go on leave when the first batch returned, but the urgency to get transport moving intervened before I could take a break. Our happy days were numbered, cooking supper at night in an old basha, and visits to the Yank camp to see film shows would be a thing of the past. The condition of the famous Ledo Road into Burma, and as far as China, would very soon be suitable for motor vehicles to negotiate the hazardous terrain when the monsoon season came to an end. At the beginning of November an order was issued, "Prepare to move in twenty-four hours!" an announcement we had been expecting setting us on the road to a rare adventure. At last we would be driving for miles on a famous highway praised for its remarkable triumph of engineering, built by hundreds of labourers suffering hardship and appalling conditions. I was excited to be driving with the first convoy to travel on the new Burma Road[21], knowing it would be an exhilarating experience taking far longer than a few days to accomplish. With high spirits, I sat in the cab acting as second driver[22], alongside the official driver responsible for his six wheels 30cwt Dodge truck. At the end of the journey we would be meeting our boys in 36 Division, who were making headline news printed in the papers and broadcasts on India's radio almost every day, reporting the successful actions fighting the Japanese,.

What a journey! What a road! There were so many different contrasting changes of scenery; one day we would be climbing steadily upwards the whole day, and the next travelling down. We crossed a small plain heading towards more mountains that would dwarf the Pennines. Driving up the mountains was a breath taking experience, moving higher, and higher, on a twisting narrow roadway with hundreds of feet of nothing on one side and densely wooded slopes ascending on the other side. Sometimes, we would round the edge of a mountain to glimpse the tail of the convoy writhing like a snake on the road below us in bold contrast to the green mountain side. Often entering thick clouds of heavy mist, visibility was poor, the temperature dropping lower and lower, suddenly emerging into brilliant sunshine and blue sky. Below us, floating white clouds bathed in sunshine casting grey blankets of shadow on the undulating mountains as far as the eye could see. On the third day I took over driving the truck, and again later before reaching our destination. The road surface was well finished and in good condition for plain Mother Earth. We were on the move during the hours of daylight, sleeping at night by the roadside. Any attempt to write letters was out of the question.

Journeying for more than a week, we bypassed Myitkyina, where a short while previous there had been heavy fighting to capture the town. Myitkyina was now well behind the lines of our boys who were moving steadily forward. We caught up with their line of advance at Sahmaw, but they were still some way ahead. Pushing forward further we passed a region that had suffered the devastation of war, scattered dug-outs and bombed native villages. Our objective was to reach the Railway Corridor, a railway line linking north and south Burma. We followed the railway line leaving it only for short distances when we came across an easier route as we drove on. The monsoon had left the top surface of the road through the jungle powder dry. Clouds of dust whipped up by the trucks in front created an invisible screen that persisted until we were once again driving on a solid road surface. Our bodies were thickly covered in dust. We thrashed our clothes vigorously each time we halted, removing as much dust as we possibly could. Eventually we picked up a guide sent to escort us to the Battery lines, giving some hope we would arrive the next day. Next day came and still no sign of the Battery, they had again moved forward to a new gun position. One more day on our journey we reached Mogaung, where there was excitement and jubilation when at last we were reunited with the unit and all our pals. Ahead was our next objective, the railhead town of Pinwe where Japanese forces put up fierce resistance before it was captured by the Division.

After capturing Pinwe we took *the point,* and again began to push forward attacking the retreating Japanese. This was our longest advance in a single move without a halt, a distance of twenty miles that took us to Katha, the only decent town I had seen in Burma. It appeared to have welcomed civilisation and was very different from the small villages we had passed with houses built of bamboo. There were concrete roads I had never found anywhere since leaving Shillong. We were given the good news that Christmas was to be celebrated at Katha. One of the town buildings was a Toc H that eventually became a W.A.S.(B) canteen. An ENSA concert was organised over Christmas but I did not attend. The midnight Christmas service was held in the local Parish Church, not as you may imagine an impressive sturdy architectural stone structure with spire, it was constructed of four wooden walls under an apex roof. At Katha I watched the Burmese girls dancing in their colourful costumes, and another evening the comical footwork of the Indian troops. The town is an important river port on the bank of the Irrawaddy River and this was our first chance to see this magnificent waterway.

On Boxing Day I took a steady stroll towards a temple attracted by the golden dome glistening in the sunlight. It was like stumbling on a long lost tomb that writers of fiction have a compulsion to describe, enhancing their stories of mystery. Wandering along pathways that were wildly overgrown with jungle scrub, I at last came upon the main gate. Beyond the gate, almost hidden in tall grass and scrub, was a row of hideous stone idols thronging the way ahead. On either side of the gateway were two huge carved stone elephants in a kneeling position, each elephant had a single ivory tusk, the other tusks appeared to have been desecrated. The whole place held an uncanny atmosphere, and as much as I wanted to set foot inside the gate my willpower would allow me to go no further. I turned away from the solemnity of the scene, leaving its mysteries to the deities who regard its sanctity.

2 January   *BLUE AIR LETTER CARD*

It is 3.15am and I am on duty my hours of sleep are passed and I shall get none until nightfall, you are probably about to go to bed. My previous switchboard operator has left me a lovely cup of coffee and there is tea in a flask. We clubbed together to buy the flask from canteen stores for night time use. We get uncommon and useful luxuries like this offered to us occasionally; remember the fountain pen? I think that you will agree the pen is performing well. It takes a great amount of ink to charge fully, but dries out very quickly in the heat. I experience the same problem with my cigarette lighter. A fill of petrol is short lived, evaporating with the heat and lasts no more than about two days. I do not use it regularly, except when matches are scarce.

You would marvel at the box I constructed for the camera and photographic materials. I made it from a small arms ammunition box cut down to half the depth, a wooden outer case with inner lining of tin, and lid sealing tightly in a lipped groove. The Inside is well padded with the original ¼in thick felt to protect ammunition from heat and hard knocks. This I am certain will hold the camera, plate holders, plates and chemicals safely, and will be secure in all types of weather and humidity.

I recently sketched two sepia colour drawings illustrating 36 Division's actions during the campaign fighting the Japanese; there are five altogether and I would like to do more.

It must have been grand when you once again saw fruit at Christmas time. Wild bananas are growing here but they are inedible, tangerine oranges come in at intervals and there is plenty of tinned fruit, pears, peaches and pineapple. Yesterday for dinner I ate two pieces of steak with fried onions. When the rations do get through to us we fare pretty well, three good meals each day.

3 January   *BLUE AIR LETTER CARD*

About three or four months ago I mentioned having to replace several watch straps, the one I have now is a flexible rolled gold metal strap made by Bentex, it often suffers harsh treatment and a broken link is easily repaired making it serviceable once again.

5 January

I asked Mrs. Carrington to please forward the camera; it is now with me having arrived in perfect condition. I can not put into words the joy I felt when I saw the registered package. The plates were well packed and sealed, they are Selochrome backed, marked with the exposure speed. The package of developing materials has yet to arrive. An air mail letter received from Auntie Molly lists all the water colours she has posted. Mail is haphazard and I hope it can be straightened out soon.

The underpants I wear have been made from coloured parachutes, one pair yellow and the other blue, tied at the waist with tapes woven tubular that lay flat. The tapes are from the support lines on the coloured parachutes, the white chutes have a different type of twisted cotton cord. For extra comfort part of my bedding on which I sleep is a third of a whole red parachute that goes everywhere with me.

8 January   *BLUE AIR LETTER CARD*

Those photographs I was expecting by sea mail arrived this morning and I am impressed to see Harry smartly dressed in uniform with a crease in his trousers. I have long ago forgotten to be proud of such a personal touch.

11 January   *To my brother Harry BLUE AIR LETTER CARD*

I received mother's letter yesterday with the carbon pencil and rubber, I don't know why it has got here so quickly. Yesterday a fellow received a 1½ pence sea mail letter dated 27 December, which is remarkable; maybe there have been air mail planes cruising around with cargo space available.

You still hit the high spots when you tell me you go dancing. I wish I was there with you, but of course we first must sort out our problem here, as you must at your end. I can believe your home station spit and polish must get wearisome; I have completely lost touch with this army tradition, except now and again somebody thinks to remind us and exercise a bit of discipline, often ignored with little respect for it.

The time is 7.30, and morning mist is hanging around close to the ground. I can hear the cooks bustling about preparing the first of three meals for the day. You may wonder why I am beginning this letter so early in the morning, no lights are allowed during darkness and I must take advantage of whatever spare time I can find to write letters. I would like to post this today.

It is pretty nippy these mornings when I dip into the wash bucket, its *shiver my timbers*, and the days are not unbearably hot. I spend the sleep of night on part of a parachute on my camp bed with a couple of blankets over me, and a change of clothes to get into bed, a little different to what is usually undressed. I put on a pair of slacks kept specially clean reserved for the job, two pullovers and my socks, and I can wake in the morning feeling cold. I recall the days lying nude beneath a mosquito net with sweat trickling in streams over my skin and sleep impossible until tiredness takes over.

I am going back to my old office job today, Johnny the bombardier is leaving this morning for home leave. Maurice has been working in the office and I shall be helping for about two months, until Johnny returns. Cheerio, Sunshine.

16 January *BLUE AIR LETTER CARD*

There was no way that that I could write during the past few days, the postage stamp situation is nil, but today the ration of one 4 annas stamp per man came in. I got to work on Maurice and George to help me out, and bought from them their ration of stamps. Once again I am on exchange duty, and although this letter is dated 16th, there are just two hours of the day gone by. Drawing is on the sideline and I have nothing further to add to the collection.

18 January *BLUE AIR LETTER CARD*

The postal dates on the mail are not arriving in a consecutive order, what is more important it is getting through. Christmas was a time of making merry, and we were able to spend it at a much better place than we could ever have anticipated, the details have already been told.

20 January *BLUE AIR LETTER CARD*

Yesterday I received five Air Letter Cards, two from dad and one each from Harry, Auntie Ethel, and Faye in Cape Town. I like the good reports you gave me about Major's health.

I noticed an advert for Burroughs Wellcome, Bombay, in the photo catalogue you sent to me and I shall write to them asking for a price list of photographic chemicals.

23 January *To my brother Harry*

After scratching about with my pencil here are some recent efforts you may like to have but I am afraid right now I can do no better than this. They are small simple ideas to fit this envelope, any larger it would need to go sea mail. I received a photograph of you from mother, taken on your 21st birthday on the Isle of Wight. I must say you look pretty tough.

23 January *BLUE AIR LETTER CARD*

There was a nice batch of mail yesterday, two air letters from you, one from Harry, 200 State Express from the Observer Cigarette Fund and the local Rag. I have no idea who may have sent the cigarettes, I have not found any identification with them.

Fortunately, since I had to leave this letter five air mail letters, two from mother, two from dad and one from Lilian were handed to me. There is nothing I require at the moment, a variety of items can be bought in the Battery canteen that is kept fairly well supplied with certain items. Sweets I can occasionally buy and tend to nibble them sparingly.

28 January   *BLUE AIR LETTER CARD*

Yesterday came a letter from Mrs. Carrington telling me she had posted three parcels, but I have received two only. It is a mystery when all three parcels were posted together.

Very shortly my relief will arrive and I shall be away to get some *shut eye*. It is 9.0pm and for the moment everywhere around is peaceful and I hope it stays that way throughout the night. My watch decided to stop about a week ago for no good reason, unless it was because I have been very busy doing a lot of digging. I took a look inside and it is working as good as new, perhaps the inspection removed some uninvited foreign matter.

Today's news sheet says the cold weather in England has been pretty bad, I hope you came through without any overwhelming setbacks. My duty relief has turned up and I am now free to taste a cup of char before getting into my bed.

1 February   *BLUE AIR LETTER CARD*

The parcel of developer and chemicals arrived from Mrs. Carrington, it had not been registered and during its travels received a bashing. Fortunately the contents seem to be fine, a tin containing fixative powder, two familiar yellow cartons of Tabloid Rytol developer, and a small bottle of tropical hardener liquid. They conform perfectly in size to fit the carrying box. One of the lads made me two tin trays, one for developing the plates and another for the fixing solution, both fit neatly together saving space. I shall be able to develop two plates only at one time, but this should meet my needs.

I see I have burned a hole in the paper with the cigarette I am smoking. I now know you sent me the cigarettes when I found the pink slip tucked between the wrapper and the carton with the words – Keep Smiling. You must not worry about the watercolour landscape sketch, 'Monsoon,' which has been stolen. I wish the coppers every success to recover it, and good luck to Mr. Beecham for his prompt attention to the case and willingness to do his best to help.

It is good news Harry has been using his brains at last seeing the doctor about his ears, perhaps he suffered serious injury, or permanent damage from the exploding bomb.

3 February   *BLUE AIR LETTER CARD*

Yesterday I received yet another parcel of State Express 555 cigarettes, this time the pink slip was on top of the tin in Harry's handwriting. It will not take me long to smoke the few cigarettes left from the previous batch. I do not rush through them smoking the good ones the moment they arrive. I light up a Woodbine at intervals to help the decent cigarettes go further.

On telephone exchange again and it is 2.0am, I don't mind night time duties it gives me the opportunity to write letters in a well protected dugout, with the aid of a very simple electric light. I hope you will somehow be able to get for me a small supply of photographic printing paper so that I can make reference prints from each negative.

Two days ago, two fellows serving in the Regiment left on 28 days leave after their names were drawn from a list; both men are from my Battery, and my unit B.H.Q!

I was glad to hear you have found my mouth organ. It will be relaxing to entertain ourselves during brief moments of stalemate when we are out of harm's way, or a long advance as we were when driving to Katha, sitting on top of a truck singing carols before Christmas. I though at the time how nice it would have been if I could have played the tunes on my mouth organ.

5 February

I made an unwitting mistake putting the 5th on this letter, I am on duty and it is 0245 hours, past midnight and February 6, with no idea what day it is. Please forgive any mistakes you find; it is not the best time to be writing letters rolling out of bed at 2 o'clock in the morning.

Yesterday after digging and eating a well earned lunch, the cry – "Mail up!" sent everyone scurrying to the sergeant distributing letters. All the happy smiling faces pricked up their ears and looked on as he began shouting out names. With every confidence I knew there would be something for me judging by the unusual size of the catch. Six Air Letter Cards was the number I turned away with. About an hour before the mail arrived a W.A.S.(B) mobile canteen drove into the gun perimeter and two white girls started selling the usual luxury supplies. They certainly made our eyes pop out, coming through the wooded jungle to our forward position. I was busy digging my slit trench as was almost everyone, our sweating bronze bodies dappled with patches of dirt, but who cared? We carried on digging while they were dishing out their wares from the back of the wagon. Frequently there was the whine of shells flying through the air; thankfully they were all going in the right direction. They were also well entertained by a group of dive bombers putting on a display giving the Japanese a headache.

In a few days it will be exactly one year since we left India on a long journey to where nobody knew? It was to Arakan, and our first *action* against the Japanese. From Poona we travelled by train to Calcutta, enjoying for a few hours my greatest thrill on the footplate and driving the train. We saw nothing of the big city crossing the famous Ganges River straight into Calcutta docks to board a ship, the S.S. *Jalagopal*. During the two day sea voyage I painted the portraits of the Sikh, and the Gurkha. Landing at Chittagong we spent the night far away from the town, and in the morning boarded a paddle steamer for Cox's Bazar. Once again on land we moved into Arakan by road, then came that fateful day, February 29, when I sprained my ankle. It was on March 8, the first *fire orders* were sent singing over the air. I was hard at work digging in when a wireless operator nearby suddenly displayed an expression of bewilderment and happiness as he passed the *fire orders* to the Battery. Without delay our very first shell from the guns went whizzing over and I glanced at my watch, it registered exactly 12 o'clock midday. Advancing to Razabil there was some hard fighting by the infantry, and with our support they captured the tunnels at Maungdaw and Buthidaung. Taking into account the circumstances we had to deal with, the barrage put down was larger in comparison to the great artillery barrage in North Africa. I came across a news article where a special unit was ordered to rescue an R.A. mob, cut off by the Japs. Later I learned the unit had moved into a position we had previously occupied a short time before. If by chance we had delayed our plans to advance we would have found ourselves in that situation. When we were stationed at Ledo, one fellow received some periodicals with pictures of the fighting in Arakan. On a front cover was a photograph of Razabil, taken after we had occupied the area. Razabil was a strongly defended Japanese fortress and I could mark on the picture the exact spot of my slit trench. You have probably read accounts of the fierce fighting to capture two tunnels held by the enemy. There were many pictures in newspapers of a large Japanese gun the Division captured in one of the tunnels. I was not fortunate to see the gun, but many of my pals were. I was busy in the office at the time and could not get away. The tiffy[23] went to examine the gun, and reported destructive souvenir hunters had removed the maker's nameplates. The gun was sent to India and put on show as the largest gun captured from the Japanese. It was at the bottom of the Ngakyedauk Pass I spent my 22nd birthday. Leaving Arakan by road on our way to Shillong, we spent a night at Chittagong. This was our second visit when I had an opportunity to see the grand Technicolor film, *Arabian Nights*, tasting what could be classed as civilisation, after several weeks hard fighting against Japanese forces in Arakan.

I bought the rolled gold watch band at Shillong for £1.7shillings, it is more serviceable than any leather strap, and the cloth bands are useless in this climate. The Japanese occupation money I sent home was given to me by a Burmese who was carrying around a stack of notes.

I have not answered any part of your letters; however, everything you have written has been noted. I am pleased Major is getting along fine and enjoying the snow. I remember he loved to be rolled in the snow, snapping at it when I threw it in his face. I show his photograph to many people who remark what a swell dog he is, but admit to holding little love for Alsatians. We are keeping fit digging as this remark will verify, uttered by one of the boys emerging from his slit trench and peering into its depths to survey his work, "A special design, for nervous people!"

Our guns are giving the Japanese a good bashing and the reverberations have knocked out the flimsy light in the dug-out where I am on duty writing!

8 February   *BLUE AIR LETTER CARD*

I come off exchange duty in quarter of an hour at 10.0pm, and then to bed. The earlier period I spent writing to Harry. We are at last able to send home air mail letters free of postage. I am pleased you found so much interest in the stories of my travels. Relaxed censorship has permitted me to write about past experiences, the details are out of sequence and a little jumbled, I am sure you can piece it together to make sense of it. Everything here is tik hi[24].

12 February   *BLUE AIR LETTER CARD*

The results of the poster competition were published in SEAC Newspaper and I am sorry to say I was not among the lucky ones. I wrote a letter to Burroughs Wellcome in Bombay asking for a price list, they replied saying they can not supply photographic chemicals owing to war time export controls in England.

15 February   *BLUE AIR LETTER CARD*

I have not yet seen the light of day, it is 4 o'clock in the morning and last night before '*stand to*' I was able to read three air letters, one each from you and one from Harry. He told me of his visit to the specialist who plugged his ears, and they must remain that way for three weeks. The treatment appears drastic making his life very difficult being unable to hear.

Now I know the £8 has reached you safely, I shall send more money home when we get the forms to complete. Each month a number of names are drawn from a hat, the lucky ones can choose to have a parcel sent home through an organisation in Cape Town. The cost is 3Rs 8ans, eventually everyone should get a chance to partake in the scheme. It has not been operating very long but you can be sure the contents from South Africa will be well worth the money. Two more lucky guys are going home to England on leave; one in my Battery, to Marshside, Lancashire, and the other chap is from a different Battery in the Regiment.

17 February   *BLUE AIR LETTER CARD*
I have been getting together another batch of sketches ready for posting. The food these days is pretty decent and yesterday everyone received a bar of Cadbury's chocolate and a few sweets. It was grand to enjoy really good chocolate, but since leaving South Africa I have forgotten the nice taste of my favourite sweets, Liquorice All Sorts.

17 February   *To my brother Harry BLUE AIR LETTER CARD*
I gather from your report the specialist has a new patient on his list and he is using your ears like a dust bin, putting everything into them except the Hoover. With your ears plugged, you will not be enjoying films for a while. This letter will not get finished tonight Harry, I am on exchange duty and my turn is almost completed.

Continued 18 February
Today is like a nice early summer morning at home; as the day grows older it will get much warmer but nothing like the temperatures during the hot season. I hope you are in the best of health and your ears will soon be OK again.   — • • —
   NEWS FLASH – Friendly dive bombers are creating one hell of a row near to our gun position giving the Japanese a nasty pounding; one more problem for the enemy to cope with.

21 February   *BLUE AIR LETTER CARD*
Scribbling another letter with lots to say, however, I can not give all the news but will write a long letter tonight when I expect to be on duty. I have taken my first photograph, and the other thing I have to say concerns some of my sketches. You may remember I mentioned I had made several sepia monochrome paintings, scenes of the campaign. These drawings have been taken in hand by an officer who assures me he will get them published somewhere. The parcel of paintings I packed to be sent to you has been posted. Thank you for ordering more photographic plates.

22 February
I shall give you a summary of the sketches posted two days ago, providing I can remember them all. They have been gathered together

since October; involvement in fighting this war has prevented me from producing as many as I would wish. The earliest is the portrait painted at Ledo of an Indian M.P., a moonlight scene; and the same night I sketched the boys making supper in the basha. A design in colour inspired by a song the first time I heard it sung called *Paper Doll*. A scene of the wagons halted for the night on the Burma Road, painted with only the aid of headlights from our vehicles. Two pencil sketches of Burmese chicos. A painting of a Burmese temple at Bahe. Two portraits of Maurice, one in carbon pencil, the other in pencil. I promised him one of the drawings. I hope you will forward the sketch to his home, the address I shall give to you in a later letter.

My monochrome sketches in sepia, depicting incidents involving 36 Division during the campaign in Burma are to be sent away for publication by the Public Relations Officer. There are about eight scenes of our activities. Had I guessed the drawings would be so much appreciated I might have produced many more.

The parcel of paintings recently posted could only be censored some miles back at Division HQ, and taking them there I passed through the village of Bahe, where earlier we had been dug in at a gun position, and I made a painting of the temple. I had with me the camera and decided the same temple was worth a photograph. The night previous, I loaded four plates into holders in total darkness, squatting uncomfortably in a slit trench with a blanket covering me. To economize on my limited supply of plates I made only one exposure, I must wait until I can take a second photograph before developing both the negatives together. The photograph was taken in bright sunshine with clear blue sky at 10.30 in the morning. I could not pick and choose the setting during the brief moment I spent there.

24 February   *BLUE AIR LETTER CARD*

My job in the office has come to an end, a bombardier clerk has been posted to the Battery, and Maurice has a new partner working with him. Officially I am doing signalling and telephone duties, but other work sometimes takes priority. I am often asked to letter direction signs indicating a safe route to follow when the Battery moves forward. It makes a change from doing my regular job and offers a chance to take things easy for a spell.

A bunch of new guys joined us a few days ago and have been working in the hot sun with backs bare, if only you could see the condition of their skin. They will have had no sleep for the past three nights. I notice many examples of sunburn, but these fellows are by far the worst, suffering from exposure to the blazing hot sun. I am walking around wearing a pullover until the sun gets up then bare to the waist for the rest of the day with no ill effects. It was funny to see white skins amidst a pack of brown bodies when they first arrived.

Many lads have fashioned a neck scarf from coloured parachutes and one I wear has been made from a turquoise blue parachute. A friend acquired a few precious gems from a local native and he has given me a lozenge shaped goldstone that would look well set in a ring.

28 February   *BLUE AIR LETTER CARD*

I took another photograph yesterday when I met a group of Indian soldiers squatting around a small fire in the jungle cooking a midday meal.

Tonight we have been treated to a mobile cinema, the first film show since we were at Ledo. I had time only to see half the performance before coming on duty at 10 o'clock. The film is Bing Crosby in *Going My Way*, and from my position inside the dug-out I can clearly hear the sound track from the speakers. The newsreel before the main film was amusing, causing loud cheers among the audience showing past achievements of 36 Division in Burma. Bing is singing the famous song *Avec Maria* on one side of me, and on the other side the deafening roar of our guns shelling Japanese positions. I am feeling fine as usual, the *grub* not too bad, sleep about the right number of hours, plenty of exercise digging, baths laid on in a bucket, mail coming in OK, loads of sunshine, some people would pay pounds for this, what more could I want? Of course, I could say to be home enjoying all the comforts that go with it.

4 March   *BLUE AIR LETTER CARD*

The two negatives I exposed have been developed and they appear to be fine. The photograph of the temple was hard to remove from the holder and I carelessly broke the corner off the glass, fortunately the main part of the image is not affected. The second negative is OK but has a minute scratch on the emulsion that can be corrected.

You wish to know how I deal with darning holes in my socks? Fighting a war in the middle of a jungle there is no time to spend darning socks. I possess about half a dozen pairs, when they get religious (holey), I throw them away. I am certain to be one of a crowd when new socks are handed out, there is not the usual red tape exchanging old or worn out kit for new.

My mouth organ will give a good deal of pleasure when the enemy is not nearby listening. Yesterday I was not feeling so good, my temperature was normal thank goodness, two days ago I had a vaccination and this, plus a strenuous work load yesterday night has given me heat exhaustion. Nothing to worry about, I am feeling OK now.

5 March

Once again I am back on office work, the bombardier has left us and I don't know how long I will keep the job this time. Developing plates was successfully carried out in my slit trench at night covered by a tarpaulin. The water temperature was 65°, and timed 4½ minutes to develop using normal strength developer. At half strength, I calculated the time at 11 minutes to develop. I mixed one pair of tablets with 6ozs water timed 15 minutes, but because I added tropical hardener, developed them for 16 minutes. After fixing and washing the negatives in several changes of water, I stood them on a drying rack covered with a piece of fine cotton cloth to keep out dust and placed the rack under the lid of my camera box. After two hours I was packing them safely away.

I made a few drawings from memory in carbon pencil recently of our actions against the Japanese, and found ten minutes free to sketch a portrait of one of the lads on a small piece of drawing paper he could fit inside an envelope to send home.

8 March   *BLUE AIR LETTER CARD*

My pen has run dry; therefore I am using a pencil as you can see, and sat in comfort leaning against a huge teak tree, the fat stalwart trunk shading my back from the hot sun. Diving into my pack checking the time, it is ten minutes past three. I never wear my watch when digging.

The sun has begun its downward path and the excessive heat of the day is lessening. The days have been growing steadily warmer over the past weeks, and overnight the dew is not so heavy, or the nights as cold as they were a month ago.

Thank you for getting more chemicals, the 8oz tin of fixing salts I have will only give me 16 measures of solution, the bottle of hardener even less than this. I know it can be reused but I have not the means to conserve a larger quantity once it has been diluted.

9 March   *To my dad*

I wish you Many Happy Returns on your birthday dad, with special thoughts on 26 March. I was able to make this birthday card for you some time ago. The table you sent to measure fluid ounces will be helpful. I must possess a queer desert spoon, when tested with a liquid measure in the M.Os. kit, a little over two spoonfuls is a good guide equal to one ounce.

11 March   *BLUE AIR LETTER CARD*

I could increase my allowance home each week but have no wish to do so at the moment, I think it far wiser to arrange to send a fair amount when it has accumulated. You can expect to receive £15 in about two months, the usual form to send home this amount of money has just been completed.

Yesterday I took another photograph and two more today. I am impatient to see prints from the negatives and would like you to get me either *daylight,* or *gaslight,* printing paper. You might send it by air. It is not necessary to include a letter but be sure to mark it 'Printing Paper – To be opened only in a darkroom.'

Recently I have found very little spare time to write to Harry, we are constantly pushing back the Japanese and we must use every effort to keep him on the run. It was good news to learn the specialist is hopeful he can salvage one of Harry's ears, and a restful break for him if he can get a few days leave at home.

58. Audience for a Dancer

59. Opportunists Pilfering Oil

60. "Baksheesh Sahib?"

61. Teaching the Tricks of the Trade

62. Trade Depression, Poona

63. India's Young Generation

64. Measure for Measure, Poona

65. Solemn Celebration

Above: 66. Monsoon – The Other Enemy
The Royal Artillery Commemorative Book, p. 112.

Left: 67. Innocence

Right: 68. Sikh

Below: 69. Photographed by a Gurkha, Burma

Left: 70. Mochi (cobbler), Jhansi

Right: 71. Midday Sun, Jhansi

Left: 72. Lokhan Wallah (metal worker), Jhansi

Right: 73. Flags of Convenience, Bombay

Above: 74. Taj Mahal, Agra

Left: 75. The Tomb of Mumtaz Mahal, Agra

Right: 76. The Red Fort (detail), Agra

77, 78 & 79: Japanese Sword Surrender Ceremony, Johore Bahru

80. R.A. Christmas Card 1946 (centrefold)
Surrounding the Victory Parade Salute, are scenes of repatriation, and Release Training Programmes to rehabilitate veterans awaiting demobilisation.
The badge of the Royal Artillery was emblazoned on the front cover.

Right: 81. SEAC Newspaper Cartoon "He's going to live in Civvy Street but does not say which number."

Far Right: 82. SEAC Newspaper Cartoon "Hello, Intelligence here."

Below: 83. Royal Artillery Cap Badge

Above Left: 84. Triumphal Arch, Haw Par Villa, Singapore

Above: 85. Rampant Dragon, Haw Par Villa, Singapore

Left: 86. Johore Bahru

Right: 87. Gathering Shellfish, Singapore

88. The Flotsam of War, Johore Straits, Malaya

Left 89. Awaiting Repatriation, Transit Camp, Singapore

Below 90. 'G' Branch Intelligence Staff. Two veterans of the Burma campaign are holding Japanese swords presented as war trophies.

91. Lilian

Overleaf: 92. Bumboats on the Suez Canal

CHAPTER 11

A New Move

G Branch Intelligence, HQ 36 Division

13 March *BLUE AIR LETTER CARD*

It is March 13 but certainly not an unlucky day for me, you will have
noticed my change of address. When I handed over my sketches to the
Public Relations Officer to send away, he was so full of praise for my
work as he looked over the sketches, he left me wondering if there was
more to his admiration than words. A few days later, the Battery captain
asked about my art school studies and qualifications I obtained in art,
details of which were sent to Regimental Headquarters. The information
must have been sent higher, straight to the top of the line.

Yesterday came news I was to report to Division Headquarters, G
Branch Intelligence, as a draughtsman. This morning, I settled in to begin
my new job. I am attached to Div HQ, not posted, this will be made
permanent after a short period of time, but I shall remain in the Royal
Artillery. I feel a bit queer among all the *brass hats* I meet around the
place.

There are three of us working together, the other two guys are N.C.O.
draughtsmen, both were overjoyed to learn an artist had been sent to join
them. I feel browned off at the moment with complete strangers, leaving
behind my good friends, George and Maurice. My two new companions
are decent guys. Everyone in the Battery wished me well, they were as
sorry to see me go as I was to leave. I know this might be a good break
for me, and a safer move farther back behind forward positions out of
range from Japanese artillery. I am now in my third year abroad counting
from the date of embarkation, 12 March 1943. Sometimes looking back
it seems like the months have passed quickly, and other times it feels like
twenty years.

17 March   *BLUE AIR LETTER CARD*

Photographs I took recently were a pictorial scene of a deep red sandstone ravine, and a composed study of a statue of Buddha. My chance came to photograph Buddha when I discovered several statues placed in a slit trench, probably for protection. They were in various sizes ranging from 9 inches to 3 feet tall, made of different materials. Selecting a magnificent heavy bronze casting about 18 inches high, I arranged the statue of Buddha in the centre of a still life group, adding a Burmese bronze pot, a piece of white cotton parachute draped in the foreground and a large fan shaped cactus leaf in the background.

I have been chatting to a U.S. army official photographer; he made contact reference prints from my negatives, and gave me several sheets of cut film and printing paper. The sheet film will need trimming to size and special adaptors made to fit into the plate holders.

24 March

My mouth organ came recently with a batch of readdressed letters from the Battery. I am getting on well in my new job; it is the type of work I like, and easy for me to do. Often there is a mad rush when we have an emergency, working into the night, twice only so far and no later than 10.30. Since arriving I have been called upon to do one sentry duty. It is not so scary as night guard duty close to Japanese positions; with the Battery, that came around frequently. You must have read reports about what it is like throughout the night in the Burma jungle, sometimes you think the whole Jap army is making a desperate attack.

I have made more exposures with the camera, but some plates have broken. There is no trouble loading the plates, the problem is getting them out of the holders with sweaty fingers in this hot, clammy climate. I may be able to find a solution to overcome the problem. I would like to have as many photographic plates sent to me that you can manage. Incidentally, I was carrying the camera when the front sprung open accidentally and I lost the cable release.

31 March, Easter Saturday   *BLUE AIR LETTER CARD*

The enemy is moving out at a good pace and we have to catch up with him causing delays with mail finding us. Tonight, I was able to visit the Battery a little more than a few minutes walk from Div HQ, and George the post orderly handed me three letters. You need not send me any hypo fixing solution, the Yank photographer has given me ½lb made by Kodak.

1 April

I was with the Battery again this evening, and handed two more letters and an Observer newspaper. War news is good these days; our activities were clearly mentioned on the radio. The promise to bring repatriation down to three years service overseas is looking to be less of a myth and increasingly a possible reality in the near future.

The U.S. army photographer, Lt. Whitley Austin, SEAC Photo Unit, took a photograph of me sketching. Arranged around me were war scenes painted from memory, witnessed during the campaign. He is sending away a copy of the photo along with my drawings, hoping they will make a story to be published in America. This is the second bundle of sepia drawings floating around somewhere, scenes illustrating the fighting in Burma sent away for publication. As well as being given the hypo, he handed me a tin of developer, and that too is made by Kodak. I mention photography quite a lot in letters, but you must not think it is taking the place of art. Spare time is scarce these days, the only drawing I can do is designing, or sketching from memory, accomplished with intermittent interruptions. There is never an opportunity to get away sketching, or paint a portrait. When we are out of *action*, far away from attack by the Japanese, and settled in a camp with half day Saturday and Sunday free, that will be the time to wander off. With paint box in my pocket, and an empty milk tin to collect water, I shall be painting again at every opportunity.

A small group of Kachin Levies[25] riding elephants suddenly appeared moving slowly along the road. I hastened to get organised with the camera, fearing any attempt to take a photograph with so little time to prepare was doomed to be a failure.

I spend less time in the sun since leaving the Battery, my bronze back, arms and chest has lost some of the deep tan.

5 April   *To my brother Harry*

I can not say my next letter will be more convenient to celebrate your birthday Harry and I take this opportunity to wish you Many Happy Returns, and a pucka day. This card I was able to prepare for you in time for your birthday on 23 April, and I shall be thinking of you. My days working a ten line telephone exchange, wireless telegraphy and signalling may be gone forever since taking up my new position with the Intelligence Branch, at Division Headquarters.

An unexpected wind storm has interrupted this letter, sweeping everything away, followed by a slight fall of rain but not sufficient to wet anything. As I write I hear temple bells on the pinnacle of a sacred shrine tinkling in the breeze. You perhaps have seen their familiar appearance in the background of photographs printed in newspapers, showing scenes of war in Burma. A few precious gems, rubies and sapphires from the richest mines in this area have come my way as souvenirs, scrounged from local inhabitants.

6 April

There was a windstorm and slight rainfall yesterday; I retired to bed thinking all is well until about 1 o'clock when I became aware I was feeling rather damp. The moment I opened my eyes the white parachute serving as a make shift tent was lighted in brilliance by lightning, closely followed by a roll of thunder. Quickly out of bed I slipped on my trousers, stowed away my clothes and kit underneath the camp bed to protect them from the rain. Getting back into bed a little wetter, I pulled the blankets over my head to dodge the spray and was once more asleep, thankful I knew nothing more about the interruption until I awoke in the morning. I hear thunder again but hope there will be no repeat performance tonight.

The sheet film the Yank gave me is Agfa Ansco, 5 x 4ins, semi-pan backed. Cutting a sheet in half and trimming around a glass negative, I am able to get two negatives from each sheet, but it is not easy working beneath a blanket in total darkness. I flattened out an empty bully-beef tin and made six thin metal adaptors to hold the sheets of cut film. These I place inside the camera plate holders. A total of six photographs were taken one morning recently when out walking with my camera. In spite of the uncomfortable and difficult conditions I have to go through at night processing the negatives, they turned out OK. At 6.0am the next morning we were suddenly told, "Prepare to move forward to a new position." When I checked the negatives I had developed, I could see they were not perfectly dry. I packed them very carefully back to back, ready for a journey of almost forty miles by truck. Not until two hours after arriving at a new position was I able to unpack them, only to find damp patches had caused reticulation of the emulsion. After carefully licking the film with my tongue to gently moisten the surface, I set them to dry once more. Later, inspecting them I found to my amazement that a miracle had happened, the negatives had dried out perfectly and the treatment I gave them had solved the problem.

7 April

Sleep was again interrupted by rain, and in spite of a wet night I managed to keep myself dry.

7 April

Only a short spell of time has elapsed since I completed a letter to you, but I wish to tell you the first batch of drawings sent away by the P.R.O.

reached Calcutta safely, and from there forwarded to England. They are to be published in a paper or magazine, and this is the only information I have so far been given. I get along well with everyone in G Branch, they are a fine bunch of fellows and I am happily settled in the new job.

14 April   *BLUE AIR LETTER CARD Typewritten letter*
A parcel of cigarettes sent to the Battery has been readdressed by George, and I should get it soon unless it goes the same way as the last parcel. I was given the information at a dance during our stay at the last location. The Burmese girls were in short supply, and the floor was not the best. George was there, Maurice too, who asked if I had passed to you his home address to post his portrait and I was able to say, "Yes."

We have experienced many storms recently through the night but not much wind. Last night passed peacefully without wind or rain which makes a change.

15 April
The mail has caught up with me and I got a nice bundle of letters. I am happier in my present position doing the kind of job I much prefer rather than the type of work I was called upon to do in the Battery office. It is a funny thing Harry should mention in one of his letters our link up with a Chinese Division at Namsaw. To commemorate the event I designed a certificate about half Imperial size, lettering a citation in English. This was presented by Maj Gen F W Festing, commanding 36 Division, to the general of the Chinese Division, expressing a successful liaison between the two armies. I received personal thanks from Maj Gen Festing for the finished design. This was not the first commemorative certificate I was asked to produce.

The second certificate I designed had an illuminated colourful border incorporating battle emblems, and in the centre a dedication was carefully hand written in Burmese, by a local scribe. The commander of 36 Division presented the framed certificate to the prime minister of Mong Mit. Mong Mit is an important town in central Burma, until recently it had been overrun by the Japanese. An elaborate ceremony was organised for the presentation celebrating the town's liberation, inviting the Burmese in the surrounding hills and jungle to come out of hiding and take part. A procession headed by the prime minister dressed in dazzling robes, followed by attendants and monks, paraded along the main street of the town to the sound of music played by a group of Burmese musicians. I had with me my camera watching the whole of the spectacular celebrations. The excitement and turmoil created by the vast crowd of local villagers interfered with any opportunity to take a photograph.

The drawings sent for publication to England are scenes I witnessed during the fighting in Burma, sketched in sepia from memory. I produced them during calm moments between sudden interruptions from our unsociable enemy. They are:- A view of a Jeep leading a convoy of vehicles on the mountainous Burma Road; troops occupying Pinwe, after the town was capture by 36 Division, a spot where we had a rough time; two drawings of the Irrawaddy River at Katha, one scene loading stores into small native boats, the other scene, ferrying the Battery water cart across the river on a pontoon raft driven by an outboard motor; a Dakota aeroplane dropping supplies by parachute; a team of mules carrying equipment to forward positions; a sketch of Gyobian chaung, where there was strong opposition by the Japanese near Pinwe; a picture of The Jeep railway, vehicles fitted with special wheels to run on railway lines pulling trucks; and two sketches of the Battery's 3.7in howitzers in *action*.

I briefly mentioned in a previous letter I had been to a dance, it was organised for the local inhabitants in the village hall of a town we recently liberated. Dancing was to begin at 5 o'clock and go on until 9 o'clock in the evening. I managed to get the afternoon off work, and joined a couple of sergeants who also decided to go there. You could not call it a dance in the strictest sense of the word as one might expect to find in England, nevertheless, we tripped around the floor in army boots to dance music. It was a lucky break when we joined a happy group of young Burmese, pleased to make our acquaintance. I did a fair amount of dancing, sweating profusely in the heat of the afternoon. As darkness descended in the evening we continued dancing by candlelight, everyone having a thoroughly good time, until one or two flashes of lightning announced a warning that a storm was brewing. The previous day the rain had not started until about 4 o'clock in the morning, sound asleep and unprepared, I got a jolly good soaking before I could take evasive measures to stay dry. After having one more dance, my friends and I decided it would be wise to get back to camp before the arrival of the threatened storm. Turning away with happy hearts from the unexpected pleasure, we were lucky to catch a wagon going our way, avoiding the oncoming storm by five minutes. If after leaving, the revelry continued until the stipulated time, we missed only one more hour of the dance. The consequence was once more like old times, my nose constantly aware of an attractive aroma my shirt acquired dancing with the girls. For the next few days I was constantly aware of the scent of perfume and powder, it was so unusual I was reluctant to wash away the fragrance that brought to mind many happy memories of the past.

Major's enamel food plate I stole from him when I left home is giving excellent service and has travelled far with me. It is perhaps more chipped and battered than it was, but still intact.

Thank you for my birthday card, you will be pleased to know it arrived in good time.

15 April   *To my brother Harry, typewritten letter*

I was so pleased to get your letter today written from hospital. Your injuries appear to be worse than originally thought, unless the M.O. is not taking chances with your ailment. I sincerely hope you had plenty of attention and nursing care while you were in hospital.

I have today written a letter to mother and dad, it will be enclosed along with this in a green envelope to the Base Censor. The camera has done good work and you will learn about this when you read the other letter. You must be aware of the lonely feeling at night in camp before going to bed. A group of us gather outside my parachute tent to have a jolly good sing song sitting around a small camp fire and blackened char tin to make the usual nightcap. I play the tunes on my mouth organ, and three friends add vocal strains chasing away any depressing thoughts. An officer passing by said how cheerful and happy the sound of our little concert party was.

What do you mean, saying I should welcome the chance to sleep in clean white sheets? I do sleep in white sheets; at least they were white when they came down to earth as a parachute carrying our supplies. There is little need for blankets at night, both my blankets I place beneath me for extra comfort when sleeping. Since leaving my position in the Battery, very little of my time is spent digging up the rock hard ground of Burma.

16 April   *Typewritten letter*

There are five days still to go before my birthday and I have received no fewer than four birthday cards. I told Harry I had acquired some gems from Mogok, a few rubies and sapphires collected as souvenirs. I paid nothing for them, simply traded stuff that was of little use to me. There was some high bargaining around the camp. It was common to find a group of lads investigative a collection of precious stones a local villager was willing to sell, or exchange. Some gems I have seen on offer were real beauties. Amusing remarks can sometimes be overheard when a batch of gems are being offered, and displayed in the palm of a Burmese. Looking over the shoulders of a crowd of lads examining gems, you might hear someone say – "That's a nice piece of mepacrine bottle." Mepacrine tablets taken to combat the effects of malaria are supplied in small blue glass bottles.

18 April   *BLUE AIR LETTER CARD*

I am getting swamped with mail these days and it is fortunate I can find time to reply. Thank you for the parcel, you could not have put together a better selection of gifts for my birthday.

21 April

You can see today is my birthday, as yet there is not much work about this morning with plenty of time for the situation to change. Enclosed is a card I have made on behalf of Harry and me for your wedding anniversary, I know I shall not be with you on that special day but you will be in my thoughts. Although today is dull, with the sun striving to steal through the overhanging mist, it does not suppress the heat reaching far above what is comfortable.

I noticed a group of Burmese temples nearby and set out in earnest to take a photograph, tramping through paddy fields trying to keep my feet dry, hopping from bund[26] to bund like a goat. In spite of my endeavours I did not see a likeable composition and turned away disappointed. I have not so far exposed any of the cut film in the camera.

The variety of materials available to use in the office are amazing, one or two different colours of poster paints, every colour of waterproof inks, a variety of rulers, T squares, set squares, ruling pens, and drawing instruments one might wish to work with. The drawing paper we are issued with is not of good quality and there are no carbon pencils.

Last night some of the boys caught, and killed, a 14 foot python in their area, I was shown the skin that had been wound around a bamboo pole.

23 April   *To my brother Harry BLUE AIR LETTER CARD*

I promised myself I would write to you on your birthday, Harry, Many Happy Returns, no doubt you will have arranged to spend it with a few of your pals. All is quiet in the office this morning, it is not yet 9 o'clock but suddenly, without warning, I could be up to my eyebrows drawing diagrams and marking a load of maps. I did not celebrate my birthday except to do guard duty! I am pleased you are at last out of *dock* and hope you keep it that way.

28 April

Since I last wrote we have moved again and the envelope with the photo printing paper has caught up with me. Every morning there is a lot of discussion when the European map is displayed marking the achievements over there. Areas occupied by Allied Forces coloured red, grow larger each day, the remaining white parts alter shape gradually getting smaller.

There is a roll of SEAC Newspapers on the way to you, I am aware it will be old news you will be reading, the pictures you should find interesting and you will learn about our activities which I have not been allowed to write about. Inside the papers are a series of aerial photographs, by this date the notes and markings identifying enemy positions are past history. The photos can be arranged to show a view of Myitkyina, registering each one to overlapping in the correct sequence. My arrival in that area with the convoy from Ledo, was not until after the tough fighting to capture the town from the Japanese. Another aerial photograph is a spot where we set up gun positions. There is more Japanese occupation money with this letter.

Last night I set about developing negatives under great difficulties, the temperature of the water was 85°; I have never before had it so high. In spite of using tropical hardener, the gelatin around the edges softened and puckered the film. One of the pictures was the shot of the Kachins riding elephants which I expected to be a failure.

A chap showing me his Zeiss Ikon folding camera was mystified by a small white flare appearing in the bottom of all his photographs. Two photographers had already been consulted but could not find an answer to the phenomenon. I quickly diagnosed the problem. There was a tiny pin hole in the corner at the fold of the bellows which I temporarily sealed with black passé-partout.

Because I have not had the chance to go about sketching, I have been working on ideas for a few humorous cartoons. Two cartoon drawings have already been prepared and it is my intention to send them to either Lilliput, or Men Only magazine.

28 April   *To my brother Harry BLUE AIR LETTER CARD*
A letter yesterday tells me your weather is looking better and that is good news, you should be here now, anybody unaccustomed to endure these temperatures would be a grease spot in a couple of days. The flies find my exposed skin a very happy playground and the torment is terrible; apart from the hazards of war, it is one of the many discomforts we cope with.

Division HQ is accommodated in an old monastery building, and glancing up from my desk I can see stout tall palms with long thin pointed leaves fanning out in all directions shivering occasionally in the wisp of a breeze. The brilliance of the sun is cutting everything into light and shade, above the trees a few small clouds play in the pale blue sky. A panorama of sheer beauty with uncompromising heat leaving no doubt I am involved in this tropical scene and it is not simply a pretty picture being played out on a silver screen.

I hope you are fine, and with medical treatment your hearing will improve.

3 May

At our last position we were staying in an old monastery when one evening after dinner and before dark, I was able to make a watercolour sketch of a sub-contractor, a batman Gurkha. I caught his expression and features quite well, finishing the portrait next morning. There is little office work coming in these days and rain each day prevents me from wandering too far from base to paint a colourful scene. Sketching portraits of people in and around our position are the only type of paintings convenient to produce. Rain falls for an hour, and after taking a short rest comes again at regular intervals, often catching us unawares at meal times. A monsoon weather pattern is creeping upon us once more.

Fortunately you did not send a cable for my birthday. Cables to India are not a problem, but cables to troops in Burma are forwarded from Calcutta taking longer than a week. I have known telegrams from Bombay take two weeks to arrive to troops in the isolated jungle of Burma.

The cigarettes on issue at present are not very good, W.D. & H.O. Wills hold the contract to produce Woodbines for forces in India and they are not the quality of the original brand. The natives refused to smoke the first stock manufactured, totally rejecting them. There is an exacting formula for cigarettes manufactured for the forces, and the relative costs they impose on the war effort to be considered. If Wills were allowed to produce cigarettes for the forces to their usual standard, the costs to the British Government would be unacceptable.

The cut film I have used for the first time to take a photograph. It stands up well to the climate, better in some respects than a glass plate. The gelatin emulsion is firmer in these conditions, but the back of the film softens during processing because of the high temperature and is easily marked by fingerprint impressions which can not be removed. There are five cartoons on the way to Men Only magazine, I could find no other address that might be suitable for them. They are sketched in carbon pencil and India ink which I think may not be a satisfactory medium to reproduce in print.

5 May   *BLUE AIR LETTER CARD*

The time is almost 8 o'clock and I have just finished breakfast, the sun is shining gloriously in contrast to the past few days which have been more like monsoon weather. I was told to put 4ans postage on the cartoons that were sent away but I feel this was not enough to go by air.

As the defeat of the Japanese in Burma became inevitable, restrictions imposed on the use of unofficial cameras by front-line fighting units were

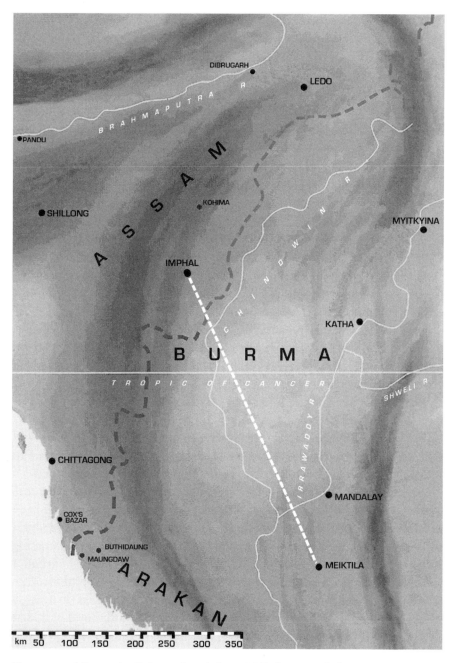

Flown out of Burma by Dakota aircraft from Meiktila to Imphal

relaxed. Following this announcement, I wasted no time asking for my Zodel Junior folding plate camera to be posted. My intentions were to record the local people and scenes that had so far been available only to my pencil and watercolour brush. With just six single metal plate holders, the scenes to photograph were carefully selected and the number of exposures strictly limited to preserve plates. Pictures were composed in the viewfinder with allowance made for inaccuracy, and each exposure calculated using tables published in a Burroughs Wellcome handbook. Dry chemicals mixed with water were used to develop and fix the negatives.

Our position was frequently under shell fire from Japanese guns, and processing was carried out at night under great difficulties. Choosing a perfectly peaceful night with little sign of trouble from the enemy, I began developing plates in a two-man slit trench, covered by a tarpaulin. Half way through the process, Japanese guns suddenly began shelling our position; my companion immediately rushed to our slit trench for protection. He was not amused when I shouted he was not to lift the cover of my temporary dark room and scurry elsewhere for shelter.

The lack of fresh air and tropical heat in a confined space caused serious discomfort. Washing negatives immediately they were developed was not a simple task. Every negative had to be carefully hand washed in several changes of clean water, taking twenty minutes or more to complete. Finding a crystal clear stream at one location, I carefully rested negatives on pebbles in a shallow part of the stream to let the slowly flowing water do the washing. Imagine my frustration when I found minute grains of sand sticking to the emulsion. It took a great deal of expert washing by hand to remove the offending material. This brilliant idea was never again tried.

With the Japanese army in full retreat to Rangoon following the capture of Mandalay by allied forces, the role of 36 Division in Burma had been successfully completed. Being flown out of Burma by Dakota from Meiktila to Imphal was the first stage of a long journey by road and rail crossing India to Poona. Travelling by road convoy from Imphal we boarded a troop train east of Pandu, taking seven days to reach our destination, often waiting on a branch line for a schedule service wanting to pass on a single track. We slept at night on hard wooden fold-away bunks, and halted at convenient times for the cooks to prepare meals on the side of the track. On arrival at Poona, we were stationed some distance outside the town at Alandi camp. The camp was on the opposite side of town to the first camp at Kharakwasla where we had undergone assault training before moving into Arakan, for our first action against the enemy. The next phase was to regroup, and combine with a large force in preparation for an assault landing on the Japanese mainland.

CHAPTER 12

Alandi Camp, Poona

By early May 1945, the role of 36 Division in Burma had been successfully completed and we were moved to Alandi Camp in Poona.

19 May *BLUE AIR LETTER CARD*

I am sorry for the absence of mail, you may have guessed I was moving out of Burma far away from enemy action, and during the long silence it is for the same reason I have received no news from you until yesterday when I was given a huge handful of mail. There is time now to rest after a job well done and hopefully I may be given a spell of leave.

It would not be honest of me to say I am sorry Harry's health has been down graded by the specialist because of the injuries he sustained from the bomb in France. Look upon it as a small blessing, the change will not permit him to be considered fit enough to help us out in this part of the world, but I do hope he will make a good recovery. I was unable to write about the signing of peace in Europe when it happened. We receive the news over the radio as the situation developed and were able to follow the successful conclusion of hostilities.

20 May

Some of the boys are going on leave in the next few days; I told the clerk in the office I would make private arrangements. Tonight I must write to Mr. and Mrs. Carrington telling them I may have the chance to visit them again very soon although no definite date has been arranged when my leave will begin. Recently I visited the Battery and was able to inform Maurice you had posted the sketch I made of him to his home address. He has chosen to spend his leave at a rest centre in Bombay, and hopes to be on his way there in three days time.

A few friends would like copies of my photographs taken in Burma to send home. A local photographer charges 4ans a print and I shall put in an order for whatever prints they chose to have. My printing paper is far too precious and for personal use only.

You celebrated V Day during the days I spent moving out of Burma. Halting overnight at a camp I awakened next morning to the familiar sound on the radio of BBC bells ringing in my ears. I lay in bed listening to the commentary between flashes of celebrations from different parts of Britain. At Hull, tugs and ships were sounding off the V Morse signal with hooters and sirens in a cacophony of discordant notes. The recording had been made one and a half hours earlier and described the King and Queen on the balcony at Buckingham Palace, appearing several times at midnight to the delight of the crowds gathered in front of the gates. We could not celebrate during our long journey across India but saw flags and decorations hanging out in many towns we passed. This happy conclusion to the war in Europe can only mean that some poor fellows will be unlucky, and ordered to join the fighting in this forgotten part of the world. It is time I was away to the canteen for my supper before it closes.

27 May

How grand it is to be getting letters once again. Harry's letter is a credit to his thoughtfulness, he writes saying that behind the V Day celebrations everyone's mind was on the job still to be done out here. We too would have celebrated the end of that terrible war if we had been there. We tried to picture the scenes but in reality for us it was just another day. I should like to have my Royal Artillery dress cap with me when I am on leave, would you please send it by air mail to Mrs. Carrington. I am invited to stay and she hopes I shall be able to get out on safari shooting game, duck and buck.

I shall pack and send home my negatives now that reference prints have been made.

30 May

I bought a box of Barnett Sensichrome, 2½ x 3½in plates, when I was in town, the shopkeeper offered me two more boxes, all the stock was well out of date and I wanted to see the results of the box I bought before buying more. Since developing a negative I note there is a pale blue tinge around the edges, the image lacks contrast and there is an overall grey caste viewed from the back. They are suitable only to record pictures for reference.

5 June   *BLUE AIR LETTER CARD*

You must have noticed this letter has my new address, 'India Command,' it is obvious I am once more in India. For reasons of security I could say nothing about this until now. I managed to get together all my kit that has been distributed at various dumps in Assam and India, in preparation for my leave. On Saturday afternoon I felt in a painting mood and made a quick sketch of a chico.

7 June

Train reservations are being arranged for my leave and I hope to get away on 21 June and return on 15 July. In preparation I bought a pair of new shoes in town, and during the visit saw the film, *Since You Went Away*, the type of film dad would say "I did have a good cry."

I am so pleased you received the food parcel from the W.V.S. in Cape Town at a convenient time to enjoy the luxuries when Harry gets home on leave.

A staff sergeant draughtsman who works with me is going on leave to visit his brother and we hope to travel together as far as Jhansi, he will continue on to Delhi.

8 June   *To my brother Harry*

I am back in India after being away 15 months, except when we moved out of Arakan for a rest period before going back into *action* in Burma. Tonight I hope I may get into town to see a film I have been told it is quite good, *A Song To Remember* is the title.

Give my regards to Joan, your new female acquaintance serving in the WREN's.

12 June

Yesterday I had a pleasant surprise when the parcel with 3 dozen Selochrome photographic plates arrived, together with four packets of glossy printing paper. It is little wonder you write saying you have not had any news from me, it was not possible to write on our way out of Burma. I can now explain the reason why. I was with Tac HQ in a forward position when we were given the news to move to Meiktila, in preparation to fly out of Burma. I spent quite a time messing about on the airstrip at Meiktila in the blazing sun before boarding a plane, (no seating), for a three hour flight to Imphal. The following two nights were spent in camp making ready for a journey more than a hundred miles by truck, much of the road over difficult ghats[27], and crossing the Brahmaputra River gave the satisfaction we were well clear of Burma. A long train journey began taking days to cross India to our final destination at Poona. The journey was broken when we boarded a small boat to ferry us over the River Ganges to a train waiting on the other side.

The photograph enclosed was taken by a Gurkha sergeant a few days before we left our most forward position south of Meiktila. He was seeking advice on photography and during our discussion wanted to take my photograph. I developed the roll of film for him and maybe out of courtesy he gave me the negative.

13 June   *BLUE AIR LETTER CARD*

The news that you have posted my dress cap to Jhansi is fast work indeed and it will be there for me when I get my leave. Wearing a bush hat in an evening to a dance can sometimes prove too cumbersome and inconvenient. Tonight there is a dance for which I have managed to get a ticket, and it is to be held at a hall I have never before been to. As usual I expect there will be far too many guys and barely enough room for dancing.

The cartoons I sent away have been returned with a note saying they would not be able to use them. I think the medium is not compatible with the type of printing process used to produce the magazine.

18 June

A letter I got from you took only seven days; mail both ways is going well, my air letters reaching you in eight days. It makes a deal of difference when the service is good, forging a closer bond in distance and time. I am amazed with your story about Major trying to catch a fly, he must be recovering in health to be so active. There are few flies here just now but some parts of Burma are riddled with them, and if Major was there he would never be still.

Last Wednesday night the dance was much better than expected, organized for B.O.R.s below the rank of sergeant limiting the numbers, not the usual one hundred men and a girl, or shoulder to shoulder. I went with a friend; the fun began at 7.30 before we got there and did not finish until 10.30. There were partners for almost everyone, and it was the best floor for dancing since Cape Town. Continental style with small tables arranged around the edge of the dance floor. Cakes, lemonade, sandwiches and cigarettes all free. Half way through the dancing we were entertained with a stage show. At the end of the dance we came away with floral garlands draped about our shoulders as if we had been on a night out in Hawaii. The garlands had been made for the cabaret but never used. To round off a perfect evening, the best for a long time, we enjoyed a late night meal in a Chinese restaurant. Friday night was an opportunity to go dancing again, but this was the usual large crowd, and not enough girls as one might expect, much less enjoyable then the previous dance. I think I will find myself taking the Liberty Truck to a dance at a canteen in town tonight. Tomorrow evening is my last chance to go shopping before making an early start on my leave the next day.

I discovered a pucka photographic dealer selling a variety of goods, drying racks, photo masks, lenses and came away with a box of a dozen plates which cost me 2Rs. They are Ilford Selochrome, exactly the same brand you sent to me. The dealer said he would try to get for me a yellow filter to fit onto the lens of my camera. The box of outdated plates I bought is not worth spending the time expecting satisfactory results, I shall dump them. There is no hope of buying printing paper; all the dealers need every bit they get for business use. The friend with whom I work is fascinated at the way my pen keeps moving along and has glanced over my shoulder to read if what I write makes sense.

20 June   *BLUE AIR LETTER CARD Typewritten letter*
It is almost ten o'clock and time for bed having made preparations for an early start tomorrow. I expect to leave camp at 7.30am to catch a train from the station an hour later. The camera plate holders are fully charged with Selochrome plates. Last night I bought a dozen Kodak panchromatic plates and a dozen sheets of Kodak XX cut film. This month's quota of new stock has arrived in the shops.

My friend who was to spend leave with his brother in Delhi has changed his plans and decided to stay in Bombay. I shall have the pleasure of his company for only a short part at the beginning of my journey. His brother has not replied to the letter he sent telling him he was arranging to visit him, and can only imagine he has been posted elsewhere.

Twenty-one days leave in Jhansi, 21 June – 15 July (including travel). Mr and Mrs Carrington had three daughters, Thelma, Norma, and Pat, and one grandson, Keith, who was Norma's son.

22 June
It is mid afternoon and not two hours since I arrived at the home of the Carringtons'. Everything is just the same, nothing has changed, but it is warmer than where I am stationed at Poona. A letter from you and my dress cap were waiting here for me. Mr. and Mrs. Carrington, Norma and Keith are all well. Pat is here also with her Alsatian dog and I have had time only to say "Hello!" Pat with her dog, are leaving in an hour to stay with her sister Thelma in Bombay. Pat has no permanent home at the present time and is finding it very difficult to look after her Alsatian dog. Right now the whole family have taken to relaxing in their beds, to avoid the uncomfortable mid afternoon heat in this part of India.

23 June   *To my brother Harry*

For quite a while I have been expecting leave, and I arrived in Jhansi yesterday to enjoy twenty one days holiday with friends, beginning officially today. This is the longest break ever given to me during the whole time I have spent abroad in the army. Oh Boy, it is warm here! I have been told the temperature is much cooler than it has been. The monsoon has not yet begun but there was a heavy downpour of rain last night, today there are no clouds to be seen in the bright blue sky.

I shall be going to a dance at the Railway Institute tonight with Norma and her friend. Mr. Carrington is a life member of the Institute through his employment with Indian Railways and has arranged an open invitation for me to visit the Institute during my stay. Tomorrow, I must be out of bed at 5 o'clock ready to go on safari. Mr. Carrington wanted to know how I could be out dancing until midnight and awake at 5 o'clock next morning before dawn, to go on a shoot. Sunday night has been booked for a visit to a picture show to see the film, *Two Worlds*, a story about which I know nothing.

Everyone has been hearing about my exploits in Burma, and all that has happened since I was last here. The family remarked I had lost weight and was looking much thinner, the obvious explanation is compounded by the time and energy spent almost every day digging in the wild jungle of Burma.

So long. — • • —

27 June

Shade from the hot sun on the front porch is a comfortable place to be scribbling this letter with a distinct change in the weather at Jhansi. The heat has been terrific, almost like Burma, the big difference is no enemy to be wary of, and no digging in the hot sun. The monsoon began in earnest yesterday when it poured down with rain. Today it is much cooler, the sky is overcast and there are no dark clouds in view that promise rain, it does not take long for them to creep up on you. Last night I saw the film, *Lassie Come Home*, it was marvellous acting by the part played by the dog, the star of the show.

In a letter to Harry I mentioned I was to going to a dance with Norma and her friend, and quickly discovered this was not the ideal temperature to be tripping round on a dance floor. I wore my dress cap, but you will be sorry to learn that some kind gentleman took a fancy to it thinking it would be more fitting for him to wear on his head. Mrs. Carrington, and Norma were shocked and sorry, I passed it off as a bit of bad luck and hope the guy who took it is well pleased.

30 June   *BLUE AIR LETTER CARD*

Thank you for the praise about the drawings that have been printed in *Soldier* magazine. Capt. Condon, the P.R.O. responsible for sending them away is no longer with us; I may try to get in touch with him, he is serving with the 14th Army. There are more drawings somewhere the Yank officer sent to the U.S.A. for publication, no news has reached me concerning what may have been planned for them, or where copies of the illustrations are likely to appear.

I shot four duck last Sunday morning on safari; two were lost when they sank into deep water before the young shikaree could recover them. We saw five buck too far distant to take an accurate shot. However, we shall see what tomorrow will bring, we may go out early again on a shoot.

Saturday today, I shall be dancing tonight in the company of Norma and her friend. I got the job driving their car one evening when Mrs. C came with Norma and me to the pictures. Mr. C would never go to see a film show. I am thinking about making a trip to Agra about the middle of next week to see the Taj Mahal, and the Red Fort, magnificent features of Indian architecture steeped in the history of the Mogul Empire.

I travelled by rail to Agra to visit the Taj Mahal and Red Fort, staying overnight in a forces rest centre. I then travelled to Bombay where I spent two nights with Thelma and Pat before returning to Poona.

15 July   *Received from the WAR OFFICE, LONDON, dated 15 June*

We have today asked the Ministry of Information to pass payment of eight guineas to you at your home address for drawings recently published in 'Soldier' magazine. Congratulations on your excellent sketches and to say that we hope to see more of your good work.

17 July

Back in the office after spending three weeks glorious leave. I left Jhansi on Thursday evening about 6 o'clock and reached Bombay a little over 24 hours later. I wanted to spend my last couple of days in Bombay with Thelma, never having met her before, and also to see Pat who was staying with her. My welcome was more than anyone could ever wish.

Pat and Julie, who share a flat with Thelma, met me as I arrived at Bombay station. Thelma is working in an office during the day otherwise she too would have been there. I felt rather proud, a gunner dressed in military uniform escorted through the streets of Bombay by two pretty young ladies, one on each arm, a rare sight in India. I must have passed within one hundred yards of Thelma's flat half a dozen times or more when I visited Bombay, never knowing the address where she was living.

Bombay was full of rain making it uncomfortable to get about. The day after I arrived, Hal, a Yank officer major, turned up to spend fifteen days leave with Thelma. He is friendly with the family and keeps Mr. Carrington well supplied with American cigarettes. On Saturday morning, the day before I left, Pat and me wandered about the shops in Bombay and I bought six Kodak Super Pan plates. Sunday afternoon my stay came to an end when I said good-bye to my friends and took the train back to Poona.

Last night I joined others on the truck going to town and took with me the skin of a buck, shot on safari, not by me, to have it treated and cured. While I was there I saw the Technicolor film, *Wilson*, and having little interest in politics it did not impress me.

This morning a mobile medical unit visited the camp seeking blood donors and I gave some of my *poison* to the cause. Right now it has left me feeling weak and apt to use the familiar expression 'a fly could knock me over.' Incidentally, of 28 names entered for only six tickets to a dance tomorrow night, I was one of the lucky ones and I shall again be flitting my feet around a dance floor.

21 July

On the night I last wrote, I developed some plates, and the next evening spent dancing which as I fully expected was likened to a crowded football match counting the number of men that were there. But moments like this are a break from official duties and pass away time.

Before I went on leave I had a gold ring hand made to my design, two snake's heads facing each other holding in their jaws the oval goldstone I acquired in Burma. The gem has little value but the ring has been admired.

There was an unfortunate accident when I broke my thermometer a short time ago, and I hope you will be able to replace it for me. I tried desperately to buy a new one in Jhansi, and Bombay. Clinical thermometers were the only ones available. It will be absolutely necessary to rely on accurate temperature readings for developing negatives during hot weather. I prepared a solution of Kodak DK20 developer to make prints from my negatives in the office tonight after dark. Please do not send me shaving soap, razor blades, tooth brushes, tooth paste or Ovaltine tablets, I can get all these items without any difficulty.

31 July *BLUE AIR LETTER CARD*

I have not had time to write to you during the past few days because I have been preparing entries for an art exhibition. A great deal of effort has been put into a pencil portrait of a Sikh soldier, which I mounted and framed. Also, I made a watercolour portrait of an Indian, a drawing in pastel of a Mohammedan wearing a red fez, and a copy of the watercolour *Monsoon* that was stolen; all have been mounted but not framed. The entries must be delivered to a college in town before next Sunday in readiness for an exhibition from 18 to 26 August.

The magazine Soldier, May 26 1945, Vol.1, No.7, arrived yesterday. My sepia sketches of Burma have been printed alongside an article about the Chindits, everyone seeing them has been reminded of the moments we were busy fighting the Japanese.

1 August

The best bit of news I can offer you is my promotion to *Bombardier*, the equivalent rank of a full corporal, two stripes. I was told about this before I went on leave but could say nothing until now when it will be officially posted on Div HQ Orders tonight. It is back dated to 1 July and the extra pay credited from that date. The army give you an increase one way and take it back another, reaching a higher level of income places me in a compulsory income tax bracket. I have been an N.C.O. for a whole month and did not know it! The rank becomes permanent after three months and can not be withdrawn except by Courts' Martial.

I already explained why my regular correspondence has been interrupted spending free time sketching, and organising drawings for an art exhibition. One afternoon I was looking for someone to sit for me and about 5 o'clock I approached a Sikh on his way into town who kindly said that he could spare half an hour. He was a perfect model, becoming quite involved, remaining absolutely still for more than two hours, taking a few short breaks to rest between sittings. Occasionally he glanced at the sketch to see what progress was being made and obligingly gave more of his time than originally planned. He was willing I should continue, but I insisted the final touches could be added later. I chose to use pencil as the medium to enhance his magnificent black beard. During this week a whole morning was spent in town looking for materials to make suitable mounts for my entries to the exhibition.

This is the weekday when all able bodied persons take a little exercise galloping across the beautiful Indian countryside. The cross country run takes place each Wednesday afternoon, over a period of about three quarters of an hour. It is the general's idea, setting an example full of enthusiasm as he took the lead testing everyone's fitness on the first run when I was away on leave. Never since then has he been seen to participate.

I was out dancing last night and surprisingly had quite a good time. Rita, a nice young lady and excellent dancing partner is making special arrangements to attend a dinner dance together on Friday night. Last week at a dance I meet a girl whose mother once lived in Church, she said the whole family moved out here in 1936. At another dance I got talking to a guy with a familiar face, and wearing the badge of the Lancashire Fusiliers, he recalled having seen me around Accrington. He is in Div HQ, and his home is in Church, and he is waiting to be repatriated. He promised he would call on you when he gets back home. Church is striving to be a famed town on the map!

Before the dance at the forces club last Friday night I played tennis with Rita, my first game for about three years. The tennis court and dance hall are within the club grounds. Racquets to play the game are readily obtainable for a refundable deposit whenever the court is available. It has a hard concrete surface that could not be described as ideal, but finding anywhere to enjoy a game of tennis makes a pleasant change

Major must be coping quite well with health problems reaching his twelfth birthday, a ripe old age for a dog of his breed. I am sure you are responsible for maintaining his fitness; paying careful attention each night to the special treatment you give him to ease his suffering, common with his age. I must close this letter immediately and postpone all work in the office to don my P.T. shorts, and gym shoes, to join the mad caper across the countryside.

7 August   *BLUE AIR LETTER CARD*

Sunday last, my four pictures were handed over to the exhibition authorities, only time will tell if they are selected. A colonel kindly offered to take my entries to the college along with pictures he was submitting. Depending whether I can get time off work he suggested we should go together on the opening day to view the exhibition.

I am in perfect health except for a badly bruised left wrist when I slipped and fell bruising my arm, now I must wear my watch on the other wrist. I was called to attend the dentist for an inspection, he reported he could find no trouble with my teeth and all is well.

9 August

There was a wonderful piece of news that came over the radio yesterday and there was more news this morning, America has dropped an atomic bomb on Japan, and the Russians have declared they too are now at war with the Japanese. Perhaps these new and sudden developments may make those yellow shrimps turn in their ambition to fight. In my opinion it will last a while longer, the Japanese soldier is not easily scared and is willing to sacrifice his life against impossible odds before accepting defeat.

I reported sick this morning for the first time since I came to Div HQ with an injury to my arm when I accidentally fell; my wrist suffered a nasty graze that is painful and troublesome. Fortunately it is my left arm that is out of action; tomorrow I shall again call on the M.O. for further consultation. Last Tuesday I attended a dance that had been given little publicity and was not a regular weekly occurrence. This was quite a different event to the usual dance for forces, for instance, there was not the normal rationing of girls to cope with and I missed very few dances. I went along with a friend and had a great time dancing to a decent R.A.F. band instead of a noisy Indian gang. Life is not altogether dull when I can get out enjoying myself.

13 August

Everything is exactly the same as usual in spite of the prospects of peace raging at the moment. We are all ears for every scrap of news, putting little faith in an immediate satisfactory outcome until we know what is official. Everybody is tense, hoping against hope that peace is brought about once again throughout the world. There will not be a soul in camp during the two days holiday that has been promised, if and when it might happen.

14 August

I hope Harry is soon settled following his new posting, he was so happy stationed in Troon.

The negatives I promised to send home are packed, but before I can address and post them the durzee[28] is stitching a substantial cloth cover around the box to protect them.

What strange weather we are having, it began raining Friday evening and for the past two days has been coming down incessantly and not a sign it is going to stop. Tonight I plan to go dancing and will surely get wet. The dance is by invitation only, Rita has promised to do her best to get me a ticket. Sunday I saw Deanna Durbin in the film, *Can't Help Singing*, which was not bad at all.

A friend with whom I often went to dances is returning home tomorrow. He is Class B, with three years four months service in the army, a bricklayer by trade, and the reason for his early release. Good luck to him! Did I say a girl was hoping to get me a ticket to a dance? I must be extra lucky, I have just been told that half a dozen tickets for the dance have been handed in to the office and one of them has been ear-marked for me.

The food is not as good as it was, I believe it is the same throughout the whole of India. My wrist is slowly healing but painful still, and I shall see the M.O. tomorrow for his opinion.

This letter has been interrupted by the 1.30, I.S.T. news broadcast announcing the Japanese Government has finally accepted the terms of surrender.

There comes a price with my two stripes each week, detailed to oversee a variety of special jobs. One is N.C.O. on duty at the canteen, and another, executive in the office; on the other hand I have never been asked to stand guard, or do any of the detestable army fatigues I have been required to carry out in the past.

19 August   *BLUE AIR LETTER CARD*

This is my first letter since the peace pact became official. Oh, what celebrations! The rowdiness was expected, but nothing like the state we learned that Britain was in. We stopped work Wednesday morning when we first heard the news. Saturday afternoon I went into town with the colonel to view the art exhibition, and two of the four works of art I entered have been placed on show. The pencil portrait of the Sikh has been 'Commended.' I shall be making more visits before it closes. All exhibitors are given a catalogue, and free pass, to view during the time the exhibition is open. This morning, Sunday, a special service for PEACE was held before a large crowd on the racecourse in Poona, attended by the Governor of Bombay. I had a job of work to do and was unable to go there. How nice to know that peace is with us once again and future prospects fighting the Japanese enemy on their homeland is no more than a frightful memory. Next year – back home!!!

A letter from Pat today asks if I can arrange accommodation in Poona for her, and husband Jim, who has been granted leave from the army in September.

My wrist is finally better, once again I am able to wear my wrist watch on the left arm as usual.

21 August

The issue of 50 cigarettes has changed for the better, English *Players* in packets of ten, the first decent cigarettes the army has issued.

Last weekend I went to see the film, *Dragon Seed*, which I thoroughly enjoyed. I prefer drama, or non fiction, or a well produced film with good music. There is a concert and dance at the forces club tonight, if I can get to town I shall make an effort to be there. A dance organised by HQ to take place on Friday should be a happy event, if enough girls can be persuaded to attend. I have already settled arrangements with my dancing partner in this respect. One evening a short time ago after dancing a Tango, a dance pro came up to my partner Rita and me, to compliment our dancing technique. He said it was "It."

A letter from Harry tells me he has moved to Catterick, and taken a step down losing his trade. He bravely accepts the change and made a prudent remark that he could have lost more than that. This may lead to a better chance for him to get his discharge from the army.

23 August *BLUE AIR LETTER CARD*
Celebrations in *Ossy* must have been quickly arranged making bunting to hang out in the street. On Thursday, 16 August, I was invited to spend the whole day at a house in town and to have dinner at night. About nine o'clock I gate crashed a Royal Air Force Cadet's dance, telling a sob story to the M.C. at the door, he took pity on my persuasive manner allowing me inside with few questions asked. I felt rather conspicuous in the dance hall, dressed in khaki among a large crowd of servicemen wearing blue uniforms.

The thermometer reached me safely, in future there will be no further need guessing the temperature of liquids when developing negatives.

27 August *Typewritten letter*
Yesterday was my first full day free of work since coming out of Burma, except for the period on leave and recent VJ celebrations. I am allowed one clear half day each week but never before have I been given a whole day. The art exhibition closed yesterday and if I can find a truck going into town tonight I shall collect my pictures.

The news is good that Uncle Fred should soon be on his way out of Sweden, I bet he will be given a very special family reunion when he eventually gets back home after the years he has spent in isolation abroad.

31 August *Typewritten letter*
My sketches are back with me in the office after collecting them from the exhibition. An officer began asking questions about the paintings when he saw me unpacking them and wanted to know if he could see more of my work. There is to be another dance arranged by HQ and I am busy designing a poster. Tonight a dance is to take place in a local canteen, it will be nothing special but arrangements with my regular dancing partner have already been made. Last night I enjoyed one of the best ENSA concerts I have seen, but confess there have been few occasions

when I could attend any type of entertainment during the months scrambling around in Arakan, and in Burma.

Your son has achieved the privilege to wear a group of medals on his chest, taking advantage to wear them when attending functions outside the camp. Not yet issued with the actual medals, a narrow bar of medal ribbons pinned on my army blouse. It has not been possible to reserve accommodation for Pat and her husband, not one of the many hotels would accept a booking so far in advance. The M.O. gave me a jab for cholera two days ago and it was my misfortune to be treated at the end of a long queue, I thought he was using a bayonet.

4 September

A letter from Harry says he is trying to arrange leave to coincide with that of his Wren girlfriend Joan. He asks me the question, "What does it feel like to be a peace time soldier?" I can tell him there is not the slightest difference at the moment. The kinsfolk have been fortunate to come through this war pretty well except Harry; he has suffered more than anyone. Cousin Ronald, a prisoner of war in Germany, and Uncle Fred stranded in Sweden are the other casualties. I could not tell you about my exploits but as far as dad saying in one of his letters there must have been thrilling moments in *action*, I can tell you that thrilling is hardly a word I would have chosen. As there is little chance I shall again be called upon to do any further fighting, I can mention incidents that might have caused the censors to go raging mad if written in my letters. And, had they got through, would have caused you to worry.

The worst day ever was on the 15 February this year at Myitson, all around this time the fighting was no pic-nic and similar encounters in Arakan. Another tough period happened shortly before Christmas when the enemy was determined to destroy us. If we had not countered his aggression, I might never have been able to write any further letters about life out here. It is strange how people are scared by different circumstances during the conflict. My nerves were affected by Japanese artillery constant shelling our position at night, other guys cursed and bore it. Many chaps would be terrified by the relentless rapping of enemy machine gun fire, but that I was never over concerned about unless I thought it was becoming too close to feel comfortable. Night time was scary when the Japanese soldier was more vicious than he was throughout the day. Our tactics were the opposite, shelling Japanese positions by day, but night time entertainment was often arranged for him too. I would glance at my watch in the late afternoon and remark to Maurice or George, "We have an hour left," (or whatever time there might be until the sun had set), then we could expect Japanese guns to open up. When we moved to set up a new gun position we worked to exhaustion before nightfall digging a slit trench for defence, and building a dug-out for protection. We needed no encouragement to complete the job before nightfall if we wished to survive another day.

I would like to relate a strange experience I had one night on leave in Jhansi. I mentioned at the time the temperatures in that area were pretty high. To get a comfortable sleep throughout the night beds were sometimes placed outside in the compound beneath the starry sky. The hot night atmosphere, the chirping of crickets and other nocturnal insects was similar to a night time scenario ever present in Burma, and I was soon asleep. Mr. Carrington would occasionally be out of bed walking around but this was not set to disturb my peaceful slumber. Suddenly, startled from my sleep, I was not dreaming, I heard the distant sound of gunfire and was out of bed immediately ready to dive for cover expecting to hear a swishing sound rising from silence to a screeching whistle as the missile came on. Slowly my senses returned when the full reality of the truth came to mind. I got back into bed with pulse racing and nerves on edge before controlling my fears and falling asleep until morning. I remember telling my story to Mr. and Mrs. Carrington at breakfast. Jhansi is a military zone and an R.A. Battery on night manoeuvres was the cause of my disturbed sleep. I previously heard spasmodic practice firing during the day; but this was the first time gunfire occurred during darkness at night.

This letter has been filled with experience of war when after all we should want to forget the horrors. High praise for the successful attacks against the Japanese enemy is well justified by the heroic actions of the infantry fighting under appalling conditions during monsoon weather, tropical heat and the dense jungle of Burma. Disease was a constant companion playing a game of chance with each soldier's life, whatever ability he struggled to fulfil. The perils of the silent enemy demanded immediate medical treatment for anyone suffering dysentery, malaria, heat exhaustion, or tropical ulcers.

At one of the dances recently I noticed a guy watching my partner and me each time we waltzed around the dance floor. I told the girl there was a guy taking a particular interest in her, she was adamant she had no idea who he was. A while later after a short break from dancing he came to me and asked, "Where do you come from?" I recognised his accent immediately and replied, "Not far from you!" His next question was to ask if I had a brother, at that point I realised he was Jack Brindle, a cricketer friend of my younger schoolboy days who never used a cricket bat, always slogged the ball with a baseball bat, a present sent to him by a relative living in America. We arranged to meet again next Sunday night.

There is yet an interesting story that could not be told during an attack on the village of Myitson where Japanese resistance was extreme. The Battery moved forward to establish a gun position near a small group of deserted Burmese houses constructed on piles with flimsily woven bamboo lattice walls under thatch roofs. The Japanese, having recently retreated, were familiar with this area and accurate artillery fire from enemy guns ranged on our position. I was operating the telephone exchange one night during the hours of darkness in a well protected dug-out when the bombardment from Japanese artillery began as usual, and enemy shells were exploding within the gun perimeter. As I came off duty at daybreak, I noticed that one of our trucks had been destroyed by a direct hit, but I was a little puzzled by the excitement and elation shown by a group of gunners sharing out coins. A shell had exploded beneath one of the native houses and a large hoard of coins secretly buried by a villager had been unearthed. I was not so quick to receive any of the spoils, but thankful we had suffered no casualties that night, or more serious damage than the vehicle that was totally wrecked.

9 September   *Typewritten letter*

You may guess by typing this letter I am in the office, doing lunch hour duty for a friend even though today it is my day off. I developed a couple of negatives after dark last night and this morning washed them. Afterwards I washed a few handkerchiefs, these I never give to the dhobi to wash they could easily become misplaced with other handkerchiefs, unlike a shirt or trousers. My friend in the office asked if he may have the drawing of the Sikh and also the watercolour portrait that was on show in the exhibition. Reluctantly, I agreed and he gave me 30Rs, I could have got much more if I really made any attempt to sell them. I certainly know why the paints Auntie Molly sent never reached me; every letter she has written has found me only by good luck. Never once has the address been correct on any items she has posted. She directed one of her letters to – 'Fenton, G Branch, H.Q. Division, S.E.A.C.' The devil must have been on holiday when I got that! In reply I politely hinted to take a little more care in future and check current details when addressing letters or parcels sent to me.

Tonight, I hope to meet Jack Brindle in town, there is sure to be a good chin-wag. Our second dance organised by the unit has been postponed for the moment, there is the usual Monday night dance tomorrow. Rumours we would be granted a holiday for the reopening of Singapore have ceased to abound during the past few days and hopes are fading fast.

11 September

I shall shortly be leaving this most marvellous and mysterious India on a journey taking me further eastwards. Attacking the Japanese mainland is no longer an option and not a murmur when the move will take place or plans concerning the future task of the Division. There will be more letters from here offering the latest information when it comes to hand.

11 September   *To my brother Harry*

I met Jack Brindle again on Sunday night, first tasting a good meal at a Chinese restaurant, then to a coffee house and a walk around the town until it was time to see the second showing of the film, *Henry V*. We covered a lot of ground chin-wagging about old times and the games of cricket played with many school friends on waste ground near home.

I drove a station wagon into town last night for a group of sergeants stranded in camp because not one of them had a licence to drive. I dropped them off and drove to a forces club to spend a happy evening dancing until midnight before collecting the sergeants as promised after their night out in town. Tonight is the night for one of the regular dances and all being well I shall be there.

At long last censorship of sensitive information has been lifted; a happy relief for Base Censors bombarded and overworked doing a job taking time to read through many letters I have written since leaving England. I wonder if any particular censor might remember me.

14 September   *Typewritten letter*

The weather is getting warmer, nothing like the temperatures in Burma or Jhansi. Yesterday we were given a whole day Victory holiday, for the reoccupation of Singapore.

17 September

Soon after my first arrival in Poona I bought a pair of shoes for casual wear to take on leave, and for dancing. I am afraid they are now past their youthful days; the mochi is resoling them for the second time. I bought a new pair costing 20Rs at a controlled price; there can be no bargaining. I remember the first pair I bought cost 18Rs and they have served me well, far too shabby for dancing, nowadays worn for comfort sitting in my office at work in preference to wearing army boots. I bought a bundle of watercolour paints spending about 30Rs on my shopping spree, *Schoolastic* quality, not as good as *Artist* quality but I was fortunate to find them. I made alterations to the posters advertising the Division's dance, now to take place on Friday, perhaps one of the last decent dances I shall attend in India. Monday today, and this evening is the usual dance at a soldier's club in Poona where there are never more than two dozen girls. I have got to know many of them, taking every opportunity not to miss finding a partner to dance. The last two evenings were spent at local cinemas watching films, *The Enchanted Cottage* was the title of one of the films.

The whole of yesterday was a free day off work spent at Kirkee, a much smaller town than Poona. Lazing away the whole morning at an open air swimming pool with a crowd of revellers enjoying ourselves, many were members of the armed forces. Everyone was relaxed and in high spirits, a feeling of contentment now the war is over. In the evening I went to the local cinema showing the film, *Laura*.

I am rolling along just fine, like the familiar quotation about 'The old river….'

23 September

The Div HQ dance on Friday evening went well and you can bet I had a marvellous time. I was with my usual partner with whom I always dance the Tango. The whole evening was a great success, and another dance is being arranged to take place next Tuesday week. I shall get to work producing another poster advertising this next event.

Pat and her husband were to arrive in Poona yesterday, I can not say if they have done so. I went to the railway station early in the morning and found the only train from Bombay was due at 12.10, lunch time. I went back to camp and returned to the station to meet the midday train but did not see them. I booked the accommodation as they asked; perhaps my letter did not reach them before they left home.

24 September

By the time I was ready to get out last night it was too late to visit Poona, I chose to go to Kirkee instead. Kirkee is a small town compared to Poona and much nearer to camp. It has a picture house and forces canteen where the Friday evening dances are held. I saw Abbott and Costello in the film, *Pardon My Sarong*, a comedy I had seen some time before. After getting back to camp I developed some exposed plates, they were pretty rotten, the emulsion has aged and the whole batch is unfit to use.

28 September

Thank you dad in anticipation, if you can find free time, for a job of maintenance on my bicycle to keep it in working order until I get back. One of the girls I am friendly with cycles to the dances on a gent's bike, and I have the good fortune to borrow it, riding back to camp instead of hanging around late at night waiting around for the Liberty truck.

At the end of the dances peddling myself to the camp, she rides on the crossbar and I drop her off at home on the way. Parking the bicycle outside my basha invites some amusing remarks, there might be more unkind suggestive comments coming from the boys if instead it was a lady's cycle!

At the end of September 1945, 36 Division was merged with 2 Division.

From this time forward I am with 2 Division, and indeed sorry as are many of the chaps to see 36 Division disbanded, and combined with 2 Division. A large number of men are going home on repatriation, or demobilisation, all my friends in G Branch office have left. Two new guys fresh out joined the office staff with the change over. I moved a short distance to another camp making it convenient to get to the towns of Kirkee and Poona. I do not understand why there is no news from Pat and Jim; my visit to their hotel was in vain.

A parcel is on its way to you that will not arrive for a month, souvenirs I bought in Agra when I visited the Taj Mahal. There are presents for each of you. For mother a trinket box and two small trays, each piece inlayed with mother of pearl motif of the Taj Mahal, carved I was told, from Indian jade. I prefer to call it marble. For dad there are a couple of ties. A neatly hand carved wooden box for Harry, useful for knick-knacks and small items. None were expensive. You may think otherwise if you glance at the description of the contents on the export label.

I am pleased Major made good friends with Joan during the time she and Harry were spending their leave together at home with you.

2 October

Dad will be enjoying his holiday from work, spending time on the *estate* (allotment), with 'Victory Grow More' campaign fresh in his mind. I should like to taste some of your home grown crops. Before every meal I pick a juicy looking tomato from the basket of the fruit wallah squatting on the floor near the entrance to the dining hall. The cost is 1anna for a tomato, oranges you can buy two for 3ans, bananas I do not fancy, they never look tempting. Our *grub* is not to the standard we ate at the last camp. I cannot say why that may be, we have our usual staff of cooks and supplies are from the same store, the reason is perhaps there are many more men to feed dining in the new mess hall.

Reading your letters leads me to think you are not aware of the vast distances you can travel in this country. It is no short journey between

Poona, and Bombay, a distance of about 125 miles, considering the great expanse of India it is relatively near. The rail journey by express mail train takes about three hours. It is easy to lose all sense of distance compared to travelling around in England. Getting a lift for twenty miles in a Liberty truck is a mere hop, fortunately the camp is only a few miles from the nearest town. I shall be going there this evening to the dance organised by my old 36 Division. I collected a ticket at their office when I delivered the posters advertising the dance. I was at the usual Monday dance last night. A social affair called a dance, held outside on a concrete floor that it is not a smooth surface.

I am smoking a State Express cigarette from the package you sent to me, after drinking a mug of tea and eating biscuits delivered by the charwallah. A letter from Pat says their plans to spend a holiday in Poona had to be changed.

8 October

Let me say something of my activities, last week I saw the film, *Rebecca*, for the third time, this film I saw first in England about three years ago. Dancing on Friday night, and on Saturday saw the film, *Song Of Bernadette*, an opportunity missed when it was being shown where I was stationed on the border of Burma a year ago. Sunday night was a time of jubilation at a Victory Ball attended by the elite of Poona and Bombay, and I shall send you the Ticket - Programme to give a true impression of this great occasion. The celebration was held in the gardens of Government House, Poona, dancing on a large tightly stretched canvas floor smothered with powder to smooth the surface. There was a cabaret show, novelty dances, and plenty of good fun. It started about 9.45 in the evening and continued throughout the night until 3 o'clock this morning. My dancing partner Rita was with me doing our best to dance on a crowded floor during the early part of the evening, as people drifted away after midnight I tried to dance out my shoes. The band was good, and the tempo for the Tango by far the best for a long time. People sitting at a nearby table complemented our dancing but they were no one we knew. I never got to bed before midnight during the past week. I am on duty tonight and hope I can catch up on lost sleep.

15 October

I promised you this programme of the Victory Ball and not wishing to exceed the postal weight you must be content with a single page letter. Last night I was again dancing but had no knowledge of it until the afternoon, the place was new to me and never before have I been there. Dancing was due to finish at 2.0am, this was the night the clocks were put

93. The Red Sari

Above: 94. Temple Gateway

Left: 95. Temple, Northern India

Top Right: 96. Dibrugarh Market

Right: 97. Dibrugarh

Above: 98. The Bridge at Dibrugarh

Left: 99. C.M.P.(I) 36 Division

Right: 100. Japanese Occupation Currency

Above: 101. Temple at Bahe by Moonlight

Left: 102. Monsoon Mud

Top Right: 103. A Night Halt on the Burma Road

Right: 104. Sentinels at Katha

105 & 106. Units of 36 Division Crossing the Shweli River, Myitson

107. Attacking Myitson

108. Convoy on the Burma Road

109. Ferrying the Battery Water-Cart Across the Irrawaddy River
The town of Katha is visible in the far distance.

110. Moving Stores Across the Irrawaddy River

111. 366 Light Battery Attacking Pinwe
While making this sketch of 3,7 howitzers in action, the gun in the foreground suddenly ejected a volcano of flame from the muzzle, setting fire to the jungle scrub. The barrage laid down was happening so fast the 'charge' had been placed in the breech without loading the shell. Dense clouds of smoke from the fire could have alerted the enemy to pin point our position, but fortunately the matter was quickly dealt with and a disaster was averted. The boys manning the gun had been paying too much attention to me sketching.

112. 36 Division Occupy Pinwe
A railroad town in the centre of Burma, particularly important for the transportation of teak logs. Chains harnessed to elephants were fastened to keyways cut into the ends of the logs after felling, and hauled through the forest to the railhead.

Above Left: 113. 'Wellcome'
Photographic Exposure
Calculator and Plate Holders

Above: 114. 'Zodel' Junior
Camera (3½ x 2½)

Left: 115. Ravages of War

Top Right: 116. Malayan Village,
Penang

Right: 117. Village Siesta,
Penang Island

118. Mending Jungle Green

119. Port Tewfik

120. St Martin in the Fields,
Trafalgar Square

121. The River Thames at Woolwich

122. The Royal Artillery Barracks, Woolwich

123. Half-Timbered Houses, Wiltshire

back gaining one hour, and the band played on. Unfortunately, I could not stay to the end of the dance, leaving before the last waltz to catch the truck back to camp, gaining almost an extra hour at the dance.

This mob is becoming more like a R.A. Battery, parading each morning at 0745 hours and every other day turning out for a half hour training period in the afternoon. Who would think this is Div HQ, a war over and won? I guess I am as happy as ever making the best of life.

20 October

A letter from dad arrived in record time, written on 14 October and post marked 7.0pm. It was handed to me yesterday about 5.30pm taking less than five full days to reach me. My spare time is spent designing a couple of Christmas cards for a competition by the Division, one is completed and another I shall soon have ready. They must be handed in by the 27th of this month. I exposed some of the panchromatic cut film bought some time ago because I was a little doubtful about the conditions under which it had been stored. A couple of pictures were self portraits to check the emulsion, one of the photographs is a write off; it had the misfortune to be given a double exposure. I shall send you a print from one of the negatives.

26 October

A couple of designs have been entered for the Division's Christmas card competition, the General and other persons judged them this morning, there is no news a winner has been chosen. Well over fifty designs have been sent in.

Thank you for 200 State Express 555 cigarettes you ordered, a separate pack of 200 State Express 333 cigarettes from the Observer Cigarette Fund came at the same time and I must acknowledge their receipt. The double exposure photograph was taken by a girl friend after I set up the camera; the fault was entirely my doing not checking each plate holder beforehand. The portrait I sent to you was taken by an army friend after again setting up and focusing the camera. He is leaving on a train for Bombay at dawn tomorrow to get a boat to England, as are many more of my good friends from 36 Division, the lucky guys.

29 October

Thank you for information about the Royal College of Art distinctions examination, my success will depend on the quality of my work that is selected and put together by Mr. Lindoe; I must leave the choice entirely in his hands. Examples of abstract creative designs are his favourite subjects at the art school; my attention has been directed to sketching watercolour portraits and landscapes, and most unfortunate many of the paintings you will never see, they have been given away to friends.

7 November

Division HQ moved again yesterday, I am back in the same old office when I was here with 36 Division. My design made third prize in the Christmas card competition and I received 5Rs, the first prize winner has not been over praised. My attempts to write letters, or turn out Christmas cards or sketching recently has suffered, overwhelmed reforming the merger of the Divisions. I ordered another food parcel, with luck it may arrive in time for Christmas.

Last night I went to the usual dance at the forces club in Poona to find it had been changed to Saturday, the alternative was to go to the pictures to see the film, *Sudan*. In my judgement likened to a fairy tale, desert rogues dashing around creating the excitement. I hope tomorrow I can go into town and see the film, *To Have And Have Not*. On Friday there is a dance at Kirkee, and Saturday night there is a dance in aid of the Poppy Appeal Fund.

10 November

I think one of your letters is missing, you briefly mention receiving the Victory Ball programme and tell me Uncle Joe is out of the navy working again in the gent's outfitters; to what you refer is meaningless and new to me.

12 November

Monday has arrived, since I began this letter two days ago while waiting for a lift into town and those few lines were all I had time to write before the Liberty truck picked me up.

Yesterday I posted a small booklet you will find extremely interesting, printed recently by H.Q. printing press and distributed to troops in the newly reformed 2 Division. It outlines separately, brief details about the origins of 2 Division, and 36 Division, describing the history of each Division. The booklet is a souvenir of past achievements and engagements in war.

On Saturday evening I won a cigarette case during a Spot Waltz at the Poppy Appeal Fund dance in Kirkee. I shall be sending it home for dad, or Harry, if he would like to have it.

15 November

I have at last seen the exalted film, *Gone With The Wind*. When it was being shown in the past I was never in the right place, at the right time to see it. The film first toured India when I was in *action* in Burma, shown in Poona for a second time while I was away on leave in Jhansi. Last week it arrived here again for the third time, no queuing for tickets, the picture house was no more than half full with a choice of comfortable seats.

India has imposed severe restrictions on exporting silk, and I am afraid from now on I am not allowed to send you more. I must consider myself very lucky to have posted the parcel containing a length of silk before the new regulations came into force.

17 November

Last night I went to the usual Friday dance at Kirkee. Recently the weather has been humid and heavy. Each evening when the sun goes down dark clouds torment the moon, rain has occasionally fallen but never continuous. At the dance it was uncomfortable because of the oppressive heat, but not as bad as it can be. This is the winter of the year with very chilly nights. Tonight I hope to visit Poona and see the film, *Waterloo Road*. One of the lads from the office has gone into town on an errand, and as a safeguard we asked him to book seats for us. It is usually a problem to find vacancies on Saturday by this late hour.

Now the war is over you can celebrate Guy Fawkes bonfire night in England once again, I recall many happy memories of those past occasions. There are no Christmas cards prepared as I usually do, owing to the big changes, I am disappointed and so too will be many relatives. I feel sure moving from here is not far in the future and it is bound to upset all our plans for Christmas festivities. We have only rumours to guide us where we may be going and told we can expect difficulties with the cigarette situation at our new destination.

Good Show! Our friend has returned from Poona with tickets for the cinema show tonight.

18 November

Thank you for comparing the standard prices of articles on sale at home. The only worthwhile item I could buy here are shoes. A comfortable pair in any style can be bought for 20Rs, the cheapest range from about 15Rs. I have bought a new pair to send home as personal effects and they have been worn once to comply with export regulations. Part of a red parachute used as bedding in Burma is now out of commission and packed to send home.

Tomorrow I shall be in no position to write letters as I am taking on a big job with other draughtsmen, preparing a map 6ft by 8ft for a lecture explaining details about moving to a new destination.

20 November

Earlier this week I gave the mochi the cured buckskin to make a pair of slippers. Under the special terms for personal items, I am wearing off the newness before posting them home duty free. They cost 7Rs (ten shillings and sixpence), and the mochi has certainly done a marvellous job. Not a single present have I bought for any relative this Christmas. I have bought a present for Lilian, she has been such a faithful friend and I wanted to show my appreciation. I chose for her a pyjama set, Chinese style made of angel silk. It has a one inch black border around the edge of the jacket and a design on the front woven in gold thread, a white neckband and padded shoulders. I paid 40Rs (£3) for the suit.

We finished drawing our large map and the General used it to give a lecture to everyone in Div HQ. I can tell you we are bound for Hong Kong, that wonderful island off the coast of mainland China. That is the last order we were given, but orders in the army, no matter how official, often have a tendency to suddenly be changed.

Last night, I was at the usual canteen dance and had a great time as can be expected, even if the night is spent dancing with one of the guys. When there is little alternative I usually take the part of the lady. Talking to a FANY at a dance recently, a girl fresh out from England, she was highly amused to see many fellows dancing together. With few girls around this is often the only way many lads can enjoy dancing.

Sitting at my desk writing and turning my head to glance through the open doorway, I see outside a beautiful moonlit scene, almost as bright as day, bringing back memories of the nights in Burma. Last night it was very cold and tonight too is going to be another cold one.

25 November   *To my mother for her birthday*

This letter and card is for your birthday, a card and a letter for grandma's birthday has already been posted to her. At last, the personal effects parcel is ready for posting which has inside a pair of brown shoes, the buckskin slippers, photo magazines, a book about dancing by Victor Silvester, a towel, a pair of K.D. shorts, the spot waltz cigarette case and a tie. The shoes and slippers are wrapped in the red parachute for added protection.

This week we were to begin a long journey to Hong Kong, but for some reason I know not why, the move has been postponed. We were given a talk about what to expect when we got to Hong Kong and I was very much looking forward to spending time there.

Have a jolly good birthday mother, and remember me to everyone.

2 December

The package of lettering nibs arrived in good condition, they will be most useful. Producing Christmas cards has taken priority over writing letters and all the cards I could make are in the post to relatives and friends. Three simple different designs, each design drawn on a wax stencil and printed on the office duplicating machine. It is only possible to print black line work, the best I could do under the circumstances. However, this turned out to be far more than I expected with so little spare time available. Four cartoons are on the way to SEAC Newspaper, I believe their rates for publishing are quite good if the submissions are accepted.

Last week I received a letter from one of the boys who served with me in 36 Division. He promised to write to me on his return home. Once he was back in England I never expected a letter, lesser still a parcel of cigarettes which he says is on the way to me. He was an M.T. clerk and took me in his truck wherever I wished to go when needing transport. I could always depend on him to pick me up after a dance.

Last night I paid the usual Saturday visit to Poona and saw quite a good film, *Blood On The Sun*. Tomorrow night I expect to be at the Monday dance, with a sorry feeling the dance next Friday night may be my last for some time.

9 December   *BLUE AIR LETTER CARD*
– Special Issue Christmas Design
Also – 2 Division Official Greetings Card (Crossed keys Div. sign)
This I am writing on your birthday mother to let you know I am thinking about you on this special day. I hope I can get to the dance in Poona tomorrow, it is doubtful, perhaps I may get the opportunity to look in and say goodbye to friends and to everyone there I have got to know.

12 December   *BLUE AIR LETTER CARD*
– Special Issue Christmas Design
This letter is dated 12 but so far only one and a half hours of the day are gone, there is little space on this special card which is all I could find readily available. You are probably well prepared for Christmas, I do not expect I shall be in any position to celebrate the occasion this time around, and mail from me will not be forthcoming for a short time ahead.

Cheerio, I am in the pink.

CHAPTER 13

The Far East

On 12 December 1945, 2 Division set sail from Bombay to Singapore.

18 December

This letter I am writing on board ship at sea, and it will not begin its journey to you for a few days; when you receive it you will understand what has caused the lack of news. I am enjoying this voyage with no unpleasant sea sickness, but we have not struck heavy seas since leaving Bombay. We are sailing alone, not in convoy with escort ships zigzagging all over the ocean, threatened by attacks from enemy submarines or aircraft. The ship is cruising ahead, leaving behind in our wake a straight trail of foam marking a steady progress eastwards.

Unfortunately, we were not given shore leave after boarding the ship in Bombay. I was hoping for an opportunity to visit Thelma, who lives near the Taj Mahal Hotel. From the docks I could clearly see the dome of the hotel, about 20 minutes walk away. During the past few days the sea has been like a mill pond, now I know what is meant by the expression, *a glossy sea*. This old tub can roll about in these conditions and it is perhaps our good fortune we have not yet had to endure severely rough weather. Something I never expected to enjoy on board was watching a film show, *The Suspect*, with Charles Laughton playing a good part as usual. We are due to dock in Singapore on Thursday 20th for a short break during our journey to Hong Kong.

There is a present on its way to you mother, a handbag I had a sudden impulse to buy after hearing from many of the lads, ladies' handbags are an expensive luxury in England. It was bought shortly before I left Poona and posted on your birthday, please regard it a fitting gift for that special occasion.

26 December

I am once again on dry land after a pleasant voyage taking all things into account. The ship anchored outside Singapore for a couple of days before disembarking last Friday. It appears we are preparing to stay here, the original plan to travel further to Hong Kong has almost been forgotten. We are stationed at the southern tip of Malaya, near a small town Johore Bahru, a few miles north of Singapore Island. The camp is pleasantly placed in the country and until we get our vehicles with us there is little chance of venturing out or getting around. Once we are settled I am sure there will be no complaining about our digs, someone has chosen the perfect location, a vacated Mental Hospital. The driveway from the main road to the camp is about a mile long, lined with palm trees leading to the top of a small hillock on which is built a group of comfortable open air wards, hospital rooms and offices. There is clear evidence Japanese soldiers have been living here during their occupation of Malaya.

I have had little opportunity to gather together information about Singapore, or Malaya, all I have seen so far has been from the back of a moving truck driving here from the docks. I noticed the markets and bazaars appear to be much cleaner than those in India. The reason perhaps is the high population of Chinese, noticeable everywhere. The people of Malaya are quite different to the Indians and appear to be better educated. One thing to be thankful for is the absence of incessant cries from persistent ragged children with outstretched hands chanting, "Baksheesh sahib?" Displayed in Chinese on the front of many shops are vertical sign boards advertising the type of business, or services offered, and alongside the equivalent in English. There are many classical buildings in Singapore, no doubt influenced by the long occupation by the British. If Accrington could boast of such grandeur it would achieve greater fame. Impressive buildings crowned with domes towering six or seven stories high overlook the harbour, clearly visible silhouetted against a clouded sky to ships arriving in Singapore. Passing along narrow streets it is hard to imagine the magnificent buildings exist, and impossible to glimpse their pinnacles. The houses and shops built either side adopt every type of material from palm leaves, metal sheets and concrete, denying the existence of the finer buildings. Much of the town has been altered by the war, and the splendour of Singapore in earlier days of peace has to be guessed.

The weather at this time of the year is beyond imagination for an Englishman arriving in the middle of Christmas. We are lucky to be here during the coolest part of the season, the island lies 2° above the equator with a changing weather pattern in sympathy with Britain, but no similarity whatsoever. It is 3 o'clock in the afternoon and I am wearing shorts, not because of the heat, I have known hotter times in Burma. Since arriving it has been dull, and each day it never fails to rain heavily, but briefly in the afternoon only. Today it has not rained, who knows what will happen in the next fifteen minutes. Following a heavy downpour, the water quickly drains away into deep gullies and in a short space of time everywhere is dry. I imagine it can get very hot during the summer months – I'm thankful that I shall no longer be here by then, I hope! There is a great variety of scenery and oriental life to be captured in paint on paper, but I am bound by opportunity and leisure time to enjoy this luxury. Street scenes are very different from those in India, and Malaya has a wonderful coastline edged with native huts and fishing villages. Palm trees appear to thrive better than others so far seen in countries elsewhere. I would most like to sketch portraits of the Malay natives, and the Chinese also. As yet I have said little about myself, leaving this for my next letter not wanting to mix personal matters with my first impressions of Malaya.

27 December

My correspondence is anything but straight and I hope I can get it under control shortly. Today I have written to Harry, and Rita in Kirkee, but there are many more replies I must write. Thank you for all the letters received on Christmas Day, they were more than welcome after being without news since leaving India. The batch of 500 cigarettes you ordered will be welcome because we can not afford the price of cigarettes sold in the shops here. We should be given a ration of 50 cigarettes each week but everything is upside down since our arrival in Singapore. Cigarettes on sale in the shops are expensive, 7 dollars, and 8 dollars, for a tin of 50; the Malay dollar is equal to 2 shillings and four pence English money.

We received a message from General Slim when the 14th Army was disbanded, thanking us for our contribution and successes achieved in Burma, although officially the 36 Division was only attached to the 14th Army. We were under American Command, and rumours reached our ears we might be obliged to wear the China-Burma-India badge. This is a large American shoulder badge in the form of a shield with a thick blue horizontal band at the top bearing the Star of India, and Chinese Star. Beneath the band are vertical red and white stripes. Later towards the end of the campaign there was an indication we would receive a medal granted by America for our support, but neither of these promised decorations materialized, and nothing more has been said about the affair.

Once again these eight pages are filled with news of my activities skipping answers to questions you ask in your letters. For this reason I hate getting mail in large batches trying to organise my replies, don't give up hope, I shall put it all to rights eventually.

– 1946 –

1 January

This morning I was awakened about seven thirty by a sergeant asking, 'Would you like a mug of char?' Breakfast was served at eight thirty, and quite nice too considering the quality of the rations on which we had been living recently. Transport was arranged for anyone who wished to go swimming in the sea; having sparse knowledge about the existence of any nearby sandy beaches I passed over the opportunity. This afternoon a Horse Racing game is being set up to entertain would be gamblers, about which I know very little. I had no interest in the game when it was played on board ship, and never let it occupy my time. I shall most likely venture into Singapore along with Charlie, a new partner in my office, if we do not get there this afternoon we will certainly make our way there tonight.

New Year's Eve last night was full of interest and would read like a book if I were to try to capture the atmosphere, telling every little detail about the native bazaars and streets I walked along. Charlie and I went first to the Union Jack Club for char and sandwiches, aware we had missed the beginning of all three film shows in town, free for persons serving in the armed forces. Instead, we set about finding the New World Amusement Park we had been told was a complex bursting with oriental entertainment and mystery. Ambling along busy streets, passing market stalls crammed with goods, taking note of all manner of native life, mainly Chinese and Malayan, looking all the while for an enormous arena of excitement designed to attract pleasure seekers, similar to a fair-ground at popular sea-side resorts. We walked around searching for twenty minutes before discovering the place of intrigue we had set our minds to explore. There were no gigantic Ferris-wheels, or Noah's Arks, all around was an abundance of side shows, a few picture houses and two Chinese theatres. We found everything fascinating, casually strolling around absorbed in the colourful oriental atmosphere. I can honestly say we saw many good looking Chinese women and girls about the place. Their dress is most distinct, you might at first glance think they were walking outdoors in pyjamas, lightweight garments, matching trousers and sleeveless jackets white or pastel colours. I never met a Chinaman wearing a symbolic pig-tail, or saw an elaborately dressed Mandarin with a lengthy flowing black moustache. Returning from the entertainment park, the town appeared calm, currently occupied with the same scenes of night life everywhere. Arriving once again in the centre of the city I noted the pale illuminated town clock told it was 11 o'clock. Passing a Y.M.C.A., Charlie casually made the remark a dance was in progress, before he could say more I had crossed the road ascending the steps to the door. I talked our way inside, Charlie was not one for dancing, he was happy to stand at the side listening to the music and watching the dancers. A large crowd crammed the floor but I wasted no time choosing a partner for an 'Excuse me' dance. With time only for one last dance, we made our way towards the car park to wait for the Liberty truck and return to camp. My last dance of the year 1945 was with a Chinese girl in Singapore; my partner for my first dance of the year was a Burmese girl at the candlelight dance in Mamyo.

The New Year came in as we waited in Singapore for the truck to collect wanderers returning to camp. Suddenly, sirens and whistles blasted the air, and searchlight beams dashed about the sky announcing the arrival of the New Year. Three fellows nearby cared not the slightest for the hullabaloo, a Good Samaritan had lined them up neatly on the pavement, flat out on their backs with hands crossed on their breast, feet dangling over the edge of the road. You will have seen little of the New Year in England at this moment, it is almost midday and within the hour everyone will make their way to the dining hall for Christmas dinner. A few days late, but HQ, 2 Division is celebrating Christmas Day today, the official feast day having been totally disrupted by our untimely arrival in Singapore.

2 January

Now the day of the New Year has passed, I can tell you more about our celebrations postponed from Christmas. The whole complement of men in Division Headquarters collected in the dining hall at 12.30 for Christmas dinner, alongside each place were set a few sweets, two bars of chocolate, twenty cigarettes, and dates. The smiling faces for such an occasion were to be seen everywhere as jokes created laughter above the rowdiness, singing and banging of plates. The most humorous and fitting of all were the loud cries, "Let me out!" (Remember, we are housed in a mental hospital). Before dinner was served, Major General Nicholson gave a friendly chat and expressed his good wishes to everyone for the New Year. After the Toast, an inebriated voice shouted, – "Three cheers for owed Nick!" The general hearing the remark turned away smiling to himself.

Officers and sergeants wasted no time serving the *grub* and liquor. The meal was excellent, quite a change from food we had been living on in the recent past. I washed down my dinner with a shandy, made with beer and ginger beer. During the time of feasting, music by the Division's band drowned the noise of knives and forks scraping on plates. I thoroughly enjoyed the meal, more so because nothing so good was expected having recently arrived in a new camp with limited resources not yet fully organised.

After dinner, Charlie and me, along with a couple of G Branch clerks, hurried away to Singapore knowing we would miss a good tea meal, but looking forward to visiting the town in daylight for a change. First to the N.A.A.F.I., then a walk exploring the town before going to the Union Jack Club to spend a good two hours chatting over tea and sandwiches. The canteen was newly functioning and there was little else to choose to eat, except ice cream and minerals. As we were talking, we discovered Lord Louis Mountbatten was in the next room conducting the official opening ceremony of the club, and a dance planned to be held that evening. We stayed until the music began and soon I was dancing, none of my friends I was with could dance. The first half of the evening was pleasant, as time moved along it was difficult to dance as the floor became too crowded. The majority of women were FANY, and W.V.S., some Dutch, and a few Javanese. When the last dance was being played at 11 o'clock we made our way to the vehicle park to get a truck back to our quarters.

6 January

Two days ago SEAC Newspaper wrote to me saying they had accepted two of the four cartoons I sent them. To quote their letter, '...we will be pleased to see more,' and returning the remaining two cartoons said, '...but please keep them an inch or two above the knuckle.' I shall leave you to guess what that means. Today I received a SEAC Newspaper dated yesterday, and the first of my cartoons appeared in print. Four more cartoons are prepared and I may send them off today, or tomorrow.

I am to lose my partner Charlie, he is going to Siam, we both wanted to take up the new job offered but he is the one chosen to move. My boss decided he wanted to *hang on* to me. A position in ENSA interested me when I learned they were in need of poster artists, with Charlie gone I shall be working alone, spoiling any chances for a transfer. I shall in future be getting a heap of work to cope with, and need to enlist help with the preparation of maps.

9 January

The night before last I was in Singapore with Charlie, spending our last evening together before he left for Siam. With Charlie gone, my work load has greatly increased; he dealt with the distribution of maps, whereas all lettering, drawing, or artwork required, is done by me.

I shall buy another pair of shoes; the predominance of Malay rubber encourages the manufacturing of crepe rubber soles in preference to leather. Prices are coming down slowly and I expect this will continue as Singapore struggles to get back to normal.

The day after my first cartoon was printed in SEAC Newspaper, the second one appeared.

15 January

Since I last wrote I have been in bed with a fever, fortunately it is not malaria. Thankfully I am feeling much better and my temperature is back to normal. I had a thick head, lousy cold, and unpleasant after effects which are slowly disappearing. I am back at work taking things easy following three days sickness. The Intelligence Office was in a whirl while I was laid up, my type of work was piling up and there was nobody capable of attending to it. The office staff was more than pleased to see me back at work. What do you know? The powers that be are trying to change my unit and rank, I do not comply with Div HQ War Establishment. To keep me here I am to be transferred to the RASC, Corporal Clerk (tradesman). I shall benefit by an increase of nine pence each day, but, – 'Once a gunner, always a gunner!'

Three of the second batch of four cartoons sent to SEAC Newspaper have been accepted, one has already appeared. They returned the fourth because they had previously used a similar idea. Another selection of cartoons is almost completed; I shall wait a little while before posting them, I do not want to load the editor with too many, too quickly.

Last night again to the dance at the Union Jack Club, it was *terrible* – I had one dance and left. A canteen at the camp has been organised at last, which most certainly will improve our leisure evenings. Until this comforting luxury appeared, any sort of liquids to drink were limited to meal times, and occasionally you might find suddenly the mains water in all the buildings had been turned off. There is no extra food to be found anywhere around the camp area, we get only the rations the cooks serve at meal times. I called at the canteen to enjoy a cup of cocoa on my way to the office to write this letter, and I shall enjoy another cup of cocoa before I turn to my bed tonight.

21 January   *BLUE AIR LETTER CARD*

There is little time for me to write, within one hour I begin fourteen days leave to Penang, a small island off the west coast of the Malay Peninsula, about 400 miles north of here. Yesterday I learned about this but no arrangements were made, however, this morning I was told I would be leaving by train this evening along with two other fellows. I shall be staying in a Church of Scotland Rest Centre on Penang Island, funded and run by a charity organisation for members of the armed forces.

Fourteen days leave in Penang, 21 January – 6 February (including travel), at the Church of Scotland Rest Centre.

28 January

After receiving my pay on the morning of 21 January, I went straight to the office and told my staff they would not be seeing anything of me for almost three weeks, giving brief instructions how they should cope with work in my absence, telling them to make the best of it. Three of us from Div HQ are spending leave together, and I am lucky to have with me an old friend who served in 36 Division; sometimes attending dances together in Poona. The other fellow, an infantry man in Div HQ Defence Platoon, is unknown to me. The men in the Defence Platoon are the unlucky guys who carry out parades, and do guard duties at HQ. We left Johore Bahru by truck at 4.30 in the afternoon, arriving in Singapore with time to spare before boarding a train at 8 o'clock. We dumped our kit in a secure zone and made a bee line for the N.A.A.F.I. to feast on tea, biscuits and ice cream. I found the train as uncomfortable and unreliable as those serving the Great Indian Peninsular Railway. With us in the carriage were two Chinese women, one had a baby needing regular attention, and a jolly crowd of Dutch troops wearing army uniforms. I try to make myself as comfortable as possible when travelling under the most trying conditions, after long experience it becomes easy. During the hours throughout the night, until daylight next day, my lack of movement caused me to suffer slightly from a tender *gluteus maximus*. The train arrived at Kuala Lumpur six hours behind schedule, one half only of our journey completed. In places the terrain was too steep for the engine to steam straight ahead, zigzagging back and forth, reversing on steep inclines making slow progress gaining a few miles. We missed a scheduled connection at Kuala Lumpur and had five hours free time waiting for a train to carry us to our destination at Prai.

We made friends with three of the Dutch troops when we learned they would be travelling on our train as far as the mainland railway station at Prai, the ferry port for Penang Island. They had done this journey before. The three of us British guys and three Dutch friends made our way to the N.A.A.F.I. to pass away time until our train was due to leave. We ate cakes, drank char and lemonade, spending a good hour enjoying a game of darts. That night, we heard beer was on offer and we each treated ourselves. The Dutch troops recounted to us in fairly good English, interesting stories describing underground activities during the German occupation of Holland. They had been serving for nine months in the Dutch army since their country was liberated, spending ten days in England before moving here to Malaya. They told us the ten days in England were terrific, and said, "The British are swell people."

At the railway station our carriage once again had little room to spare, I laid myself on the floor to sleep, using my small pack for a pillow. The train plodded steadily along through the night, in the morning we gathered information about our progress at every stop and we were told the train was running to schedule, more surprising we may arrive early. The scenery that morning was beautiful, large forests of palm trees, and dotted alongside I could see native huts built on stilts. It was interesting to gaze on acres of rubber plantations as the train meandered along, tree trunks uniformly sliced extruding trails of milk white sap snaking into cups collecting precious drips of latex. At ten o'clock we stopped at a station to be given the news we would be arriving at our destination in twenty minutes. Strange or not, the train pulled into Prai station exactly on time. We exchanged good wishes with our Dutch friends before parting to go our separate ways.

A ferry steamer was waiting to carry train passengers to Penang Island, a twenty minutes sail to George Town, the main town on the island. At George Town, an M.P. on duty telephoned our arrival to the Church of Scotland leave centre, requesting transport to take us the last four miles of our long and tedious journey. Arriving in time for dinner at 1 o'clock, we were served an excellent meal, fully appreciated after scrounging whatever food we could during the many hours we spent getting here.

Dinner was far better than any we have been served at Johore Bahru, afterwards I took a much needed shower before settling down to unpack my gear. I am sharing a room with Bill, the friend I knew in 36 Division, the third fellow has moved into a room opposite. The beds are comfortable and soft, where I sit writing this letter. After slipping into swimming trunks we stepped out of the dining room onto a soft sandy beach, and might have walked a few steps to the sea if it were not for being told there was a splendid seawater swimming pool five minutes away. Swimming in the pool was good fun, then back for another shower to wash away the seawater. Tea is served at 4 o'clock, followed by supper at seven; in the evening if you wish to enjoy night life in George Town, a truck is ready to take you there.

Less than one hundred holiday-makers are staying at the rest centre, managed by a large staff capable of coping easily with catering for meals and the leisure amenities. I believe we have been very lucky to be given the opportunity to spend time here, few vacancies occur, and the rules state we MUST spend fourteen clear days leave here. This suits me just fine!!

29 January   *BLUE AIR LETTER CARD*

You must understand writing letters is not a priority right now; it is my wish to take full advantage of every minute enjoying myself. I have written to Harry, and to friends, telling them I am spending a pleasant few days on leave at a wonderful holiday resort in Malaya.

Some mornings I tried sketching and admit to nothing but failure. Friday night a dance was held in the rest centre and straight away after the last dance at one o'clock in the morning, Bill and I hastily went to our room, changed into swimming trunks and dashed into the sea for a moonlight bathe. Each day we manage to take at least one dip in the sea. Every night I have been dancing, last night for a change I saw the film, *All This And Heaven Too*. A concert has been arranged to take place tonight at the rest centre, an evening certain to be filled with amusement, followed by bathing in the sea before getting into bed.

Tomorrow night I shall be dancing again with a decent partner. Last Sunday I met a girl at a dance in town and we got along fine together, she told me I had only my dancing to thank for the date tonight. "Guys are not my hobby," she said.

Because of the temptation to laze on the nearby sandy beach constant exposure to the burning hot sun has caused the skin on my shoulders to peel, they are not sore, and my back and arms are as brown as they have ever been.

1 February

Time is rolling along and I shall feel sorrowful when the moment comes to start back to camp. Bill says it is by far the best leave he has ever had and I feel tempted to agree with him. This is so different from the occasions when I stayed at Jhansi. There I was given all the welcome of home, with people around thinking I was a relative of the family, but of course I am not. At the leave centre all manner of activities are catered for, the nearness of the beach, a swimming pool, dancing, and in the evening regular visits to a bustling town full of attractions and entertainment. This is a holiday vastly different from the lazy leisurely way of homely life at Jhansi in the company of old friends. It is impossible to choose which is the better holiday of the two extremes; both equally enjoyable in many different ways.

I did not get to the dance on Wednesday, mentioned in my last letter, that day the whole of Malaya was *topsy turvy*, engaged in strike action for whatever reason I do not know. No busses running, picture houses and dance halls closed, and very few shops open. It was presumed unsafe to allow us into the town; our presence may irritate the mood of local people causing trouble in the streets. We were advised to stay at the centre. Shortly before dinner was served at seven o'clock, plans were changed when it was decided the disruption was not as dangerous as expected and we would be allowed to spend the evening in George Town.

Yesterday morning I was out sketching, of the four attempts undertaken so far this is about the best. In the afternoon Bill and I visited friends living at a house about one hundred yards along the beach from the rest centre. We met the family a week ago when taking a stroll by the sea. They are Eurasian, and invited us to call on them whenever we wish. We spend happy times playing games with their young kiddie, teasing him until he is giddy with delight. His father is a jockey who rides horses at the racecourse on the island. Bill has just told me he is on his way to visit our Eurasian friends and asked me to follow as soon as I finish my letter. I promised to show them some of my paintings and photographs I have with me. It is Chinese New Year's Eve, and the family will be celebrating the event at a dance this evening. There have been occasions during the evenings when I visited one of the taxi dance halls in town. Any number of tickets can be bought from a kiosk on the edge of the dance floor. One ticket is handed to a hostess with whom you wish to dance. Every dance with a hostess is hardly a friendly liaison, few of the girls speak English and it is nothing more than a business transaction. If you happen to get lucky and find a partner who is not one of the girls working as a hostess, it can be a pleasant evening dancing. This brings me up to date with the brief story of my leave, time to put aside this letter to join Bill and our Eurasian friends at their home. A regular routine after tea at 4 o'clock is spending an hour in the swimming pool improving my diving technique before changing for dinner in the evening.

5 February   *BLUE AIR LETTER CARD*
The last complete day of my leave and the hours are flying steadily by. I shall depart tomorrow evening at 6 o'clock to begin a long journey to Singapore, feeling sad and reluctant to return. Singapore can not equal the pleasures enjoyed during the past couple of weeks at the rest centre, oblivious to my commitment in life serving as a soldier in the army. The Chinese New Year was celebrated during our stay, adding a surprising colourful spectacle full of fun. It is unbelievable that almost a year ago, around 15 February, we encountered the most vicious fighting during the whole of the war. That I briefly mentioned in an earlier letter. There

were many more fierce engagements, but the 15th is a date never to be forgotten.

I was fortunate to have made a date to go to a dance on Chinese New Year's Eve with a girl who could dance. The next day Saturday, the first of the Chinese year I went with the same girl to a show and saw a decent film in Technicolor, *Ali Baba And The Forty Thieves*. Sunday night I looked in at the City Lights dance hall, and last night I was again there dancing the whole evening with my new found dancing partner.

The end of this month will see the completion of three years service abroad. It makes me happy thinking of that. Returning to my unit there is one thought in my head, the abundance of mail waiting for me. But, as I have mentioned many times, it causes a headache sorting out by date and struggling to write many replies in a short space of time.

Cheerio. The next letter I shall be writing from Singapore, or Johore Bahru would be more correct.

8 February   *BLUE AIR LETTER CARD*

I am back in the Mental Hospital once again partaking of char and biscuits in the canteen. I arrived at 2 o'clock to sample good old fashioned army tack, (bully-beef), before collecting my mail. How, or where, to begin answering my correspondence is a question the dilemma poses, four letters from mother, three from dad, three from Harry, two from Charlie in Bangkok, one from Rita, one from Uncle Joe, a note from the editor of Blighty magazine, and an Observer newspaper. The note from Blighty magazine acknowledges the receipt of my cartoons, informing me payment and copies of the prints would follow.

The good news that Uncle Fred is home from Sweden after being marooned for the duration of the war years was certainly something for the family to celebrate. He should be able to cope with the cold weather you are having. Everyone I meet tells me I look well, back from my leave with a deep brown tan. Spending hours in the hot sun never troubles me; my skin is well acclimatised to the conditions. But, writing this letter within a few degrees of the equator, tormented by the humid temperature, hands clammy with sweat, and shirt sticking to my back absorbing perspiration, causes a great deal of discomfort.

11 February   *BLUE AIR LETTER CARD*

Winsor & Newton sent me two No.7 paint brushes; the quality is good but far from pre war standards. I received 200 State Express 555 cigarettes from the Observer Cigarette Fund, and 300 Churchman No1, with a label typed, *Jack*. I am sure the packers have miss read the name of Jock, a good friend who returned home from Poona. The editor of

SEAC Newspaper sent me a British Postal Order, £4.13s.6d, equal in value to $40, payment for four cartoons.

Last night I developed negatives taken at Penang, tonight I hope to make prints from them.

14 February

Once again with intentions only to write a short letter, spare time has been spent designing an embroidered motif in colour for the back of a shirt. Enclosed are copies of a portrait photograph taken in a studio at Penang, I bought the negative to make extra prints.

18 February

There has been more mail from you, and a letter from Jock, telling me he sent cigarettes that should have arrived. On the subject of cigarettes, by my reckoning you have ordered a total of 1500 sent to me. You had better put on the brake. How many cigarettes do you think I smoke? We get a free issue of 50 each week, usually Players in a sealed tin. I smoke on average less than 30 a day. Fully aware you are paying two shillings and four pence for a pack of 20 cigarettes, I must seriously consider quitting the habit when I get back to England.

The coloured design I would like to have embroidered on the back of a shirt was carefully wrapped in a rolled package and posted yesterday. The design is painted in full colour, actual size, along with it a pencil outline drawing as a guide to trace the motif onto the material. I am fully aware of the difficult task Auntie Molly has undertaken promising to do the embroidery. There is no real hurry whatsoever to complete the work, I shall be in no position to wear it for many months ahead.

I have been approached to teach art classes in the evening at an Education Centre, recently set up for occupational therapy, and a dozen guys have shown a willingness to attend. Information has reached me that my transfer to the RASC appears to be going through and it will take a while to complete.

22 February

Division HQ had the bright idea to hold a dance last Wednesday at a club in Johore Bahru. You can well imagine I was looking forward to a wonderful evening, dancing to the music of our own military band. The affair was a disaster as far as I was concerned. Ticket numbers were supposed to have been strictly limited which did not appear to be the case, the dance floor was absolutely crowded. Not enough women turned up, those that did were *old battleaxes*, overseas service volunteers looking for a good time. Some of the dames are out to catch the attention of officers, or an easy life sponging on anyone to save money, but the FANY's and W.V.S. are doing a good job out here. I had one or two dances with female partners, other dances I took *lady* dancing with my pals. An amusing incident occurred dancing with Bill during an 'Excuse me' dance, a friend came to us, tapped Bill on the shoulder and said, "Excuse me," and I danced away with a new partner.

Yesterday morning none other than Admiral Lord Louis Mountbatten, Supreme Allied Commander South East Asia paid us a visit. He dished out medals before stepping onto his soap box to give 2 Div HQ his personal appreciation for our part in the war. Thanks to our important visitor the unit was given half day holiday, the same evening I took my first art class in the education centre, three people only turned up. Other guys who should have been there found the opportunity for an extended trip into town too good to miss. However, the idea seems to be getting under way and I think it could be a success.

A fellow I met in the canteen recently wanted to know if I came from Accrington, I replied saying I did not, but from a town near by. He thought when he first saw me at Poona last year I might live around Accrington, but did not have courage to enquire. I should say he most certainly could have noticed me back home. He lives on Stevenson Street East, in Accrington. The number of years I walked and cycled that street back and forth to attend art school is uncountable, some occasions four times in one day. He also had seen me dancing at the Conservative Club, on Saturday evenings, and at the Technical College in Accrington when he was taking a course in metal work. He told me he was at home a year ago, arousing my curiosity to fire questions at him about the changes made around Accrington since I was home. "There are now no barrage balloons," he said. He joined Headquarters when the Division was reforming and is serving with the Border Regiment, Defence Platoon.

More surprising news came to me when talking to two fellows recently returned from the Church of Scotland Rest Centre, at Penang. They had been approached by a stranger in RAF uniform, staying at the rest centre, who had noticed my signature in the visitor's book. The lads asked if I knew anyone called Jack Killeya, stationed at Kuala Lumpur? Hearing the name startled and amazed me. Of course, I have known Jack for many years, a close friend from schoolboy days. Jack told the lads he is Group 31, hoping soon to begin his journey home from Singapore for demobilisation. Had I been aware he was stationed at Kuala Lumpur, I may have found time to meet him during the long delays at Kuala Lumpur, waiting for connecting trains to and from Penang. I am set to be busy meeting people in Singapore on their way home. First, Maurice said he wishes we should meet when he reports to the transit camp waiting to board a ship, and now my very good friend Jack.

The weather this evening is lovely, following the whole afternoon bursting with lightning, thunder and prolonged heavy rain.

28 February

Since returning from leave I have once been on a short spree to the Honky Tonk, (taxi dancing), an easy way for many local girls to make a meagre living since the Japanese occupation. We lads dance mainly amongst ourselves; it is too expensive paying money for every dance with a girl. I visited a picture house in Johore Bahru to see the film, *The True Glory*, a wartime historical film combining newsreels from D Day, to the fall of Berlin. Given limited access to war news isolated in the middle of the jungle, except our own business fighting the Japanese, the film extended my limited knowledge of the European war.

Four days ago in the morning of Monday, 25 February, under a blazing hot sun a big military parade was formed up in front of 2 Division Headquarters at Johore Bahru, to witness the surrendering of swords by Japanese officers. Major General Nicholson took the salute in front of officers and men of 2 Division, and about twenty Japanese officers. Each Japanese officer stepped solemnly forward in turn, saluted smartly to the assembly before placing his sword on a band of white cloth laid in a straight line on the ground in front of them. It was a lengthy ceremony, everyone standing at attention in the humid heat of the day. I can not imagine what thoughts went through the minds of the Nips when two British officers and two army blokes on parade, passed out in the middle of the show. During the entire proceedings the Japanese officers stood smartly in line like statues, fully dressed in uniform enduring the uncomfortable clammy heat without showing the slightest discomfort.

I was asked by 2 I/C of the Division to design a centrepiece to fly the Union flag for the presentation of medals by Lord Louis Mountbatten, and for the Japanese sword surrender ceremony. The monument stands in the middle of the parade ground overlooked by the offices of 2 Division Headquarters. Constructed of concrete, and emblazoned with the division's badge, two keys crossed painted in black, on the four sides of a cube mounted on a stepped plinth. The names of places where the division has served are lettered on a border above the badges, and a tall flag pole is mounted in the centre of the cube. The general was highly complimentary about my contribution to the two ceremonies in the Division's history.

We have had more lightning, thunder, and heavy rain. If it is absolutely necessary to walk out when rain is pouring down and have no wish to get your clothes wet, a simple solution is remove your shirt and expose the skin.

6 March

Another batch of mail has turned up; seven letters all to be answered give an idea of the correspondence to get through. A check of my log of letters written this year, excluding business and parcels totals 47, posted in the space of 63 days; the number received over the same period is 57! The difference is accounted for by the individual letters each of you write to me, whereas every letter of mine is to you both. One week more and it will be exactly three years since I sailed from Liverpool.

I see you have got together a selection of my work and passed it to Mr. Lindoe in preparation for submitting to the Royal College of Art distinctions award, I am sure he will do his best arranging whatever is available. I am ashamed how little sketching I have turned out these last six months, not like the old days serving with 36 Division. Normally I would have found time to produce something, but this outfit thrives on hard work and is tireless making it.

9 March

A friend slightly less in stature than me has been asking about clothes, I know he would be grateful for a suit of mine that will be too small for me when I get back. He is a decent guy, finishing a five year stretch and soon to get out of the army. His folks are not well off. I write you his address asking would you please post my grey suit to his home. His demob is Group 30 and there are only two groups on the list ahead of him.

12 March   *To my dad*

The approach of your birthday calls for a special letter to wish you Many Happy Returns and this birthday card I made for the occasion. There will be four more cartoons in the post tomorrow on the way to SEAC Newspaper. Last Saturday, and Sunday, I tried sketching in Johore Bahru but the threatened rain caused me to abandon my efforts, but I was able to take photographs. Last night I developed the negatives, tonight I shall make prints from them, first paying the canteen a visit, which has recently been declining steadily in supplies, and efficiency.

Unreported in letters, a frightening encounter happened one night while developing negatives at Johore Bahru. Each ward at the mental hospital had a separate treatment room, fully tiled with large bath, and waist high bench. The lack of windows for privacy, a secure door, and all the facilities necessary for processing negatives afforded a perfect photographic darkroom. High on the exterior wall was a narrow opening along the width of the room for ventilation, safe from extraneous light on a moonless night. In complete darkness the work was going well, suddenly, I thought

I was under attack by a ferocious tropical creature, zooming around me in the darkness missing my face and head by millimeters. Unable to see the animal and not knowing what it was, I thought at any moment I would receive a poisonous bite or suffer serious injury. But, hearing a succession of rapid squeaks I realised I was sharing the room with a bat on a night time jaunt, and my safety would be better assured if I remained calm and still, avoiding sudden movements. Putting my trust in the bat's navigation skills I completed my task, emerging unscathed and very relieved.

15 March

To see everywhere in England covered with snow must make a pretty picture, unwelcome in some way if it is very cold. I am pleased the weather will be warm when I return. If I was offered the chance to go home now it would take seconds to say "Yes!" snow, or no snow.

I shall include a few recent photographs, pictures of Penang and others of Johore Bahru. The group of pals was taken a couple of weeks ago near our quarters. The fellow standing on the right is one of the old brigade, we have been together since the days at Felixstowe, India, Arakan, Assam and Burma. He is a typical farmer's boy from Yorkshire due for repatriation at the same time as me. The fellow in the centre of the picture is the chap whose address I gave you and would like to have my civvy suit, a cobbler before joining the army and makes a special job repairing my shoes. The two chaps sitting in front are newcomers to Div HQ with little service out here. Note the two Japanese officers' swords, recently presented to veterans of the Burma campaign.

21 March

Two nights ago I saw the film, *Blythe Spirit*, it was a new style of story and I got into quite an argument with the lads about the film. One chap said it was nonsense, I tried to make them see the film as I did, they were stubborn, criticising the story for being close to spiritualism.

22 March, Friday

I expect to hear something soon from the editor of SEAC Newspaper, having noticed one of the cartoons from the last batch printed in the issue yesterday. Last night was the weekly art class and the lads are enjoying it, night duties for some can interfere with regular attendance. I made two sepia paintings recently; a native village at Penang, the other an infantry patrol with a Malay overseer inspecting trees on a rubber plantation for the illicit stealing of latex sap. The Division sends out patrols when there is suspicious activity; latex is being stolen from the plantations. I hope to enter a watercolour sunset, and landscapes painted at Penang, in an art exhibition next month in Singapore. The exhibition is to be held at the Y.M.C.A. over a period of four days, open to anyone in the Forces to submit works of art.

25 March, Monday

During a journey on the truck taking me to Singapore Friday evening, I had a long conversation with the corporal who met my friend Jack at the leave centre in Penang. All office work is my responsibility and before leaving on Sunday to visit Singapore, I checked with the clerks that everything was under control. Fortunately I did, a message had been left for me to contact the corporal with whom I had travelled into town Friday evening. He told me he had met Jack in the Shackle Club (N.A.A.F.I.), in Singapore on Saturday evening. The Shackle Club is to Singapore, as the Waldorf is to New York. Every minute you spend in the club your eyes expect to see someone you know. Furthermore, I learned I had walked past the RAF camp Friday night where Jack is staying, and while I was visiting the Shackle Club, he was ten minutes away spending an evening with friends in the Union Jack Club.

Having gained this new information I hitch hiked to Singapore and found Jack at the RAF camp playing Bridge in the canteen. We spent the early part of the evening at the Union Jack Club talking our heads off, then to the cinema to see the film, *Spitfire*. By 9 o'clock we were again in the Union Jack Club, watching a dancing class and occasionally taking to the floor to dance. Our meeting came to an end in the car park waiting for my truck to take me to Johore Bahru. We stood chatting in the calm of the evening, the bright lights of the harbour glowing between two tall buildings, and ships' signal lamps flashing messages against a starlight sky. It was almost half past eleven when we parted, vowing to see each other in England before long. The next day (today), Jack is embarking on a ship for England. He promised me he would visit you as soon as he arrived home.

Another of my cartoons appeared in SEAC Newspaper yesterday. Jack had not noticed my name on the cartoons and as we sat talking in the Union Jack Club, a friend walked past carrying under his arm a copy of the newspaper. I asked if I might glance at it, as luck would have it, I was able to show Jack a cartoon printed in the issue. Two cartoons have now been printed in the paper from the last batch sent in.

29 March *To my brother Harry*

I am sending you a souvenir of a night out in Singapore, a receipt printed in Chinese and English, for drinks bought in a taxi dance club. Everything is about the same. I saw the film, *Arsenic And Old Lace*, shown in camp last Wednesday.

3 April

Bill, the pal I spent my leave with, popped into the office to tell me his
Class B release had come through. We came out on the same convoy
and expected to go home together; he left Div HQ for the transit camp
Monday morning.

During my lunch break every day this week I have been painting
a portrait in oils of one of the boys, I may enter it for the Forces Art
Exhibition. Today I paid a visit to the dentist to get my teeth in good
shape before returning home. He dealt with three that needed attention.
I hope all potential dental problems are cleared for the immediate future.
Tomorrow, Group 29 leaves here on the first stage of the journey home,
also December 1942, and January 1943 PYTHON[29]. They are UK
embarkation dates. February 1943 PYTHON will leave next month
and after that will come my turn in March. It looks good on paper, but
allowance for extensions should be made to these predictions.

6 April   2 *Division headed notepaper*

A friend employed on the printing press in Div HQ very kindly produced
for me this special headed note paper, with 2 Division crossed keys
badge, and my address. There is no point worrying I was not successful
gaining a distinction in the Royal College of Art examination, neither am
I discouraged. It was unfortunate the type of work submitted was out
of my control, and certainly not of my choosing. Favourable progress is
being made with the portrait in oils and when my model and I are free
of work, I am busy dabbling. Yesterday I received another payment for
cartoons, there is yet more to come for others that have been accepted.
I could have said something to you about the poor quality of our *grub*
served at meal times in recent weeks, but great improvements have been
made during the past few days.

12 April   2 *Division headed notepaper*

Yours truly, without doubt, hopes to be on his way home before the
end of next month, no exact date is forecast when I shall be shedding
tears of sorrow, leaving the enchanting mysteries of the Far East! It is
some time since I wrote a lengthy letter, recently my life has been pretty
dull, the last time I visited Singapore was to meet Jack. Tomorrow I shall
take a selection of my work into town for the Art Exhibition; entries
must be handed in three days prior to the official opening on 16 April.
The paintings chosen are – the portrait in oils; an allegorical scene of
a desecrated Buddha; a sunset at Johore Bahru; and three sketches of
Malayan villages. I believe prizes are to be awarded in several different
categories.

16 April   *2 Division headed notepaper*

Today I received payment of £3 from the editor of SEAC Newspaper. This evening I have written one of my spasmodic efforts to Auntie Ada enclosing a photograph, and yesterday ordered a parcel to be sent to her under our special scheme. I think all the relatives will at some stage have received a parcel ordered by me. Also, with this consignment I arranged for a parcel to be sent to Auntie Florrie. A kind friend put his name to this because two parcels can not be ordered at the same time by one person. The last parcel was sent to Auntie Ethel. Earlier I ordered one to be sent to Auntie Molly, and to Auntie Elsie before that.

Today I filled in form AF01727A remitting payment of £20 to you. I can not give any idea when you might receive this; I believe money transfers now go by air. You must consider delays caused by various offices involved, taking about three weeks or a month to arrive.

Yesterday, I was given a vaccination and I anticipate no unpleasant effects.

21 April, Sunday

I am sure you will have noticed the date is my birthday, it has begun very well. Today is the third day of four days holiday we have been given for Easter. Four work free days at a stretch is most unusual. In the mail for me today came a Blighty magazine and printed inside was one of my cartoons. Also a BPO, value ten shillings and sixpence payment for the cartoon.

Feeling thirsty and in need of a drink, I took a break writing this letter to get a mug of char. Returning from the canteen I met a group of the boys playing cricket and wasted no time joining them. It is almost four years since I last held a cricket bat. The past three quarters of an hour has been spent enjoying myself romping around playing the game with the boys, unexpectedly interrupting writing my letter.

The art exhibition in Singapore was a great success. I went along on Wednesday night to view and found a lot of excellent and interesting work on show. Many entries were artistic, but a lot of ordinary pieces too; drawings of film stars copied from photographs, and copies of illustrations of magazine prints. General Cox reviewed the show and was one of the judges. I was present on Friday night to hear the announcement of the winners, and was pleasantly surprised when my painting of a Malayan village at Penang was chosen first prize in the exhibition. I was given a Malayan pewter Cocktail Set, a large round tray, cocktail shaker and six cups. Five prizes were presented for different categories, each prize made of Malayan pewter; mine was by far the best. After the ceremony I met one of the judges, a commercial artist from Liverpool and spent the rest of the evening with him talking shop. He entered a black and white chalk drawing of a Japanese soldier which I feel would have carried of the prize in the section for portraits, participating as a judge counted him out. He said the standard of my portrait in oils was good enough to win that section, but there was no wish to show favouritism and to give other entrants a chance.

Remember this is my birthday, and I was given the best news ten minutes after getting out of bed this morning. On Thursday next, 25 April, I move to the transit camp in Singapore beginning the first stage of my journey HOME. At the transit camp I shall be placed on a list of persons waiting to be allocated a place on board a ship, to begin my long journey by sea, never yet accomplished in less than 17 days. Regular news bulletins about the movement of ships, and information listing the priority of persons waiting to return home, will keep you up to date with the latest details. There is no point writing and answering any further letters to me, my movements will delay any attempts to find me and they may not reach me before I embark on a ship. The remainder of the four days holiday I shall devote to packing and preparing to move from here. On Tuesday, I shall have a medical and the M.O. will give me whatever jabs are needed for the journey to England.

CHAPTER 14

Homeward Bound

26 April

I said I was expecting to move on the 25th, in order to avoid an early morning rush I left Johore Bahru a day earlier, arriving at the transit camp at 4.30 in the afternoon in plenty of time for dinner in the evening. The signing of all official documentation for departure was carried out yesterday morning, since then very little has been done except putting in an appearance on parade at 9 o'clock this morning. The parade is an important daily routine to announce to everyone up to date information about shipping, or the current arrangements to get people away from here. For instance, this morning we learned that a decent size ship, the *Empire Trooper*, is due to dock in the next few days. Quite a large contingent of troops should be leaving on her, reducing the number of names on a mighty big waiting list. I recognised one fellow in camp whom I knew in 366 Battery, he has been here three weeks, one of the unlucky guys that did not manage to get passage aboard the last ship that docked here.

30 April

During the next few days I shall be unable to give you a progress report about my position in the queue, the whole camp is moving to a new location. When I am resettled and find somewhere comfortable to write letters, you will learn more about my situation. There is one hell of a mix-up here; you can thank your lucky stars I shall not be home to make trouble, noise, and extra work yet a while. There are people leaving tomorrow on the *Empire Trooper*, but the ship will not take half so many personnel from here as was planned. The *Orontes* sailed last Thursday, very few people from the transit camp were allocated to embark, priority was given to colonial and allied troops making their way to the UK, to put on a big show at the June Victory Parade in London. First in line leaving here are Victory Parade personnel, after that, B and A release. Next, 28 days UK leave, and last of all PYTHON personnel. The numbers getting out on B release (specialist occupation) is outrageous, delaying personnel on genuine repatriation. This brings my news about the present state of affairs up to date.

4 May

We made our move to the new transit camp, affording very little opportunity to get into Singapore from here. At the previous camp we were situated on the edge of a soft sandy beach where it was delightful to slip into the sea. There will be no relaxing afternoons swimming at this place; we are miles from the sea. While I am here my army pay is going to credit, the moment I step on board a ship to leave I am no longer considered to be overseas reducing my pay in accordance with home service rates.

Yesterday, I took a trip to Div HQ to check if mail was waiting for me and was handed eight letters; foolishly I came away without them. Fortunately, I read them before leaving and I expect someone turning up at the camp will pass them on to me.

Repatriation is moving very slowly, few people in the camp have been given passage to UK since I came here. I believe the next boat is due to arrive on the 10th. Looking at the number of B and A Class release waiting for a ship; I have little immediate hope of getting away. However, I am content filled with a happy thoughts I shall be home to see you soon.

9 May

More fellows in B Class, 30 Group, UK 28 days leave, and February repatriation, are getting ready to depart tomorrow. According to this schedule and providing there are no setbacks, March repatriation including my group, should be the next batch to get away from here. I hope my calculations to arrive home about the end of June will prove to not be far wrong.

Enclosed is the most recent photograph of a group of friends in Div HQ, taken before we moved from the previous transit camp. I set up the camera after we had been swimming and you can see the high tide in the background behind us. Our tent was about thirty yards from the sea. I am afraid you will not get to see the paintings I had on show in Singapore art exhibition, the Division's Padre was persuasive and determined to have four of them offering me $100. I was reluctant to part with them. The friend who asked me to paint his portrait in oils paid me for the finished painting and is sending it home as a present to his girl friend.

Many old pals in 366 Battery turned up here from Java where they have been stationed, I would have been there too if I had not been transferred to Div HQ. Maurice is here, I have been showing him the sights of Singapore. Another pal I remember well as a lance bombardier is wearing the rank of Troop sergeant major. Promotions in the Battery appear to have been handed out with the rations, many old boys are wearing tapes on their sleeves. We have been exchanging yarns about the rough days in Burma fighting the Japanese. I was reminded about the incident checking a hand grenade when I could not replace the pin, tying down the firing lever with my boot laces to make it safe.

13 May

I left Div HQ along with six friends, four of them are Group 30 due to leave tomorrow on their way home for demobilisation, me and the other two guys are awaiting our turn, hoping we will certainly be the next to leave. Demob dates for Group 30 are June 2 to June 10, they must get away now or they will be behind schedule. The next boat is due on the 18th, I am keeping my fingers crossed hoping I shall get lucky and this will be my turn to leave. Each day I enjoy a lazy life charpoy bashing, anxiously awaiting news to board a boat heading for England and to gaze at Singapore merging slowly with the distant horizon.

22 May

Yesterday I received news to be ready to leave camp this morning and embark around lunch time, or soon after. I am to sail on a Yankee Liberty ship, *Taos Victory*. We have not been told a definite departure date, it will probably be tomorrow, or the following day. The passage will take about twenty-one days to reach England, disregarding possible delays caused by bad weather, or engine breakdown. Making a rough estimate at this stage, I should be home about June 17. In a couple of week's time, you might study the shipping news printed in the papers to know the expected date of arrival of the *Taos Victory*, and to which port. Let me say emphatically, I want NO CELEBRATIONS of any kind welcoming me home, I wish everything to be absolutely normal. Perhaps when we dock at a port in England, I may be in a position to send you a wire telling of my safe arrival.

In 1943 the building of fast cargo vessels began in America to replace the slower Liberty ships. The choice of name derived from the type of ship VC2, 'V' for the type, 'C' for cargo and '2' a medium size ship. The propulsion by steam turbine gave an average speed 15-17 knots, an advantage over steam engines in the earlier Liberty ships. During the war, 414 Victory type cargo ships were built.

On 23 May I embarked on the troop ship S.S. *Taos Victory*, named after a town in New Mexico. I was finally on my way home.

26 May   *At sea – Indian Ocean*

My pen has been packed away for the moment. The heading will tell you I am on the bright blue ocean about 300 miles east of Colombo, and I find it easier writing to you in pencil. The first day out of Singapore was OK, since then the weather has taken on a dull monsoon attitude. Spasmodic showers of rain frequently drive me away from the comfort of an open deck. The sea has not been over rough, but this *salmon tin* has a horrible habit tossing about on the ocean in fairly good sailing conditions, I hate to think of her antics if the weather should turn at all nasty. Quite a few fellows are suffering sea sickness at the present time, trying hard to bring up their stomachs, I am feeling unsteady with a nauseating thick head.

In about twenty-four hours we are expecting to put in at Colombo to take on water, a delay of no more than a few hours. If a longer stay is necessary, the captain may ask the port authorities for permission to allow passengers ashore. I first estimated my arrival in the UK about 17 June, I am afraid I shall have to extend this to the 20th. The *grub* on board is pretty good and sleeping accommodation much better than other troop ships on which I sailed. This vessel is fitted with bunks, saving trouble unpacking a hammock to sling at night and stow away in the morning. My chief grumble is directed at inadequate arrangements for washing; I guess I can endure the discomfort for the next three weeks. The *Taos Victory* is a fairly new ship, manned by a Yank crew, and carrying about 1200 passengers. I shall post this letter at Ceylon; there may be other ports where letters can be posted, perhaps Aden, and Port Said. Remember, I want no ceremonies on my arrival, I shall be happy to get home!

29 May   *Colombo, Ceylon*

My feet are on terra firma in Colombo, Ceylon, and the ship is anchored near the dock area. We reached Colombo early yesterday morning (Tuesday), after slower progress than was expected. We understood there would be only a short delay, then towards evening on the day we arrived came news shore leave would be allowed tomorrow, from 7 o'clock in the morning until 6 o'clock in the evening. Anxious to see more of the world at every opportunity, I straight away wrote out a pass allowing me to go ashore for a few hours to explore Colombo.

This morning, everyone wishing to go ashore began queuing on deck, wondering what arrangements had been made to ferry a large crowd of anxious tourists ashore, eager to visit the capital town of Ceylon. Around 8 o'clock all the passenger motor launches Colombo could muster raced to the ship's side, less than one hour later I was ashore nosing into all the shops filled with attractive goods enticing a visitor's curiosity. I quickly found the N.A.A.F.I. where I could begin writing this letter in comfort, soon to go downstairs to the canteen to check what choices are listed on the menu for lunch. I have with me the camera, but nothing so far has tempted me to take any photographs. At this moment I am carrying around four different currencies in my pocket, dollars I came away with from Malaya, annas from India, Ceylonese currency we have been issued with to spend here, and English money. This really is a nice place, not quite so fast living as Bombay, the town is similar in many ways except it is much smaller. I can not make a judgement from this short visit what the rest of the island might be like. We are expecting to up anchor to continue our *holiday cruise* early tomorrow.

6 June   *Arabian Sea*

We did not leave Colombo as I expected, the day after writing my last letter; this was due to engine trouble taking time to repair. We sailed a day later at midday on Friday. I am trying my best to write this letter on the mess-deck, the ship is tossing about worse than a fishing trawler. The weather conditions since we left Colombo has been atrocious, we have encountered squalls, storms and hurricanes. Tomorrow noon will mark one week since leaving Colombo, and relying on current information we should put in at Aden on Saturday, 8 June. In no way is this certain. I shall be extremely lucky to be home on 20 June as anticipated. I must once more extend my prediction by two days; we have encountered heavy weather recently forcing the ship to make slower progress. Two days out of Colombo I was overcome by sea-sickness, suffering less trauma than I did the first time having gained my sea legs with past experience. When I came on board this ship I told you the *grub* was OK, I must now contradict that statement telling you it has taken a complete turn about for the worst. The stuff being dished up at meal times is awful, and if the guys are not sea-sick from the rolling of the ship, the cooks are doing their best to make it so.
NEWSFLASH – our position at noon today was 676 miles from Aden.

12 June   *Red Sea*

The ship is anchored at Port Tewfik, the southern end of the Suez Canal, standing by awaiting orders to proceed through the canal. This letter will be collected with a batch of mail tomorrow morning and posted during a short stop for about six hours to take stores on board at Port Said. What a lovely change it has been since we left Aden, in contrast to the suffering endured isolated in this Bovril bottle bouncing about in the Arabian Sea. Our bodies have been losing pounds in sweat on the voyage, already I feel the climate getting cooler and much more comfortable on the Troop deck (lower deck). At last we are catching up with the time difference in England, our clocks are 5½ hours ahead of Greenwich Time. I shall not be home before Monday 24 June. All the best to everyone, see you soon!

CHAPTER 15

Royal Artillery Barracks, Woolwich

I disembarked at Liverpool on 23 June and travelled by rail to the Royal Artillery Depot, Woolwich Garrison, London. Immediately on arrival at the Royal Artillery Barracks, Woolwich, I was granted twenty-eight days disembarkation leave and issued with a travel warrant to the home of my parents in Lancashire. I reported back for duty at Woolwich Barracks on 22 July.

23 July

Yesterday afternoon I arrived at Euston station about half past two after a pleasant journey, reporting my presence inside the barracks by 4 o'clock. Last night, with three other fellows I stepped outside the main gate to see Ginger Rogers in the film, *Heartbeat*. Today has been spent collecting army kit, getting familiar with the layout of the barracks to settle into my new home. The *grub* here is really good by army standards; imagine getting a fried egg slapped onto my plate. I am allowed out of barracks in the Woolwich area when not on duty, from 5 o'clock in the evening until 2359 hours, to proceed anywhere outside the town I must obtain a pass. I am told this is a straight forward simple matter. When I have 'got to know the ropes,' I shall apply for a pass to visit Harry; I could be with him in central London by 6 o'clock in the evening, or soon after. It is a glorious day, very warm indeed and a day perfectly suited for blancoing webbing! Do not write to me until I can give you a full postal address.

My brother Harry, serving with No.1 War Office Signals, was billeted in private premises at 94 Eaton Square, a Government requisitioned Georgian property in Central London. A small group of Royal Signals staff conducted operations from offices on the ground floor, sleeping in rooms upstairs. A few of the occupants, including my brother, tell many strange tales firmly believing the house to be haunted. I was never lucky to witness any signs of psychic phenomenon during the nights I often slept there visiting my brother.

24 July

Here is my address, it is important to include 'Field Wing' there are also A.A., and R.H.A., in the barracks. I have written a letter to Harry telling him I am trying to get time off this weekend to see him. Tomorrow I begin work as assistant art instructor in the Education Centre. It may not be a permanent job; I shall see what becomes of it.

30 July, Tuesday

I was able to get a pass to visit Harry on Sunday, and after eating lunch together in a canteen we both were busy writing letters before heading to Hyde Park Corner to listen to the oratory, and humour, of the soap box entertainers. We stood a while among the crowd surrounding Harry's favourite speaker who was causing volumes of laughter with his wit. Getting our fill of criticism and comments about current topics, we made our way into the park to sit on the grass, listening to the band for the remainder of the afternoon. At the beginning of the evening we enjoyed dancing in the Stage Door Canteen, until the large number of different branches of military personnel in uniform drifting in towards 9 o'clock made it impossible to dance. There was a floor show at ten o'clock, compèred by Sally Rogers of the BBC. We left Piccadilly after the show and walked to Charring Cross station, Harry waited with me until I boarded a train taking me back to Woolwich. I am more than happy my transfer to the RASC, by the higher command at 2 Division HQ in Malaya, has turned out to be misguided judgement.

1 August, Thursday

It is August Bank Holiday weekend, and I received a letter from Harry saying he was expecting to visit me after duty on Saturday. If he was thinking of coming here I don't know where I could fix up a place for him to sleep. The R.A. barracks is not like his free and easy billet, you can not wander in, or out, without a pass, and there are no forces clubs with accommodation where he could stay. When we were last together I mentioned to him I may not get a pass for the holiday weekend, I was wrong. Yesterday I telephoned Harry explaining everything. My leave pass begins Friday evening. I hope to meet him in the Lion Club tomorrow evening soon after 6 o'clock when we can talk things over, deciding what we wish to do. Perhaps I might bring him here for a day and show him around. Harry's pass expires Monday; I do not have to be back in barracks until 7 o'clock Tuesday morning.

6 August, Tuesday

I got back to Woolwich this morning before 8 o'clock having enjoyed a pleasant weekend with Harry, we did not spend every minute together; I hitched up with a WAAF to go dancing. Gee Whiz – it was HOT! Dancing during the evening inside a crowded hall, wearing thick army battledress was reminiscent of temperatures abroad.

8 August

Since the long weekend the weather has not been very good, rain has persisted in the afternoon, but evenings have been fine. I look forward to spending an undecided programme next weekend with Harry; he will visit me, or vice versa. I was pleased to see him wearing stripes again increasing his regular army pay.

I like my job and hope I can hang on to it until demob. It is very much akin to the routine at art school, working the same hours, spending every minute teaching drawing and painting. I have my mind set on finding a job in commercial design when I get out of this army.

10 August, Saturday

Usually on Saturday morning I arrange a teaching programme to visit art galleries in London, taking students on Release Training Course to study classical art. This morning I collected railway warrants for my students to take them on an official visit to central London. Finding the British Museum opened at 10 o'clock; I decided we should spend time there. Obviously lacking the scope of pre war days, touring the museum was an interesting exercise. Many exhibits removed during the war for safe keeping are gradually being returned. At lunch time I left the guys in the museum and went to meet Harry. I am with him near his billet sharing a table in the Lion Club, he is writing a letter to Joan his Wren girl friend. I am in a better position to roam anywhere at leisure having been issued with an official staff pass permitting me to leave the confines of the barracks whenever I choose. Yesterday, I met Harry about 7 o'clock to spend a pleasant evening together at the Stage Door Canteen. I had to leave before the floor show started to catch a late bus to take me to Woolwich, only to discover I missed the last one, testing me to use devious means along with good luck to get back to barracks safely, but very wet!

After tea this evening we shall once again visit the Stage Door Canteen and have a few dances before the floor becomes crowded, then make our way to the Columbia Club to round off the evening. I am not sure if all the guys in Harry's office are sleeping there this weekend. If I cannot find an unoccupied bed, there is space on the floor where I shall settle down for the night. I must sign off; chico is itching to grab hold of my pen to add a comment.

Addition to my letter by Harry – We are having another swell weekend, or at least we hope though the weather is inclement. A brush with the Red Caps last night when Jim had to bear the humiliation of being addressed, "Corporal." When he was asked his rank he drew himself up to his full 5 feet 2 inches, and proudly replied, "BOMBARDIER!" – Harry.

12 August

To continue the events from Saturday afternoon, – in the evening we were dancing at the Stage Door Canteen, and again Sunday evening where I met the WAAF I had before been dancing with. This time it was a lucky encounter, not a pre arranged date. Sunday morning Harry and me strolled in St. James's Park and watched the changing of the guard at Buckingham Palace. I left Harry at 11 o'clock that night at Charring Cross and was in the barracks by mid-night. Harry is coming to Woolwich tomorrow; we are hoping to attend the regular weekly dance.

13 August

I telephoned Harry to find out if he is coming here tonight and spoke to George who was on duty in the office. He told me Harry was getting ready to leave, and perhaps even at this moment he was already on his way to meet me in Woolwich.

15 August

On Tuesday evening Harry paid his first visit here, after conducting him on a short tour of the town, the rest of the evening claimed our full attention at a local dance hall. Harry looks smart in battle dress wearing a Royal Signals light blue dress cap. I bet we present the appearance of a bonnie pair strolling around London, a corporal and a bombardier in army uniforms wearing brightly coloured dress caps.

I met the secretary to a brigadier last night from my old 366 Battery; he contacted me about a book to be published by the War Office. The brigadier has taken on the task of writing an account of the Royal Artillery's activities in Burma. My pal mentioned to his boss I had made several sketches of wartime scenes in *action* against the Japanese, and some of my paintings had been printed in Soldier magazine. He wanted to know if I would be prepared to produce a series of thumbnail sketches to illustrate passages in the book.

15 August

I think it is about time I applied for a 48 hour weekend pass. I would like to arrange for Harry to get a pass at the same time. However, knowing the way things are, it seems unlikely he will be in a position to get time off judging by the busy work load I often find in his office.

From enquiries made recently, and information gathered about commercial art, it is a progressing business. When I leave the army it may be worth considering my future as a graphic artist working in a studio. London is a place thriving with opportunities in this type of commerce where I should take steps to begin earning my living.

Last evening I saw Harry at his office spending very little time with him. A girl living in Abbey Wood I have previously been dating at the local dances in Woolwich had an appointment in London yesterday afternoon. I arranged to meet her after visiting Harry, returning with her to Woolwich to spend the evening at the popular Wednesday dance. After the dance I escorted her on the trolley-bus to her home at Abbey Wood.

I have been asked to make a black and white pen and wash drawing of a colonel's house in Hampstead. Bitty painting jobs find their way into my department interrupting teaching regular classes. I should be thankful and refrain from complaining about my pleasant and easy job in the army, allowing me many opportunities to visit Harry.

17 August

Writing once again in the Lion Club, using Harry's letter pad and waiting for him to finish work in his office before joining me. I was about to sit down when a young fellow dressed in Merchant Navy uniform looked up from his letter writing and exclaimed, "Hello Jim!" I took a second look at the person before realising it was Arnold Rushton, a friend who attended Oswaldtwistle Central School, the same years with me, and joined the forces about one month before I did. The reason I did not immediately recognise him I could see his face was badly disfigured. From threads of our conversation I learned he was getting out of the service with a war pension. I thought it prudent not to press him to know what caused his injuries; it was obvious he had been through quite a horrendous ordeal.

20 August

The weekend in London with Harry went well, and I caught the last train back on Sunday night. I say Sunday, but in fact it was ten minutes to one in the morning. I started work on one or two black and white illustrations for the book the War Office is producing, and began planning further ideas that may be suitable.

26 August

Four illustrations for the R.A. book are finished, I shall contact my friend at the War Office and let him know they are ready for his boss to see when he returns from leave in two weeks. I am glad you found the ration card I sent to you useful. I am afraid I can only be given one when I am away from the barracks on a weekend break, as I was August Bank Holiday.

4 September, Wednesday

The comfort of Harry's bed is a good spot to write this letter. I came here to suggest we might get together this weekend to pay a visit to Auntie Molly at Woodley, unfortunately as I was leaving the barracks, I was notified for office duty on Saturday and Sunday. The whole of this week my sergeant is on leave, loading me with extra work. Next Tuesday, we begin art classes in the evenings for the Band Boys[30] at the Depot, I have been given the job of taking the first class. Last night I enjoyed an excellent film at a picture house in Woolwich, the title of the film was, *The Strange Love Of Martha Ivers*. Tonight, I shall spend time with Harry at the Columbia Club.

<u>Addition to my letter by Harry</u> – Jim is making free with my cleaning gear again. He says Auntie Ada received a Postal Order for 5 shillings, instead of the Forces food parcel scheme; discontinued since ordering it to be sent when he was stationed in Singapore. The news was in a letter Jim received from Auntie Ada, and Uncle Herbert. – *Harry*.

8 September

The colonel in charge of the Education Section asked me to design the centre-fold for a Christmas card, suggesting he would like it to portray scenes of release training at work, and the Victory Parade. He was pleased with my pen and ink drawing of his house when I handed him my finished effort. I wrote a letter to the brigadier's secretary, asking to arrange a meeting to show him illustrations I had prepared for the R.A. War History. On two occasions last week when the weather was good, I closed the school at 12 o'clock, and each day the class ate lunch at a café in Woolwich before spending the afternoon sketching by the River Thames.

This evening I plan to take my girl friend Lilian to see the film, *Four Jill's In A Jeep*, showing at the Odeon cinema in Woolwich, it is an old film neither of us has seen.

11 September

Last night I took my first class teaching the Band Boys drawing techniques. A group of eight bright young students, thoroughly absorbed in a new subject added to their school curriculum. This weekend I have the opportunity to get a 48 hour pass; depending how long it takes me to complete all the important work before getting away, it may be well past 8 o'clock Friday night when I get home. Tonight I shall try to visit Harry, not having made contact with him for more than a week.

Weekend home leave with my parents, 13 – 15 September.

18 September

I got to Preston soon after 10.00pm Sunday night with time for a cup of tea before taking the 10.35 train to London. The train was not overcrowded, making one stop at Crewe, arriving Euston station at 4.15 Monday morning. I began a steady walk from the station along deserted streets to Harry's place, passing Madame Tussaud's in Marylebone Road, stopping there for a moment at that early hour to look at photographs on display. Strolling along Baker Street, onto Oxford Street and through the park, I headed straight for 94 Eaton Square, and was inside the house climbing the stairs shortly after 5 o'clock as the faint streaks of dawn were beginning to light the sky. Harry was fast asleep in bed when I steadily shook him, and spoke quietly in his ear, "Get up you are on guard," before he opened his eyes to know who the joker was that had awakened him. I began dishing out the goodies brought from home like it was a lucky bag. In spite of our whispers, Jimmy, sleeping in the bunk above turned over, opened one eye from beneath his blankets and exclaimed, "Oh it's you!" I took time to rest on one of the beds until 6.30 before washing and shaving, to return to barracks in Woolwich. I left Harry half asleep, saying I would probably see him Wednesday night, which is tonight.

Yesterday morning I collected my work from the Royal College of Art. It was packed ready, and handed to me by the porter, along with a note from an old friend who attended the art school in Accrington when I was there. He was studying at the college and noticed my name on the package. The note asked me to call at his flat nearby, but I did not find him there. He had failed the medical examination for military service and was able to continue his studies at the college throughout the war. Only now when I see my work, it is far from my best and not examples I would have chosen. If I could have arranged the submission I would have treated the matter differently, included more paintings, paying less attention to design, which I am sure would have been successful. In the evening I saw the film, *Caesar And Cleopatra*, at the Odeon in Woolwich. Not a bad film, I would rate it below the high standard it has attained.

The various branches of release training units are arranging an exhibition in the barracks at the weekend to show the different types of work we do. My class will be displaying watercolour and oil paintings, drawings, commercial art and design. I am teaching a class tonight until 7 o'clock, it will be later than usual before I can get away to see Harry in London.

23 September

I felt a bit lost this weekend Harry being at home on leave, Sunday morning I took paints and paper into London to make a watercolour painting, wandering about for a while before finally settling down in Tottenham Court Road on a sturdy fruit box, kindly lent to me by a newspaper seller. Before very long, I was in the midst of a throng of inquisitive people looking over my shoulder. London Transport bus drivers must have been tempted to utter derogatory remarks, doing their best to avoid a mob of inquisitive onlookers lining the edge of the pavement. I continued painting for most of the day except for a short break for lunch. 'I packed my traps' at 6 o'clock to spend a relaxing hour at the Stage Door Canteen.

The release training exhibition was well received, and our display was classed as the best of the different groups on show. This evening I shall be teaching a class until 7 o'clock before getting away to meet Lilian in Abbey Wood.

1 October

When I arrived back at Woolwich yesterday morning after spending the weekend with Harry, I realised I had left my wallet on the bed, beneath the pillow where I slept. A regular habit to keep my wallet secure while sleeping. Harry retrieved it after I rang him at the office explaining what had happened. Now I am stranded without money. I managed to borrow enough cash to keep me going until I see Harry tonight or tomorrow, and collect my wallet.

On Saturday morning I seated myself on a wall to make a watercolour sketch of St. Martin in the Fields, in Trafalgar Square. I spent quite some time on the painting, but I was unable to complete it by late afternoon. I sat in the art room in barracks yesterday adding the final touches to it.

During lunch break, I was listening to court proceedings of war crimes against the Nazis at Nuremberg, broadcast on the radio.

10 October

My address has changed as you can see at the head of this letter, posted from B Battery, to O & I Wing, a move placing me in a new position on permanent staff with Officers and Instructors. Before this change, I could at any time be sent to an Artillery Regiment, now I am here to stay until demobilisation comes through. Today, I was kindly informed I was overdue for leave, my last was four months ago 23 June. I had considered making another quick trip home this weekend, knowing I shall see you soon this changes everything and I may instead get away and visit Auntie Molly, at Woodley.

The house transaction appears to be making good progress, I am sure when all the formalities have been completed, and you are in a position to move into the new home, the outcome will prove to be comfortable and pleasant for you both in your retirement.

Last night I was again with Harry, instead of spending the evening together in the centre of London, there was a change of venue visiting a dance at New Cross, where we had been the previous Sunday. Taking a short walk in the street outside the dance hall during the interval, we came upon a hand cart selling roasted potatoes, and bought a bag of them. How very nice they were too. Tonight I shall go to the regular dance at the Polytechnic in Woolwich, and need to hurry and finish this letter if I am to be there at 8 o'clock, in time to meet Lilian.

14 October

In the post today was a letter from my friend at the War Office, telling me the brigadier was highly pleased with the drawings I left for him to see, and I am to await further news about them.

I visited Auntie Molly this past weekend, getting to Woodley about 4 o'clock on Friday afternoon without having given any previous warning. To my surprise, I found Uncle Arnold was there for the weekend, another piece of luck when Pat turned up later that night. The four of us visited the shopping centre in Reading on Saturday afternoon browsing around the town. Auntie Molly showed me the embroidery she has so far done on my shirt; her attention to detail is truly magnificent, exact to a style I visualised. She requires silks to blend together the various colours of the snake, and would like to have them in hand before beginning any work on that particular part of it. I left Woodley Sunday morning to keep a date with Lilian in Woolwich, at 2 o'clock in the afternoon. On my way through London I called on Harry and we had lunch together at the Lion Club. Needless to say, I spent a wonderful weekend with everyone at Lanes Farm House, and Uncle Arnold was as facetious as ever.

15 October NUFFIELD CENTRE, LONDON *headed note paper*
Using the headed note paper will confirm I am in once again visiting the centre of London. I have been teaching extra evening classes this week, standing in for an instructor on leave, and for that I am taking advantage

of an afternoon free of work. Before coming here to write I wandered around the rooms at the National Gallery, studying the paintings on exhibition. Harry is unaware I am in town and I do not expect to be seeing him. Lilian is working in an office in London and we arranged to meet after she finishes work and go to a theatre this evening.

My photograph was taken today by one of the instructors in the photography section and we straight away developed the negative in the darkroom, the result looks fine.

17 October

It is marvellous news knowing the sale of the house is finally fixed up on paper, surely dad appreciates how good it will turn out, living in a cosy home much easier to manage. You will quickly overcome the trauma of moving and everything should be fine once your lives are back to normal again.

This is the end a scratchy note, with little time to spare if I am to keep my date with Lilian in ten minutes, at 7 o'clock.

Ten days home leave with my parents, 2 – 13 November. I was unaware at the time of writing this letter it was to be my first letter to the girl I was to marry.

7 November

Dear Lilian

As I promised, here is a letter to you taking advantage to fill a few moments in a quiet life at home, telling you what has happened to me since I last saw you.

I phoned Harry at his office telling him I could not meet him to travel home together, I would be late leaving Woolwich on Saturday afternoon and he should start his journey without me. It was 3 o'clock by the time I got away from the barracks, and almost midnight when I arrived home to find Harry had been here a few hours, along with his girl friend Joan. As soon as Joan knew Harry had definitely been granted leave, she travelled from Liverpool to be here with him.

Major was looking fit for his age, welcoming me with his usual boisterous affection the moment we met, and I had a heart to heart talk with him, which you would not understand.

Sunday was spent peacefully at home doing very little. Monday evening I joined Harry and Joan when they decided to go to a dance in Blackburn, making a dash to catch the last bus back home before the end of the dance. Tuesday the 5th of November, I visited my young cousin Josie, celebrating the traditional Guy Fawkes Night, sitting round a bonfire eating roasted potatoes. Life has been pretty quiet for me since I was last with you almost a week ago, there is yet another week ahead before I shall see you again.

Cheerio sweet one. Love, Jim

13 November   *Y.M.C.A. headed note paper*
I flatter this Y.M.C.A. in Woolwich likening it to a *dump*, there is little fondness for it compared to similar canteens elsewhere. Even more surprising, it is the only canteen outside the barracks serving the vast number of troops confined in this town.

I reported back for duty about two hours ago. Waiting on Church station shortly before 10 o'clock for a train to Preston, I discovered none was due for an hour and a half; however, there was a train to Preston from Accrington at 10.05, passing through Church station non stop. As I waited, a train to Accrington came in on the opposite platform. Dashing through the underpass I was able to find a seat, knowing I had only the slimmest chance to get to Accrington in time to make the connection. My luck was in; I saw my train pulling in just as I was arriving. With haste and good fortune I managed to scramble aboard. At Preston, the Edinburgh to London 11.05 special express, stopping only at Crewe and Stafford, got me to Euston a little after 4 o'clock, one hour later I was in the barracks. My first task was collecting my kit together and making ready my bed, and then straight away I was out of the barracks tucking in to a meal of sausages, mash and peas. I rang Harry at the office, Taffy the exchange operator said he thought Harry had not yet arrived back from his leave. I had arranged to meet Lilian tomorrow, never expecting to be back in time to meet her this evening.

I saw little of Major this morning before leaving; he was well out of the picture, guilty and ashamed for having stolen a piece of meat. Usually he is actively dashing around under my feet each time he is aware I am getting ready to leave home.

18 November, Promoted Sergeant – 15 November
A glance at the top of my letter will tell you I have been promoted to the rank of sergeant!

Searching the bookstall on Preston station, also at London Bridge when returning from leave, I could not find the booklet titled, *The Campaign in Burma*, published by HM Stationery Office; perhaps the print run is sold out. I am pleased you managed to get a copy for me. I knew nothing about the publication of this booklet until Lilian mentioned it to me.

I am teaching evening class tonight. Tomorrow morning I shall be taking my class to the National Gallery in London, staying on in town afterwards to telephone Harry and to know if we can meet in the evening. The demob programme is getting worse; I will not be out of the army by Christmas, perhaps by the end of January. I hope you remembered to have my suits cleaned; it may be possible I shall get leave to celebrate Christmas at home with you.

23 November

Saturday afternoon with nothing special to do, I came to the art room to write this letter. At lunch time I rang Harry, George was on duty and said Harry had gone to get a meal, and there would be no time to see Harry today; they had a very heavy work load this afternoon.

Last Tuesday, two instructors and I had the whole day off. In the morning we decided to take a look around the National Gallery, later I went to Harry's office and found it appeared to be under control and more placid than usual. I told Harry I had arranged to meet Lilian after work, hoping I could get Forces theatre tickets from the Trafalgar Square kiosk to see a show, and asked, "Would he like to come along?" He said, "That would be fine." When I went to collect the tickets, I discovered that no more than two free Forces tickets are issued to one person. By enlisting the help of an instructor friend who was also seeking tickets, I overcame the dilemma when he gave me one of his tickets.

I met Lilian from work, we then picked up Harry and set out for the theatre at Walham Green to see a performance of, *This Happy Breed*. It was a good show and a complete change from watching a film. Since that day I have made no attempt to see Harry, I am in the middle of a severe cold, the folly of spending a terribly wet day in town and visiting a theatre later in the evening.

Strolling around Woolwich shopping centre I saw a nice overcoat in Burton's priced 120 shillings, is that expensive? There was also a pile of army blankets for sale in a shop at 8/2d each without coupons, and if dad is interested, flannel underwear vests costing five shillings each, and underpants three shillings also without coupons. There appears to be a much better selection of goods arriving in many of the shops at last.

Monday, 25 November

My letter was not posted this morning allowing me to add more. I did not see Harry this weekend but spoke to him on the telephone Saturday afternoon. Yesterday, I was invited to afternoon tea at Lilian's home; we would have gone to see a film show in the evening if it had not been such bad weather. My cold is much better and has almost disappeared.

28 November

Would you please buy a pair of fur gloves size 3-4, if you think they are reasonably priced, they would make an excellent Christmas present for Lilian? As an alternative, you might let me have four, or six, clothing coupons and I could purchase a present for her. Also, I have seen a very nice tie I should like to buy for myself, this I can not do without clothing coupons. I shall see you get them replaced as soon as I am demobbed.

2 December

Thank you for the prompt action sending on the clothing coupons, I have noticed a good selection of gloves in the shops in Woolwich where prices are more reasonable than you find in the centre of London. I shall ask Lilian's mother what she thinks about the idea. You can say goodbye to one coupon at least, I shall buy myself that tie, even though the cost is 9/6d and cannot be considered very cheap.

Friday night I saw a strange film, *Angel On My Shoulder*, an unusual story and not to everyone's taste. I made a hurried dash into London Saturday morning to see Harry in his office. There was much sweat, toil and tension about the place, I drew up a chair to Harry's desk and propped up a specially printed card I found lying nearby which read, 'Conference – Keep Out.' We had a fifteen minute chin wag before I left to spend the evening with Lilian at her home. Sunday afternoon I was again at home with Lilian. When Harry learned about my frequent visits to Lilian's home he casually remarked, "Oh, you are now on the ration strength there are you?" Today is a nice wintry day and very cold.

7 December

Many Happy Returns of your birthday, mother, I have not done much to make it feel like your birthday, and this card is trivial from an artistic point of view. I talked with Harry on the telephone about buying you something for your birthday and we decided it would be much better to wait until we are home. I am afraid I am in a position to give you no further news until I find more writing paper; I have used the last sheet on this pad.

Sunday, 8 December   MEMORANDUM – *official army note pad*

This is the only paper I can lay my hands on. A little while ago I phoned Harry, a friend had to wake him and get him out of bed before I could talk to him. We had a long chat, it is a week since I last saw him and he told me he is going to write letters as soon he has had breakfast at the Lion Club. To be eating a meal at this time of day I would call it 'Lunch'.

On Friday I was given an interesting note from my officer whom I have not seen for two weeks. I opened the official letter and was shocked to read,

Release and Occupational Training classes would cease from Friday, 6 December, except drawing and painting evening classes. All the instructors were shocked when they got the details never expecting this to happen so suddenly. The likely reason we are closing down is because Monty[31] is moving into this area in the New Year. This will make no difference to my release with Group 46; very soon I shall be making preparations for de-kitting, signing release papers, and told the date I can expect to get out of the army. Group 45 is moving out now; Group 46 will follow close behind. Christmas leave is being granted to a large number of the men here. I cannot yet say if I too will be lucky to get Christmas leave at home.

My activities this week, – Monday, I stayed in barracks. Tuesday, I took the afternoon off to met Lilian and her mother in London, Christmas shopping. In the evening we saw the film, *Stolen Life*, starring Bette Davis at a theatre in Leicester Square. Lilian and I visited one of her school friends on Wednesday. Thursday evening I arranged to see Lilian in Woolwich, but was surprised when her mother turned up, telling me Lilian had come home from work with a nasty cold and was confined indoors. Friday evening I was again with Lilian at home. Saturday night I saw the film, *Without Reservations*. Today, I have a load of work to get through, compelling me to turn down a kind invitation to join Lilian and her family for Sunday dinner.

17 December

Cold is not the right word for the weather at the present moment, yesterday I almost froze to death, today the temperature is no higher. The sun is making a weak effort to brighten the outlook and as yet there are no signs of a heavy snowfall like we had to suffer yesterday. I could do no work whatsoever; my fingers were so cold the pencil refused to obey my wishes, preferring to go its own way. Everybody gathered around a stove in the centre of the large art room trying to keep warm. Early in the afternoon we were forced to abandon all work and spend the remaining few hours huddled closer to the stove.

Lilian and I were invited to a birthday party last Saturday by one of Lilian's friends. It was a joyful celebration involving everyone in hilarious party games. Lots of nice things to eat, sandwiches, cakes, a delicious sweet and birthday cake too. Goodness only knows where all the extra rations came from. Sunday was to have been spent visiting the street market stalls and shops in *Petticoat Lane*, Middlesex Street; the day was far too cold. I was given a taste of Christmas pudding, sampling the pudding Lilian's mother has prepared and cooked ready for Christmas Day. Tonight, Harry is planning to join Lilian and me at the Polytechnic in Woolwich for the regular Tuesday evening dance, and we shall meet there.

A request for Christmas leave has been sent in to the main office hoping it will be granted.

This is the last letter written to my parents during my service in the army.

18 December

Since writing yesterday I have been contemplating whether I might invite Lilian home with me, if I should I be lucky and get Christmas leave. There is little time left to make any decision, what do you think about my suggestion? Last night Harry, me, Lilian and her friend Doris, spent a very pleasant evening together at the dance in Woolwich.

I was given Christmas leave at home with my parents, 24 – 31 December. All the letters following are written to my girlfriend Lilian.

25 December

I went directly to Euston station without calling on Harry at his office, and caught a train leaving in the afternoon at 1.10. The train made good time until we got to Crewe, from there onwards I was driven mad by its slow progress. The cause was thick fog everywhere, testing my patience and delaying my arrival home until almost 9 o'clock. Mother was sorry you did not come with me, but fully appreciated Christmas is a time to be celebrated at home in the midst of one's own family.

This morning I met cousin John Clark, whom I have not seen since we served together in the Home Guard, four and a half years ago. Tomorrow, mother, dad and I are paying a visit to Liverpool to see Joan and meet her family, and to see Harry who is spending Christmas leave there. I have made no arrangements to go elsewhere during the rest of my holiday and expect to be back with you on Sunday night.

28 December, Saturday

I am sorry I shall not be returning tomorrow as I intended, no doubt you heard the announcement over the radio about two days extension, granted to all military personnel on Christmas leave. This changes the planned arrangement to be with you on Sunday, I shall instead be turning up on Tuesday like the proverbial 'bad penny.'

Mother, dad and me travelled to Liverpool on Boxing Day to visit Joan, her family, and to see Harry who was staying there for the last days of his leave. Early yesterday morning Harry returned to London to tackle urgent office work to be completed during the afternoon. I was at a dance in the evening but found it quite dull and came home well before the end. My parents were in bed. Aware Harry was back at the office in London, and noticing Joan's coat hanging on the hall stand was a sure sign Joan decided to come and stay here over the weekend. Tonight I hope to see the film, *The Return Of The Vampire*.

I trust you are suffering no ill effects following days of Christmas feasting. Yesterday morning I pictured you joining crowds of dejected commuters reluctantly returning to work after the holiday. At this moment I would like nothing better than to give you a big hug.

When I returned to Woolwich barracks after the Christmas break, I was immediately informed proceedings were going ahead to terminate my military service with the army. Learning this sudden and surprising news, letters to my parents were minimal, concerned only with reporting details about the progress of my impending release.

All the final documents pertaining to my release were signed and endorsed at Aldershot on January 31, 1947, authorizing my discharge from military service. With part payment of the final total of army release pay in my pocket, a free issue of clothing – civilian suit, shirt and tie, hat, new shoes, and railway warrant to Oswaldtwistle, I was at last free of army life ... or was I?

During the next few weeks I continued to be classified as military personnel, regularly drawing army pay through the Post Office until the 6 May, my last day of service. On 7 May, transfer to the 'Army Reserve List' was routine procedure, and liable for recall to the army in the event of a National crisis. Correspondence with Lilian continued whilst I was at home making preparations to begin a new career as an artist and graphic designer in the world of advertising, having spent almost the entire last five years of my life in military service.

– 1947 –

Army release leave at home, 31 January – 6 May.

13 February

Major has not been well these past few days and was much worse yesterday. I did not get to bed until long after midnight, mother stayed with him throughout the night. This morning I telephoned the vet, saying I thought it would be better if he quickened his end. There has been a veil of sadness about the house since the vet left. I must write to Harry giving him the sad news, Dad will not learn about it until he gets home from work later this afternoon.

It is exactly six months tonight, since I first met you at the Polytechnic dance in Woolwich when I asked to see you home. I did not know then how happy you would make me feel when we are together, falling in love and missing you so much when you are not near, like the words in the song, *Miss You*.

I can almost consider myself a civilian once again, collecting my Identity Card, and Ration Book, from the food office last Tuesday. Tell your mother to make use of the ration card I am enclosing, and thank her for her kindness making me more than welcome in your home.

16 February

Thank you for your letter, and the cutting from the paper about the job in Glasgow. A very alert observation you made to an excellent position, but way out of my latitude. It is my intention to find work in London where there are better prospects, and a job in town would allow me to see more of you than if I was to settle down elsewhere.

Thursday night I went to the pictures with mother and dad to see, *Anna And The King Of Siam*. You know I have seen this film but thought it would help to overcome the ordeal of losing Major. Friday night I went to a local dance, meeting people I have not seen for years.

18 February

When I was given my ration book I noted there was a whole month's supply of sweet coupons. There should have been coupons for two weeks only, the clerk in the office had obviously taken pity on me not cutting them out, and just as well I did not take up the offer to accept your sweet coupons. All other ration coupons had been carefully removed up to date.

Yesterday morning I was thinking about you keeping the appointment and interview for a new job. You certainly appear to be fed up working at Radiospares, aware there is little chance of advancement in your present position. I must be thoroughly absorbed writing to you, mother has dashed in from the washhouse to check a meal that was cooking, turning to me said, "Could you not smell the meat was burning?" After mother made an inspection came the verdict, "I think it will not be too bad, Jim." Last night mother went out to a meeting and I took dad to the pictures to see a film I had seen years ago and enjoyed it much as ever.

20 February

Preparations are under way for Harry's wedding to take place two weeks on Monday and he has invited me to serve as Best Man. His decision to be married in army uniform avoids any question about what clothes to wear. My uniform has never been worn since I arrived home.

23 February

Thank you for forwarding the vacancies for jobs. Fashion design is not my line of work, the other position you sent to me I may reply to. I have responded to two advertisements you sent me. Do not feel despondent because I have chosen to deal with so few, commercial art is a broad subject. I shall not entirely depend on positions advertised; a varied selection of original work carefully prepared and presented would gain more attention.

Yesterday evening Dad and I went to a concert for Ladies Weekend, Mother was taking part dressed in my army uniform and bush hat. After the show I collected props used on the stage and an easy way to carry a silk top hat was on my head. Walking home wearing the hat and dad's silver top ebony stick in my hand, we met people convinced I had visited several pubs.

25 February

I shall convey to Joan your sincere thanks and tell her you are sorry to be declining the invitation to the wedding; I know she realizes it would be difficult for you to get time off work for a long arduous journey to attend the ceremony for such a brief visit. Since I last wrote to you my time has been spent preparing for presentation, a portfolio of examples of lettering, drawing and painting. You may think I am getting a bundle of work together, the reality is different; I can spend two days, sometimes longer to finish a drawing.

28 February

Quite an assortment of prospective jobs you typed with your last letter. The first on the list, an opening for a copy artist does not mean what you may think, the position for a window display designer, again not quite my line. However, I am grateful to you for finding these openings, knowing full well you are missing nothing you consider might be of interest.

Harry will be here tomorrow and from that moment on there will be much to do, every minute occupied getting ready for his big day. He and

I are going to Liverpool on Sunday and spending the night there to avoid an early morning start on the day of the wedding. I shall return home with my parents after the conclusion of the celebrations that evening,

2 March, Sunday

Harry arrived here last night, from that moment every minute has been chaos around the house. We must be dressed in army uniforms, ready to leave and catch the train to Liverpool in two hours. When you read this news, the poor fellow will be happily married, and I shall be at home with an opportunity to write to you.

4 March

After writing that hurried note to you on Sunday, I began hastily eating dinner with one hand and trying to dress with the other, the time running short for Harry and I to get to the station to catch a train to Liverpool. Imagine our frustration finding priority was being given to goods wagons carrying coal to replenish stocks denuded by the cold weather. Our train would be an hour behind schedule, all we could do was pace up and down the platform in an effort to keep warm Eventually we reached Liverpool a little cosier, sitting comfortably in a carriage better heated on steam trains than the electrified Southern Railway specials. At Liverpool station a taxi driver pounced on two smartly dressed soldiers wearing the King's uniform, dress hats and medal ribbons, asking our destination. When he learned Harry was getting married, he drove us to Walton generously refusing to accept payment for the taxi fare.

Harry and I stayed the night with a friend of Joan's family, enjoying breakfast next morning of bacon and egg before making final preparations for the big day. My time was spent running around photographing the cake, collecting flowers that had been ordered and attending to odd jobs. Harry and I made our way to the church, once again gradually feeling the effects of the severe cold weather. The organist played, *I'm always chasing rainbows*, and other familiar pieces before Joan tripped down the aisle for the start of the wedding service. After the minister had done his job, and all formalities completed, the clicking of cameras could be heard outside the church as the happy couple were showered with confetti. At the reception I gave my little speech, inviting the guests to toast the health of the bride and groom with Port wine, and scrounging for myself a second glass. More speeches followed, and the names of persons who had sent telegrams and cards bearing good wishes were announced. The card you sent was one of the first to be read out.

After the reception, me and my family made our way to the railway station to get home to Oswaldtwistle, unexpectedly finding ourselves travelling to Preston on the same train as the happy couple. The newlyweds had planned to spend their honeymoon at Blackpool. Harry with his usual wit remarked, "It must be a rare event having father, mother, brother, and grandma on honeymoon." For the next thirty minutes, until parting on Preston station, the uproar coming from our compartment must have intrigued travellers in adjoining carriages.

Shortly after lunch today, I received a telegram from Harry, asking if I could send on to him a camera. I replied immediately saying I would personally deliver the camera to Blackpool tomorrow. He reported they are experiencing pleasant winter weather except for a keen night frost which seems to prevail throughout the whole country. The couple is coming here to Oswaldtwistle on Friday for a few days, and then staying in Liverpool until Harry is due to report back for duty in London. If you could see my bathroom there would be no doubt someone had been to a wedding, the floor is littered with confetti. At last all the excitement is behind me, I shall settle down in earnest once again doing some serious art work with an eye to exploiting what the future may hold in store for me.

6 March

It was about midday when I arrived in Blackpool yesterday with the camera; Harry and Joan were already waiting at the station to meet me. We had lunch at their hotel, and walked along the promenade to take souvenir photographs for their wedding album. I made every effort to buy a picture postcard of Blackpool to send to you, diligently searching until I learned it was half day closing, and postcards of any type were nowhere to be found. This happened to be the worst day of their honeymoon, the breezy air dusted with fine sleet was continuous, except for a short period after lunch, allowing time for me to take pictures on the promenade. We decided to go to the cinema and see Gary Cooper in the film, *Cloak And Dagger*, a typical war story of espionage. Following our visit to the cinema we stayed away from the bad weather dancing in the Winter Gardens, I had no more than a couple of dances with Joan, all the time wishing you were with me. This was my first visit, once again dancing in the Winter Gardens since I joined the army.

9 March

I would like to make arrangements to return to London next weekend to begin searching for a position with an advertising agency, or commercial art studio. The severe bad weather and preparations for attending Harry and Joan's wedding has restricted the number of hours I could spend compiling a collection of work. However, I plan taking a folio of art and design with me to London next Friday, 14 March. I would like to be with you on the 16th, for your birthday. Please thank your mother for the invitation to stay at your home; I shall be there for the weekend only. I can arrange accommodation during the rest of my stay at a Forces Club. I am classified as army personnel until the expiration of Release Leave in May. I hope to give you final details about my plans a little later, it will be late afternoon or evening when I expect to arrive in London.

11 March

Harry and Joan left here yesterday for Liverpool, once again peace and quiet reigns supreme around the place. It has been convenient to work at my desk throughout the day and at night easier to concentrate after my parents are fast asleep in bed.

I do not expect I shall find the time to write to you again before leaving on Friday morning. My train is due in Euston station about 4 o'clock; I hope this will give me enough time to telephone you at your office before you leave work. It would not be a good plan for us to meet in London, we would be caught up in the mad rush hour scramble, and I will have luggage with me. I am looking forward so much to seeing you, especially your mother and dad, and once again meeting old friends.

For almost two weeks I stayed at Lilian's home in Abbey Wood, during that period I made many appointments to call on art studios and advertising companies in London, applying for a position as an artist and graphic designer, carrying with me a portfolio of examples and wide variety of artistic work. During the course of many interviews I received hopeful promises of future employment, and assurances I would soon receive notification of any decisions made. I left Lilian's home and returned to Oswaldtwistle to await the outcome, anticipating my effort to reach as many businesses as possible would be rewarded. At home I continued corresponding with Lilian as before.

27 March

The punctuality of LMS Railways has given me the lucky chance to write to you during the next half an hour to catch the last post of the day, collected at 6 o'clock this evening. After parting this morning my journey was uneventful, the train from London arrived Preston at 3.15, I had time to wait before catching a connection to get me home safe and well. There was a letter from Smees Advertising Agency, waiting for me, offering a position to join the firm as a layout artist and graphic designer.

Please pass my grateful thanks to your mother and father, Lilian, for the welcome and generosity shown to me during the time I stayed at your home.

28 March

Yesterday evening, mother and dad made plans to see the film, *The Magic Bow*, a film we so much enjoyed seeing together at the cinema. I decided I would go with them and see it again. Throughout the film I could only think about the time I was watching it with you close by my side. I find I have time on my hands now the presentation folio is no longer a priority.

31 March

I decided to reply to Smees Advertising accepting the position offered to me, it is a well established small family business in Southampton Row. I shall be employed in a studio as a creative layout artist where my work will have the incentive to be noticed, doing exactly the type of job I always hoped for. Living and working in London will allow me every opportunity to spend my leisure time in the evenings and week-ends with you.

This is one day closer to again being with you, see you soon. All my love.

The position in Smees Advertising was exactly the type of work I had been looking for. The agency handled accounts advertising a varied assortment of products by well-established manufacturers, sauces, jams, biscuits, industrial electric tools and motor engineering accessories. I would be working as a creative layout artist in the design department, earning a living as a civilian for the first time in my life. I straight away returned to London and found lodgings with a family in Plumstead, not far from Lilian's home. Each morning Lilian and I travelled together on the same train into London, returning in the evening jostling with homeward-bound commuters searching to find a space in a crowded carriage aboard Southern Electric Railway.

Army release leave ended 6 May 1947, the next day I was transferred automatically to the Army Reserve List, expecting to avoid all further entanglement with military matters. Years of my young life as an ordinary citizen had been torn from me, the recollections of army routine would be nothing more than a memory. I could at long last settle down to begin a normal existence, denied me for almost five years, serving as a soldier far away from home in a hostile war. Lilian and I were married on 25 June 1948, in St. Mark's Church, Plumstead Common, and moved into a small top floor flat in Tulse Hill. Two years later, my son Michael was born.

Postscript

The Suez Crisis, 1951

The threatened occupation of the Suez Canal in 1951, by the Egyptian Government, increased tension between Egypt and Great Britain, raising fears of an impending war between the two countries. The British Government acted quickly to introduce measures of preparedness to meet the threat, recalling a number of Army Reserve personnel to retrain with military units. Married, with a baby son, it was my misfortune to be one of a limited number chosen to undergo a refresher course with the Royal Artillery, after four years living a life as an ordinary citizen. My orders were to serve with 'Q' Battery, 345 Medium Regiment, Royal Artillery, a South London-based Territorial Army unit. The Regiment was to undergo annual summer manoeuvres over a period of two weeks in a tented camp near Tilshead, on Salisbury Plain. Unfortunately, my rank as a sergeant had not been fully established on demobilization, and I was recalled as a bombardier.

Some months earlier I had bought a second-hand small car, and it would be convenient to drive to Tilshead claiming travel allowance, instead of using a travel warrant. Also, I could get about easily when allowed out of camp to look for scenes that might be suitable for sketching. During the time I was away from home, speaking to my wife on the telephone obviated writing letters regularly.

Training was to take place over two weeks, beginning on May 26. However, it was my good fortune to notice the period of service on my documents ended on June 6, three days short of the official two weeks. I checked the papers of other lads that had been recalled and their papers bore the correct date June 9, two full weeks. When the unit was well into the training programme I informed the Battery Office about the date error on my papers and was firmly told I would have to serve the full term. This I most certainly did not intend to do, regardless of the consequences.

Happy to cut short my recall on June 6, and return home to my wife and baby son, the Battery Office refused payment for the time served. Two weeks later the full amount was posted to my address by money order, the decision to forfeit my pay having been overruled by the army paymaster.

Two letters to my wife are the last to be written during my final days serving as a soldier in His Majesty's Forces

R. A. Training Camp, Tilshead, Wiltshire, 26 May – 6 June 1951

2 June, Saturday

My Darling Wife

My fountain pen has been playing tricks the past few days and needs a lot of persuasion to write, I hope you will forgive this letter in pencil. The most important thing I have to say is thank you for your letter received a short while ago. Michael's first birthday today, and all the time I have been thinking about the poor little fellow, I am so glad he is settling down at last. I should love to have seen him wearing his fancy new bed jacket, I bet he looked sweet.

This afternoon I shall drive to Devises, a town about ten miles from camp, taking three of the chaps with me in the car. The first thing to do when I get there is find a shop where I can buy a new refill for my pen. I would like to try sketching in the village if time and good weather will allow. We have been told, *The Flame And The Arrow*, is showing at the picture house this evening, we are meeting one or two other fellows later on to see the film. I hope to talk with you on the telephone Sunday morning, if I am able to get through. I intend finishing my service with this outfit on June 6, but can not say when you might expect to see me arrive home. Maybe I will not get away before we finish the day's training at tea-time, or whenever I can collect my service pay from the Battery office.

Sunday, 3 June

As you can see, I bought a refill for my pen yesterday, once more able to use it for writing. One of the soldiers on recall came with me to a small picturesque village about two miles outside Devises, where I made a watercolour sketch of a small group of cottages. He sat in the car with the hood down getting sunburnt while I was busy painting. The other two fellows did not come with us, they decided to take the bus to town and meet in the evening to see the film. About 6.30 I packed up my paints, it was time to meet the other fellows in Devises and to have tea. After the film show we all returned to camp in the car. When I first reported to the Battery office at Tilshead, I did not hand into the stores the suitcase holding all my gear, I was told I would not have access to it until it was time to leave. I take advantage to get my civvies out of the suitcase to wear when outside the camp. Dressed in a suit helps me to forget I am again in the army, subject to its many rules and regulations. Also, avoids attention from the military police roaming around. The nearest large town is Salisbury with no short supply of military police, but getting there is too far to travel in the evening.

I paid little thought to the special call rate when I said I would telephone Sunday morning until I remembered it does not come into force until 6.30pm. I will try and get through on the phone tonight, telling most of what I am writing in this letter. Everyone attended Church parade this morning. Recreational sporting events have been laid on for the afternoon; yours truly will not be taking part. The weather has been very good; otherwise this tented camp would be in a terrible state following heavy rain, situated as we are in a large open field.

4 June

How nice it was for Michael to receive so very many cards for his birthday, I look forward to seeing them when I get home. There was no way I could get a card for him in time for his birthday, last Saturday afternoon was my first chance to get away from camp and to visit shops. If I could have found a suitable card, posting over the weekend would cause more delay. I loved to hear your voice on the telephone last night my darling, I may try to phone you tomorrow evening to say when I hope to get away from here. Thank you for the parcel of chocolate and biscuits, I am in need of nothing, many luxury goods are available in the N.A.A.F.I. You will be able to draw the usual quota of food on my Ration Book, it has never been touched, all back dated coupons remain intact.

This morning I informed the Battery office my training enlistment was due to end on Wednesday the 6th, giving plenty of warning I would be handing in all my kit and expect to draw my pay before leaving. A fellow, with whom I have been friendly since coming here is the only person I told about my intentions; many of the chaps on recall would be likely to go mad if they learned about the wrong date on my papers! In darkness tonight after 9 o'clock, the Battery is planning to go on a training scheme for a few hours. On Wednesday, an exercise is to take place throughout the whole night, practice firing the guns, returning to camp with the dawn. I thank my lucky stars I shall miss the whole of this exciting action.

I finished the sketch started on Saturday, and on Sunday I was able to begin another watercolour of a local scene I can finish later.

It will not be long my dearest before I am home, and that moment can not come soon enough. This will be my last letter from here, there is no point writing to you tomorrow, I shall be leaving the following day no matter what!

Your loving husband, Jim.

The total number of letters written during my army career was never recorded, many more letters than those seen here was sent to my brother, and to a large family of relatives and friends.

The Home Guard

The crisis facing Britain in nineteen thirty-nine,
Provoked a war with Germany to bring her into line.
As France was overwhelmed and chose capitulation
A serious threat to England became a Hun invasion.
With Hitler at the channel ports, and Britain unprepared,
The prospects of survival were assessed with due regard.
To counteract the danger a grandiose scheme was planned.
That local groups form units into watchful bands
And train as novice soldiers, with bayonets, guns, and bombs.
Establishing defences of beaches, farms, and homes.
Throughout the entire country Premier Churchill's aim
Requested boys and elders to forge a stalwart chain.
Response from every quarter by young and old commenced,
Instilled ecstatic ardour for Britain's self defence.
Men denied enlistment in specialist occupation,
And youths awaiting 'call-up' keen to see some action,
Unfit for active service, but with willingness at heart,
All thronged recruitment centres intent to play their part.
Throughout the hours of daylight most were working hard,
With night-time leisure forfeit when they were sent to guard.
No uniforms were issued, or weapons close to hand,
But right from the beginning faith throughout the land,
Prevailed to save the nation if enemies should come
To trespass in the boundaries of Britain's island home.
A simple khaki armband with letters L D V,
Was worn with proud distinction for all about to see.
'Local' and 'Defence' the logo, 'V' for 'Volunteers,'
A skittish name 'Dad's Army,' encouraged smiles and jeers.
Veterans of the last war recalled their fighting skill,
Some appointed 'sergeant' to train squads and to drill.

Wholehearted dedication strengthened day by day
Inspired to fight for freedom dispelling all dismay,
And should invaders venture forth to occupy and ravish?
A clownish joke was banded round, 'Look - Duck - Vanish!'
The project gained momentum and plans for its success
At last gave way to uniforms, and military dress.
But only worn on duty or outposts through the night,
Expecting men like Nelson, 'Do your duty stand and fight.'
'Home Guard' became a name change for military unction,
'King's Rules and Regulations' were adopted without option.
'Shoulder flash,' and 'badges,' all worn with obvious pride
Distinguishing the counties where defenders did reside.
Grenades, and guns, were issued five bullets for each man,
Live shooting practise woeful "...just do the best you can."
"Aircraft recognition and the art of camouflage."
"Silent sentry duty laced with subterfuge."
"Cocktails made with petrol sealed in bottles with a wick."
"Hand to hand close combat," was yet another trick.
All practised to perfection at evening and weekend,
Enthusiasm flourished with Britain to defend.
Churches, and cathedral's bells, forbidden they should peal,
But if assault troops landed to ring out with great zeal.
A link-line by the telephone between each guarded post
Sighted where an enemy attack would suffer most.
And several groups of sentries dispersed around the towns,
Offered some protection when the sun went down.
Signals spelling danger were expressed in colour codes,
Relayed throughout all units to keep them on their toes.
'Purple' was the first alert, and then the next code 'red,'
Warning all defenders expect the enemy overhead.
Soon the droning bombers shed incendiaries and H.E.
Causing mass destruction in the hope that we would plea
For peace, and give Herr Hitler power throughout the land
To rule the entire country with his infamous hand.
When the raid was over, the relief was quite profound
If the signal 'white' prevailed until the dawn came round.
Each twelve-hour guard was tedious, for sentries stood in pairs,
And on the darkest nights were uttered many silent prayers.
Two hours on, and four hours off, the leisure time was spent
Playing cards and gambling till everyone was skint
Except for one, the winner, with a gambler's lucky streak
Trudging home to breakfast without a good night's sleep.

Trepidation for the Home Guard was the threat that air invasion
Might overpower defenders to accomplish full submission.
But, never in full glory was it called upon to act
To do what it was trained for in wartime to react
And resist a foreign enemy; or ever sought to brag,
That it helped to save the Nation, and the Union flag.
As allies conquered Europe with the enemy in retreat,
The Home Guard's role in Britain was rendered obsolete.

Endnotes

1	HMS *Liddesdale*	escort destroyer of Hunt Type II class, commissioned February 1941, broken up 1948
2	Charwallah	Indian trader serving hot tea
3	Chico	young person
4	Dhobi	laundryman
5	Mochi	cobbler
6	Shikaree	hunter of game
7	Chokree	infant child
8	Chota	small (Hindi)
9	K.D.	khaki drill, lightweight tropical dress
10	Garry	two-wheeled rickshaw
11	R. A. Lanyard	regulation dress for the Royal Artillery worn on the right shoulder. Apparel that can be used to fire an artillery piece
12	36 Division Badge	a white and a red circle interlocked on a black rectangle
13	Pucka	the best (Hindi)
14	Shillong	an area sharing the reputation as one of the wettest places on earth
15	Mepacrine	introduced to combat malaria in the 1930s as a substitute for quinine. It inhibits the development of malaria caused by parasites in the blood. Administered orally, the treatment has some unpleasant side effects; they include headaches, dizziness, nausea, abdominal cramps and yellowing of the skin
16	Chaung	riverbed, or small ravine
17	Indo-China	censored in the letter
18	Sonja Henie	Olympic skater gold medal winner, and movie star
19	Butch	battery head cook

20	Toc H	Talbot House. Charitable service centres
21	Burma Road	renamed Stillwell Road. The first convoy to China left Ledo on 12 January 1945
22	Driver	military vehicles were only permitted to be driven by the holder of a military licence
23	Tiffy	artificer to the guns
24	Tik hi	OK (Hindi)
25	Kachin Levies	Burmese resistance fighters
26	Bund	a raised embankment (Hindi)
27	Ghats	mountainous terrain
28	Durzee	Indian tailor
29	PYTHON	groups of personnel completing three years service overseas
30	Band Boys	schoolboy sons of regular soldiers living in married quarters within the confines of the barracks, learning to read music, and play musical instruments. Their ambition to train as career soldiers in the army, and to serve with a Royal Artillery Regimental Band
31	Monty	Field Marshal Montgomery

Abbreviations

N.A.A.F.I.	Navy Army Air Force Institutions
P.T.	Physical Training
Y.M.C.A.	Young Men's Christian Association
C.B.	Confined to Barracks
M.O.	Medical Officer
Q.M.	Quartermaster
A.T.S.	Auxiliary Territorial Service
M.T.	Motor Transport
R.T.O.	Rail Transport Officer
Red Cap	Military Police
N.C.O.	Non-commissioned officer
R.P.	Regimental Police
B.C.	Battery Commander
O.C.	Officer Commanding
P/A	Paid acting rank
2 I/C	Second in Command
M.I.	Medical Inspection
E.F.M.	Electronic Forces Mail
W.A.S.(B)	Women's Auxiliary Service (Burma)
ENSA	Entertainments National Service Association
WREN	Women's Royal Naval Service
Tac HQ	Tactical Headquarters
B.O.R.	British Other Ranks
I.S.T.	India Standard Time
FANY	First Aid Nursing Yeomanry
RASC	Royal Army Service Corps
A.A.	Anti-aircraft
R.H.A.	Royal Horse Artillery
WAAF	Women's Auxiliary Air Force